DOWN BY THE MARKES

MIKE GOUGH

First published 2016

by Mike Gough MGDBTM@gmail.com

© 2016 Mike Gough

The right of Mike Gough to be identified as author of this work has been asserted by him in accordance with sections 77 and 78 of the Copyright, Designs and Patents Act 1988.

All rights reserved. No part of this book may be reprinted or reproduced or utilised in any form or by any electronic, mechanical, or other means, now known or hereafter invented, including photocopying and recording, or in any information storage or retrieval system, without permission in writing from the author.

Trademark notice: Product or corporate names may be trademarks or registered trademarks, and are used only for identification and explanation without intent to infringe.

ISBN: 978-0-9572954-6-9 (pbk)

ISBN: 978-0-9572954-7-6 (ebk)

Typeset in Palatino Linotype

Printed by Fisk Printers Ltd, Kingston Upon Hull.

This book is dedicated to the hundreds of Apprentices and Cadets that served with Buries Markes Ltd during the nineteen fifties and sixties.

Some of them went on to become masters of huge merchant ships, and some never made it past their first ship during the time when Buries Markes went from

Beyond Misery

to

Bloody Marvellous

Acknowledgements

Special thanks go to my wife, Margaret, without whom this book would never have happened.

Cover design: Fisk Printers Ltd, Kingston Upon Hull, HU19 1SD

Cover photo: FotoFlight, Ashford, Kent TN23 4FB

Editing: The Proof Angel www.the-proof-angel.co.uk

CHAPTER 1

JANUARY 1958

Mike watched as the large black Austin reversed slowly down the road until it reached his home. Mr Bampton had arrived, as he had so many times before to bear his Father away on his journey to a new ship. Only this time the taxi, tumbrel like, had come for him. He told himself that this was the day he had been awaiting for some ten years. The day that life would really start, and that he could follow in his Father's footsteps by going away to sea.

The goodbyes having all been said, his Mother, brothers and sister helped him carry all the suitcases and kitbag to the car. With a last quick look, he was finally on his way. The instructions accompanying the rail-warrant were to join the M/V *La Cordillera* in Southampton's No 5 dry dock. There was no indication of where she would be going, or for how long he would be gone. Neither of these things mattered on that day. Nothing could be allowed to spoil the adventure.

Mike looked resplendent in his doeskin uniform with its cadet's insignia on the lapels and gold buttons on the sleeve. His white cap bore the gold wire crown and anchor badge of the Merchant Navy. On the short journey to Bridlington railway station, Mr Bampton attempted polite conversation, quizzing him on the forthcoming voyage and that of his Father, who at the time was on a voyage up the Amazon. The attempt was to ensure that he would remember to use his taxi in the same way that the family had used it all the time they had lived in Bridlington. He kept up the attempt as they travelled along Queensgate and onto Quay Road, before turning down towards the railway station. Already the enormity of what was happening was beginning to sink in, and by the time he boarded the train to Hull, the bravado and cockiness, which had been evident during the past weeks, was slowly turning to cold fear.

Mike boarded the diesel rail car that would take him to Hull, and then in Hull transferred to *The Yorkshire Pullman* for its journey to London Kings Cross. He booked luncheon with the feeling that this might be the last good meal he would eat for some time. He still vividly remembered his last excursion to sea when he was just thirteen.

It had all started with the Headmaster of Bridlington School placing a letter on the school notice board to the effect that any boy wishing to spend part of his summer holiday trawling in the Arctic should put their names on the foot of the letter. For as long as he could remember, he had taken every opportunity to visit his Father's ships and to spend as much time as possible on the water. From a school of 550 boys, where just five boys added their names to the letter, it was not surprising that his was the first.

When the time arrived in August, he and a boy called Keith were taken to Hull to join the trawler by a gentleman from the Round Table, who had organised the voyage with the trawler owners. As he had been to St Andrew's Dock many times to see the trawlers, either with a school party, or with his Father, he had the advantage over his companion. He was able to speak knowledgeably about the latest design in Hull based deep-water trawlers. He knew how luxurious they were in comparison to the old steam sidewinders. He had even been to the Beverley shipyard of Cook Welton & Gemmell, the birthplace of all the modern trawlers, and so knew exactly what he was looking for when they surveyed the twenty or more trawlers tied up on the quay.

His last visit had been an outing with the school Geographical Society when they had been shown over the almost new *M/T Lammermuir*, the most beautiful vessel he had ever been aboard, and the epitome of modern British trawlers. Unfortunately, the *S/T Rossallian* did not in any way resemble the wonderful *Lammermuir*. She was built in 1927 and coal-fired, and that was only the first shock to his system.

They were deposited on the quay by the gentleman who had brought them from Bridlington, with the promise that he would be back in three weeks' time to collect them. He did not add "should they survive", but the thought was certainly there. Mike found it inconceivable that this rusting hulk was going to put to sea. Even worse, that he would be aboard it! After clambering aboard the modern trawler that the *Rossallian* was tied up to, they made their way across the deck in the hope that this was some awful joke that was being played upon them. Alternatively that they had misread the name on the bow, but there it was: H164 *Rossallian*.

Arriving at the *Rossallian's* galley door, they announced themselves to anyone who was interested, half hoping that they were not expected, and could go home. But they were joined by the Mate who introduced himself and several of the crew. The Mate told them briefly that they would sail at high tide and were bound for the White Sea, or Bear Island. The Skipper would talk to them when they were clear of the Humber. He then showed them to their quarters. That represented the second shock. Instead of being amidships in some cosy cabin, they were berthed with the crew in the forecastle head. They climbed down the ladder into the forecastle, and were greeted with the sight of something out of Hollywood's version of *Moby Dick*. The bunks were two high on both sides. In the centre of the accommodation, a pot-bellied coke burning stove was surrounded by two hawse pipes taking the anchor chains to the cable locker below them.

The smell even then was unusual; a mixture of long dried sweat, wet weather gear, old ropes and sea boots. Mike chose an upper bunk on the port side, as far away from the stove as was possible, and looked around for some bedding. He grabbed a straw stuffed mattress. He was informed that if he wanted a pillow he would have to use the same as everyone else, a kapok lifejacket. Fortunately, they had been told to bring blankets. When he asked about sheets, it was pointed out that as they would not be out of their clothes for three weeks, they would not need sheets.

At first, he thought they were joking, but soon realised that there were no washing facilities on board, and only two lavatories, one forward and one aft. The thought that there was still time to get ashore flashed through both their minds but was quashed by the announcement that the Skipper had arrived.

On the quay, a solid looking man in his forties was saying goodbye to his wife, sitting in a beautiful Daimler. With a final quick kiss and a shout of "stand by fore and aft," he was aboard the *Rossallian* and on his way up to the bridge. A few minutes later came the ring of the engine room telegraph, a hiss, a second hiss and then a rumble as the large steam engine burst into life. With a "Let go fore and aft" from the Skipper, they were on their way to the lock gates. It was high tide, so the gates were open to give clear access to the River Humber beyond them. With a final wave to the assembled wives and girlfriends on the lock side, and the clang of the telegraph as "Full ahead" was rung, the rumble became more pronounced and they were out into the Humber heading for the fishing grounds.

She started to pitch ever so slightly in the choppy waters of the river as she past first Alexandra and then King George docks, then on past the oil terminal at Saltend. Eventually she entered the open sea after altering course around Spurn Point to a northerly direction, heading for the Arctic Circle. By this time, she had developed a steady roll, and the kippers being cooked on the galley stove became less and less appetising with every roll. The confined space of the forecastle did very little to improve the situation, with the coke stove giving off its fumes. This combined badly with the chain smoking of the majority of the crew, and the fact that the door, which was their only source of fresh air, had been battened down. He spent some considerable time up on deck, and felt terribly homesick as they passed Flamborough Head and the lights of Bridlington across the bay. Somehow, Mike made it through the night by telling himself that this was what had excited him for the past three months, and the many years before.

By morning, somehow it all seemed much better. Whilst the ship was still rolling, it was a glorious late August morning and he thought nothing could spoil it. He ate a hearty breakfast, and then he and Keith went onto the bridge to meet the Skipper. The Skipper was a very likeable sort of person, with a dry sense of humour, who obviously wondered what he had done to deserve two thirteen year olds on his trawler. But as long as they were there, he thought he might as well get something out of them.

He told them that if they worked alongside the crew during the voyage, the collection on payday, if it were a good voyage, would bring them money beyond their wildest dreams. Mike and Keith needed no further bidding. They set to work with a will.

The first job was to rescue all the meat for the voyage from its icy grave in the forward fish hold. To do this one needed a very large fire-axe. When the trawler took on its ice for the voyage, it set in the fish holds into a seventy-ton lump of solid ice. Set into this was the fresh meat and other fresh food, and the only way to retrieve it was to make a hole big enough for a man, or boy, to stand in and wield the axe. It was an awful job, as each blow produced a shower of ice particles, which flew in the face and found their way down the neck and up the sleeves of whatever was worn. After an hour or two of this, even the promise of large sums of money had a much reduced effect, but much worse was to come.

In the old coal burning trawlers, the forward coalbunkers doubled as fish holds. As the great fires burnt the coal, the next coal had to be carried from the forward bunker to the stokehold in order to make room for storing the fish. If they had been wet and cold cracking the ice, they were now very hot, dry and dirty as they shovelled the coal, and the offer of continual employment from the Chief Engineer was politely declined. As a small thank you for their help, one of the stokers produced a bucket of water that had been heated by steam from the boiler for them to wash their hands and faces. It was still eighteen days away from a proper wash.

By the sixth day, they were into the Arctic Ocean, past the Lofoten Islands and rounding the northern coastline of Norway, the North Cape, and into the Barents Sea. Much of the ice had been broken up and spread around the fish holds, and the forward coalbunker emptied and hosed down. They now helped in the preparation of the trawl and the erection of the fish pounds on the deck. This was the last normal working day before arriving at the fishing grounds, when all hands would be working around the clock hauling nets and gutting fish.

Using information via the radiotelephone from other Skippers, the decision had been made to fish the area around the White Sea and Cape Kanin. A lot of the time, they would be within sight of the Russian coastline, an exciting thought for a thirteen year old.

The first trawl was shot on the eighth day and an air of expectancy hung over the ship. Had the Skipper got it right? How many bags would the first trawl bring? Would they be able to fill the holds quickly and return to Hull? The first haul was good. The trawl surfaced fifty feet away from the side of the ship, a huge wriggling silver mass. Gradually it was brought alongside and the huge trawl net turned into a manageable load whilst keeping the rest of the fish in the main net. The first bag, made up of the trawl "cod end" was winched up above the fish pounds. The Mate darted underneath and released the "cod end" showering the nearest fish pounds with a huge silver stream of fish, mainly cod and haddock, with some very strange, evil looking, fish amongst them. These were in the main catfish, some up to four feet long, with large snapping jaws.

The crew set about gutting the fish which were piled up to their waists, first thrusting their hands into the jaws of the cod or haddock then quickly slitting their stomachs open and dragging out their entrails. The guts, with the exception of the cod livers, were either thrown over the side or into the next pound ready to be shovelled overboard.

The cod livers were thrown into a basket prior to being taken to a previously unnoticed locker near the stern. The locker consisted almost entirely of a large boiler into which the livers were poured and eventually rendered down to produce a revolting smelling soup. This would be collected by tanker when they returned to Hull and processed into cod liver oil.

The Mate meanwhile had tied the cod end with its special knot for quick release. This section of the trawl was thrown back over the side and filled up with the fish still in the remainder of the trawl alongside. The whole process was repeated three times, leaving virtually every pound on the deck a seething wriggling mass. Only then could the trawl be shot again, and the crew on deck left to gut all the fish currently on deck, before it was time to haul again.

It was not long before they were each offered a sharp knife and a set of gloves, and had to climb into the nearest pound to learn the art of gutting. The fish were nearly up to their chests, so they selected the smallest cod or haddock. Taking hold of them by the mouth, they stabbed the knife into the fish's belly and slit them open cleanly. The next part was the more difficult, as Mike was instructed to thrust his hand into the fish's abdomen and rip out everything he found in there. If it were a cod, he had to remember to throw the liver in the basket, throw the fish into the washing pound, and get rid of the rest of the entrails.

He gagged slightly on the first one, shut his eyes and got on with it. By the time the daylight had disappeared, he had started to get used to it. With standing continually in the water and fish, he was numb and cold, and he could not feel his fingers at all. He had despatched so many fish that his knife was almost totally blunt. He needed to learn how to keep the blade razor sharp.

He walked aft to the galley to get some dinner, and found for the first time in the voyage that the dinner consisted of very fresh fish. Every cooked meal apart from Sunday would be fish until they returned to Hull. This explained why they found so little meat in amongst the ice.

Mike and Keith were exhausted and ready for their bunks, but the work on deck carried on, so they jumped back into the pound to continue with the never ending gutting. The wind had started to pick up by this time and the rolling was becoming a little more pronounced. An ice cold spray of Arctic water blew over them every time she rolled to port. After a couple of hours they were very cold, their sea boots full of water, and they could no longer feel their fingers. Money or not, they headed for the forecastle. The crew worked eight hours on and four hours off, and would be out there for the next six days at least.

The forecastle was more unpleasant than usual. Large amounts of wet gear hung on lines around the glowing stove. The sea boots in front of it were steaming gently with their mix of heated sweat and sea water. The rolling caused the anchor cables passing through the forecastle to clang loudly against their metal hawse pipes, first to starboard and then to port. Mike reflected that even sharing a large bedroom with his two brothers just did not compare with this, and vowed to be more tolerant of them if he returned to Bridlington.

In the morning, the storm had increased in its intensity and the wind was on the port bow, causing the trawler to pitch slightly as well as roll. With each pitch, the water came cascading over the whaleback, making the work on deck even more unpleasant and dangerous. It threw anybody who was tired and not paying attention into the wall of the pound, with half a ton of fish following them. After two hours of this, the Mate suggested they would be safer watching from the bridge. They needed no second bidding.

Where the deck had been bitterly cold and wet, the wheelhouse was warm and dry. It was the hub of the whole of the operation. On one side, clicking away, the echo sounder gave a wonderful picture of what lay beneath them, with occasional faint smudges that the Skipper assured them were fish shoals. The Skipper sat on his stool in the centre of the wheelhouse where he had been virtually non-stop since the first trawl was shot, keeping a watchful eye over the operations on deck. At the same time, he was listening to the short wave radio for signs that other Skippers may give as to where they were fishing successfully. Most were careful to conceal their whereabouts, but occasionally homeward bound Skippers would be more forthcoming.

He was also keeping an eye on the Russian warship, which had been following them from a distance. He warned them not to be seen photographing it, and told lurid details of the trawlers that had been escorted into a White Sea port, never to be seen again. Whilst Mike was gradually becoming accustomed to the Skipper's dry sense of humour, they never the less kept an eye on the warship.

After several hours on the bridge, Mike decided that this was the only place on earth to be, and longed for the day when he could stand in a wheelhouse in total command of all the things going on around him. He had made his mind up many years before that all he wanted in life was to go to sea. This was based on many visits to his Father's ships in Hull and London, and everything that he had seen and done on this voyage confirmed that decision.

The Skipper was reasonably happy with the catch to date, mainly cod or haddock, but with a few plaice and very large catfish. However, he was concerned about the weather forecast for later in the week, when the force six or seven wind would increase to gale force, making life on deck intolerable. This could force them to take shelter, and eventually terminate the fishing, and possibly the voyage.

The ice spread in the fish holds on each layer of fish laid neatly below it had a limited life, and to guarantee the freshness of the fish they would have to head for home in four or five days' time. It was therefore imperative that they took as many bags of fish out of each trawl as possible. The continual heavy spray, coupled with tiredness, was beginning to tell on the crew. A day ago, there had been lots of talking and joking; now the jokes had gone and the talking was down to the minimum.

The crew of an old sidewinder like *Rossallian* was were only too well aware of what a gale in the Barents Sea could mean. The bodies of many good Hull and Grimsby fishermen lay in the waters beneath them: a testament to the hardest job on earth. A sudden wave could wash them straight off the deck and into the stormy waters. When that happened in the Arctic waters, there were no happy stories of people being found alive and well.

The survival time in water that cold, even in August, would be measured in seconds rather than minutes, but it was impossible to work in life jackets, or with lifelines. Working on deck had to be one of the most frightening jobs known. It was here, in this terrifying location, nearly fifty years later that the Russian nuclear submarine *Kursk* was to sink with all hands.

They continued around the clock for another three days, steaming back and forth along the Russian coast with reasonable success. The catches were satisfactory, and in general the quality good. The weather had temporarily improved, making the work less arduous. Although spirits had been raised slightly, exhaustion was setting in. Most of the crew came into the saloon at the end of each spell on deck for a meal. They ate as quickly as possible, with little or no enthusiasm for the food. They then headed for the forecastle, and after throwing off their wet weather gear, dived fully dressed into their bunks and were asleep within a second or two.

Mike and his companion Keith had spent much of the

previous few days in the wheelhouse, as the Skipper was not anxious to have his charges washed over the side. But with the improving weather they had been gutting, and carrying the cod livers to the boiler. They, along with everybody else, were now ready for the time when the decision would be made to head for home. The money they had been promised on arrival far surpassed their wildest dreams; in fact most of the conversation between them consisted of ideas on how it would be possible to spend it all.

CHAPTER 2

On the thirteenth day, the gale struck with a vengeance. The trawler was battened down, and the decision made to head homeward. The two thirteen year olds were confined to the forecastle due to the heavy seas pounding onto the deck, washing everything that was not fastened down overboard. The conditions were now truly awful. There were ten unwashed people, eight of whom were smoking most of the time, with wet oilskins, sweaty sea boots and socks, gear scattered all over the deck, and the door to the fresh air battened down to avoid shipping any seawater into the accommodation. As if this were not bad enough, the whole lot was being shaken and thrown around like a rattle.

The continuous pounding into the sea and the shudder as the water poured over the whaleback before she started to lift again became normal after a time. For the first time in the voyage, he began to feel a little frightened. Time after time he was thrown against the bulkhead as he tried to move around the forecastle. Each time the bow went down into the sea with an enormous crash, he started to count the seconds before she started to lift. Each time it seemed to take longer, and the huge waves were taking longer before they smashed onto the deck. There was no respite whatsoever. He wondered how long an old ship like

Rossallian could withstand this treatment. Could they make land before the seemingly inevitable happened?

Eventually he decided the only safe place to be was in his bunk with one leg against the bulkhead and the other against the bunk board to hold him firmly into the bunk. He was still determined that this experience would not put him off going to sea, assuming that he arrived safely back in Hull from this voyage. With each crash into the thirty-foot waves, the chances of doing this seemed more remote. He silently prayed that they would reach the shelter of one of the fjords before the mountainous seas swallowed them up forever.

Even with the lifelines rigged, the Skipper would not let either of the boys on deck for fear of being washed away. As they were unable to go to the galley for food, they survived on fresh fish doorstep sandwiches brought forward by the crew, and large steaming mugs of strong tea, with lots of sugar and condensed milk. Initially their appetites had been somewhat lacking, but as the gale continued without any sign of abating, the feeling of hunger overcame the nausea caused by the motion of the ship and the conditions in the forecastle. Besides, if they were going to be sick they might as well have something inside to bring up! By the time night fell again, he was beginning to master the conditions and, despite the clanging of the anchor chains and the rolling, he passed into oblivion and slept soundly.

When he awoke there was one awful moment when he wondered what had happened. Were they still alive or what? The ship was absolutely still and the engine, which had been running continuously since leaving St Andrew's dock, had stopped. Mike raced for the forecastle ladder, and climbed onto the deck, to be rewarded with the most wonderful sight of his life. A green mountain, just a few feet away, rose hundreds of feet vertically from the fjord in which they lay. Never had land been as welcome as this breathtakingly beautiful scene.

They were tied up at a small wooden pier near Hammerfest in Norway's most northerly fjord, awaiting a Pilot to take them through the fjords. Without waiting to be told that they could not go ashore, Mike stepped onto the pier. He was able to claim many times thereafter that he had been ashore within the Norwegian Arctic Circle. The trip ashore lasted seconds before the Mate told him that he would have to stay there and go into quarantine. He rejoined *Rossallian* even faster than he had gone ashore.

The Pilot joined them shortly afterwards, and they began the journey through the astonishingly enchanting islands with their white-capped mountains and glass like sea. He had seen photographs of the fjords before, but nothing had prepared him for the splendid reality. He would willingly have spent weeks cruising through them before facing the Norwegian Sea and the possibility of more gales.

The villages with their beautifully painted houses past one by one, set in small inlets with the fjord as their only connection to the rest of the world. Eventually they rounded a bend to be confronted with Tromso, the capital of northern Norway. After not seeing land for nearly two weeks this came as an oasis like surprise. Once again, the neat brightly painted houses and businesses along the quayside brought an almost toy like quality to the already beautiful scene. As night started to fall, they passed the entrance to the Fjord where the wreck of the German battleship *Tirpitz* lay. A discordant note in the scenic perfection, its only use to the people of Tromso being that one of its generators supplied the whole of their lighting.

Mike noticed many red lights around the fjord, and enquired innocently as to their purpose. The Third Hand who was at the wheel immediately answered "Brothels."

"What's a brothel?" asked Mike. There was a silence as the Third Hand looked at the Mate and the Mate looked at the Skipper. Eventually the Skipper claimed that a brothel was a form of soup kitchen. The question as to why so many soup kitchens were needed formed in Mike's mind. He didn't bother voicing it after seeing the Mate doubled up in the corner of the wheelhouse.

All too quickly, they reached the Lofoten Islands, and then back into the Norwegian Sea. The gale had abated somewhat, and although she was moving about fairly dramatically, she was not shipping any seas over the whaleback. By the following morning, the wind was down to force four or five. Normal life was resumed, with regular hot meals being prepared in the galley. Work to clear the ship's deck began, with all the fishing gear being stowed away below ready for the next voyage.

After the break travelling through the fjord, conversation resumed. What day would they arrive in Hull? How many other trawlers would arrive back that day? What prices would the catch fetch? The hope was that, as a result of the bad weather, there would be a significant shortage of the cod and haddock that formed the majority of their catch.

As the boys listened to the stories of the prices fetched, their expectations of the amount of money they would collect grew. Virtually everybody from the Skipper down had promised them money for the help they had given during the voyage. Mike was already thinking in terms of a new bike and having enough for a motorbike when he was old enough to ride one. The crew were planning all the ways their money would be spent. How much living could they put into the forty-eight hours before they sailed again for the fishing grounds? Certainly, Hull Brewery were in for a substantially increased turnover.

Early next morning work began on emptying the rope locker under the whaleback. As they had spent the past day stowing things away, this puzzled Mike. This was to be the washroom for everyone to get clean before arriving in the Humber. They boiled a bucketful of water on the galley range, carried it forward to the rope locker, stripped off and had a full wash. Then they dressed for entering port in the uniquely styled suits with huge bell-bottomed trousers worn by all trawler crews.

By the time Keith and Mike's turn arrived, they were already in the Humber. The excitement was mounting as they passed Sunk Island, Paull and then the Saltend refinery with its usual accompanying huge tanker discharging its oil cargo from the Gulf. The size of the tanker appealed to Mike after the voyage they had just endured. He could not envisage something of that size being thrown around by a gale lashed sea. As he had that thought, they were passed by the trawler *Primella* outward bound on her maiden voyage.

Although she was still a sidewinder, the crew were accommodated amidships in quite luxurious cabins. Deck clothing was not allowed in the accommodation, and the whole of the after end of the trawler was enclosed. No pot-bellied stoves in the forecastle, no anchor cables clanging with every movement of the ship, no cleaning out of bunkers for fish stowage, no searching in the ice for the fresh provisions. Even the fish had a mechanical washer to clean them before being deposited into the fish-room. Maybe trawlers weren't so bad after all!

Night was falling by the time they had passed Albert Dock and were making their approach to the St Andrew's Dock lock pit. As she pulled alongside the lock walls, all the crew not required for berthing jumped onto the quayside. With a final wave and a promise to see the boys at the pay off on the next day they were gone. The remainder of the crew left as soon as she was tied up on the fish market wall, once again promising to see them the following morning.

As soon as they were alongside, the boys were told that the gentleman from Bridlington who had brought them to Hull at the beginning of the voyage would not be able to collect them until the following morning. They would have to spend a further night aboard *Rossallian*. This in fact fitted perfectly into the plan for collecting their windfall at the fishing company's office. The cook had left them plenty of food to see them through the night, and they settled down in the main cabin before falling asleep in the luxury of a stationary bunk, their minds full of nothing but the riches they were to receive in the morning.

At midnight it appeared that all hell had broken lose, as the bobbers coming to rig the pulleys and lines that would be used to unload the fish besieged the trawler. At 0200 hrs, dozens more joined them as the covers were thrown off the fish-room hatches and most of the bobbers descended into the fish-room. Then the produce of the past three weeks was gradually transferred by baskets winched out of the hold and swung onto the dock. They were emptied into ten stone metal kits supervised by a weigher-off.

Within a short time hundreds of kits were spread out over the quay separated into lines of cod, haddock, plaice and assorted others. The fish hold boards were washed and stored away, and the trawlers deck hosed down. As quickly as they arrived the bobbers moved on. The whole of the fish quay was a sea of full kits awaiting the arrival of the auctioneers and wholesale buyers.

Shortly after daylight, a strange vessel pulled alongside. This was the tanker barge calling for the rendered cod liver oil. The evil smelling mixture, which had taken so much hard work to produce, was pumped over the side into the barge's tanks for transferring to the factory on Hedon Road, from whence it would emerge as Seven Seas Cod Liver Oil.

It became apparent soon after the auction started that good fish was in short supply as a result of the storm they had endured. Prices were higher than usual. The two boys reflected on how much more money this was going to bring them when the crew were paid at 1000 hrs and continued the dreams of how they were going to spend this massive windfall. New bikes were top of the list, with presents for parents and siblings following on. They drifted back to sleep in the mess room and slept soundly again until 8am, when they searched the galley for some breakfast.

A representative of the trawler owners, who advised them

that the gentleman who originally brought them to join the trawler three weeks ago would be collecting them at 0930 hrs, joined them shortly after. This message instilled instant panic in the two boys. What about the pay off? Would they be able to hold on until 1000 hrs? Was this the end of all their dreams?

They had hardly had the time to digest the bad news when the nightmare became horrible reality; the gentleman arrived to collect them. Being a busy man, he was unable to wait for the crew to pay off. The boys returned to Bridlington much older, very much wiser, but alas considerably poorer than they had expected.

Four years later the memory of all the lost money still needled Mike, but now the time had come to start a career that would make up for that disappointment. He was to be paid the wonderful sum of £9 3s 4d per month for the first year, rising to £20 per month in the fourth year of his indentures. After completing his indentures, the sky could be the limit, or at least it could for someone who was then just sixteen years old. It was nowhere near the amount of money he would make by joining the trawler fleet. Modern trawlers had been launched since his voyage, and he had been down a coal mine with the school Geographical Society, but he still believed it was the hardest job on earth. The loss just four short months later of the Hull trawlers *Lorella* and *Roderigo* with all hands convinced him that he had made the right decision.

He reflected on this as *The Yorkshire Pullman* pulled into Kings Cross. Then he tried to remember, from when he had visited London to join his Father on his ship in Millwall docks, how to use the Underground. He looked at the number of cases, and decided that the only way he was going to Waterloo was by taxi, and to hell with the expense!

He hardly noticed the journey to Southampton or the taxi ride to the docks. His mind was so filled with the enormity of what was happening. Was it too late to turn back? What would happen if he did? What would he do with himself if he weren't to go to sea? He was jerked back to reality when the taxi driver announced that they had reached No 5 dry dock. Lying there was the start of his new life: *La Cordillera.*

CHAPTER 3

Apart from the warships he had been aboard during his time in the school Combined Cadet Force, and the Festival of Britain ship *Campania, La Cordillera* was the largest ship he had seen. She lay, all 330 feet of her, high and dry in the dry dock, illuminated in the dusk by the dockyard arc lamps and her own deck lights. The panic he had felt before had turned into something far worse. He was reluctant to take all his baggage from the taxi and pay the driver. It felt as if his last contact with the normal world was about to disappear.

Eventually he steeled himself for the inevitable and piled the cases at the end of the gangway. The taxi drove off and he was left with his thoughts long enough for an officer to walk up the gangway and ask if he could be of assistance. The epaulettes on his shoulder denoted that he was the Third Officer. Mike introduced himself, and together they carried the bags aboard to comments like "How long are you planning to be away for?" and "God almighty what have you got in here?"

If Mike was to be kind, the Third Mate was quite heavily built and far older than normal for a Third Officer, due, as he was to find out much later, to his inability to pass his Second Mates Certificate. He took Mike into the midships accommodation block. Half way down the starboard alleyway, he stopped outside a cabin. This was to be Mike's home for possibly the next two years.

The cabin was about twelve foot square with a single porthole facing him, beneath which was a desk with a settee to the right and double lockers to the left. On the alleyway bulkhead were two bunks, the top one of which was to be his. His cabin mate, who had just entered the cabin together with two other shipmates, had already claimed the lower bunk.

The first of the three newcomers introduced himself and his two companions. He appeared to be older than the other two, and in fact was the Senior Apprentice, Tony Eames. He was twenty years of age, three years of his indentures completed, and just one year to go. He was slightly taller than the other two; thin with an almost cadaverous face and giving Mike the initial impression that no one was going to forget that he was the Senior Apprentice. He had attended a nautical training school run on Royal Naval lines near his home on the south coast, and appeared to believe that an apprenticeship with Buries Markes was a long way beneath him. Almost certainly, he could not wait to complete his indentures and join a more illustrious company. On his right was the other apprentice Paul, and on his left Phil, a tall Londoner who Mike would be sharing the cabin with, and a cadet like himself. Tony and Paul shared the next cabin along the alleyway, with their communal bathroom in between.

Paul Nicholson, the other apprentice, was an extremely affable Geordie, well built and of average height. He was the more welcoming of the three. He had completed a previous voyage with Buries Markes, on their *M/V La Hacienda*, and therefore knew the ropes. Phil Hammond had only arrived one hour before Mike, and as this was his first ship was just as nervous, and at a loss as to what happened next. Tony advised them to stow all their luggage away before taking them forward to the saloon for dinner. It was a makeshift meal for a skeleton crew on board whilst in dry dock, but it was very welcome coming some twelve hours after leaving home. After dinner, they sat in the cabins and speculated on where the ship was going to after they left Southampton.

As a general cargo company, most of the Buries Markes ships operated as tramp ships, loading a cargo in one port for delivery maybe on the other side of the world. The cargo could be bought and sold whilst the ship was at sea, so in reality nobody knew where they were going to end up. After discharging that cargo, another cargo would be loaded either in that port or another port in a different part of the world and the whole thing would start again.

For anyone wanting to see the world, a tramp steamer was probably the best way of visiting a large variety of different countries. As the process could take up to two years without coming back to England, it was not recommended for family men. Mike had not realised that each time he

MIKE **G**OUGH **P**UBLICATIONS

With Compliments

Web: www.mikegoughpublications.co.uk
Email: mike@mikegoughpublications.co.uk
Mobile: 07739 188041

signed ship's articles he might have to stay on that ship for the full two years. Visions of press gangs dragging innocent men and boys away to sea pervaded his thoughts. The knowledge that should the ship enter a British port the articles would be terminated cheered him immensely.

The speculation on where they were going by the time they climbed into their bunks to sleep had ranged from the United States and Canada to Japan, India and Australia. Heady stuff for someone whose sole trip to sea had been on a Hull trawler. With that, Mike was one up on Phil who had not previously been to sea, or even left England before. Mike was wondering what he was doing there. Was it going to be the great adventure it had promised to be, or something to finish as soon as possible before trading the life in for a normal job ashore?

The working day in port started at 0700 hrs with a full breakfast at 0800 hrs, working then from 0900 hrs to 1200 hrs with a one-hour break for lunch and then working until 1700 hrs prior to dinner. As they were still working with a skeleton crew, meals were taken when and where possible. On the instructions of the Chief Officer, a seemingly genial man of Irish descent, the four boys spent a large part of the first day finding their way around the ship and taking the unique opportunity to walk down into the dry dock to see the ship in her entirety. If she had seemed large when first approached on the quayside, from the bottom of the dry dock she was truly enormous. The dockyard workers had nearly finished painting the whole of her underside a deep red, and her huge propeller appeared to be burnished gold following its spring clean.

The remainder of the painting would be finished by the next day and, her survey complete, the dry dock would be flooded. They would be ready to sail to wherever the cargo was that was waiting for them.

Having looked around the outside of *La Cordillera* they set about looking at the holds and storage areas. She had five large cargo holds, two on the foredeck, one amidships and two on the afterdeck. When empty, the holds were cavernous: fifty to sixty feet long, thirty feet wide and forty feet high. A tween deck ran round twelve feet below the main deck level to give the opportunity of stowing special cargo separately and to give the ship far more rigidity.

Strapped to the bulkheads in the tween deck were large planks of timber together with steel framework, "Shifting-boards," said Tony. Mike and Phil were none the wiser, but would be experts on the subject before too long. After inspecting all the holds, they started on the accommodation. *La Cordillera* was a three-island ship with the bridge, Captain, Chief Officer and Radio Officer cabins all situated between No 2 and No 3. All other officers, together with apprentices, cadets, Chief Steward, the dining saloon and galley were in the amidships accommodation between No 3 and No 4 holds.

The crew, together with donkey men and stewards, were in the after accommodation section, situated at the stern. The donkey men worked in the engine room, primarily looking after the donkey boiler, which provide all the power needed when the main engine was not running. By far the best cabins were six passenger cabins in the bridge section. The ship had been designed to carry a small number of passengers, but no one could remember when she had ever carried any. Later they would find out that an experiment had taken place using ex Wrens as stewardesses, but it was short-lived. The cabins stood exactly as they were when first built, with the protective covers on the furniture still intact. They were to become a source of vexation to many of the officers in the amidships accommodation, who had to share their space with a huge five cylinder Doxford engine. The engine produced a large amount of heat and vibration. It was the size of two semi-detached houses, and therefore impossible to ignore.

The next morning, Mike was greeted by the most incredible sight when he walked out onto the deck. To the right of the dry dock in which they lay was the Ocean Terminal. Towering above the terminal were the three gigantic black and red funnels of *RMS Queen Mary*, which had arrived during the night. He called his three colleagues, and they walked round to the other dock to have a closer look at this amazing ship. Together with *RMS Queen Elizabeth*, it was still running the regular service to New York.

If they had ever thought that their ship was large, this put everything into perspective. She dominated the whole skyline, and was several times longer and bigger in every department than *La Cordillera*. He wondered what it would have been like to join a ship of that size as a cadet and have to spend all your time in full uniform attempting to keep passengers happy. The thought of the passengers made him realise that he had probably made the right decision.

By the time they had eaten breakfast, the stores for the voyage had arrived on a large lorry. Together with the crew, stewards and engine room staff who were arriving in ones and twos to join the ship, they set about stowing everything away. They were occupied mostly with the deck stores; new huge manila and wire rope combinations had to be dragged forward to the rope lockers under the forecastle head. This was a mammoth task, as it was impossible to drag more than ten or twelve feet at a time. Then they had to go back for the next section, until the whole rope had been moved some two hundred feet up the deck.

Following the ropes into the forecastle head stores was a huge quantity of paint in five-gallon drums. Red lead and red oxide primers, undercoat for the white superstructure, cream for the accommodation and drum after drum of black and white gloss and dark red deck paint. All the drums were extremely heavy, but the red and white lead was almost impossible to lift. Somehow, they managed.

Mike told himself that this was an unusual time, when everybody had to pull together. Soon he would be able to start in his position as a Deck Officer Cadet and wouldn't need to involve himself in this heavy manual type of work. He had not had chance yet to talk to Tony or Paul about the normal routine, but suspected that it was far different from the work they were doing now. If he had been psychic, he would have been down the gangplank as fast as his legs would carry him. As they had now completed the provisioning of the ship, they sank onto the cabin settee in a state of near collapse, and prepared for the next day when the dock would be flooded and they would be on their way.

First thing on the next morning, they started battening down the hatches. All the hatch covers had been taken off the holds, and the metal beams that supported them removed, whilst the ship was surveyed for her Board of Trade Certificate. Now they all had to be replaced before leaving port.

This was to prove to be one of the more dangerous jobs. Each of the holds had five rows of hatch boards, which had to be replaced. Each board was solid three inch wood, six feet long by three feet wide, with an indented handle at each end. These had to be slotted into the steel beams, which were lifted back with the ship's derricks into position across the hold from one side to the other. The only way to replace the boards was for two people to sit astride the steel beams, gripping them with their knees and push the very heavy boards out in front of them, coming back each time for the next board. At all times there was a 40 foot drop onto a steel deck below them.

Mike worked with Paul, and between them they built up a very tiring rhythm, which eventually covered No 1 hold without accidents. The four of them pulled the green canvas hatch cover over the boards, which was a momentous achievement given the weight of the heavy-duty canvas covers. Next, they placed the locking bars in the cleats after the canvas had been folded carefully into the hold sides, before hammering wooden wedges into each cleat. This ensured that the cover would not move before they were ready to take on cargo in their next port. Each of the two huge derricks were lowered with the winches and clamped down. They moved on to hold No 2 to repeat the operation there. Eventually they arrived at hold No 3 and met up with the crew who had started at holds No 4 and 5.

During the afternoon they were called into the saloon to sign articles, and there met for the first time the rest of the crew, mostly the engineers and their staff, and the stewards and cooks, a motley crowd making up a ship's company of forty-one. Sitting at the centre of the table with the ship's agent and Board of Trade officials on either side was Captain Pearson, a very thin man in his late forties, looking as miserable as sin. If Mike had any doubts in his mind, this was the last chance to do anything about it, but he meekly signed on the dotted line and sincerely hoped that they were not going out for two years.

Outside the dining saloon he casually glanced over the side rail into the dry dock, only it was a dry dock no longer. Water was swirling around the lower step and slowly rising to cover the next one. Without him realising, they had started the flooding of the dock some time ago. They were getting nearer to the one thing he had wanted all his life, to go to sea. He raced to the stern to have a better view of what was happening. He saw the water pouring in, and the two tugs outside the dock waiting to take them out into the Solent.

In a time that seemed like days, but in reality was only about three hours, the dock was full and the dry dock gates opened. Before he could contemplate the significance, they were deafened by one of the most magnificent sounds ever heard, the *Queen Mary* was saying goodbye to Southampton in the traditional way before starting her latest voyage to New York. The deck, the air, and everything around them vibrated to the blasts on her whistle, as she moved very slowly, stern first, out of the dock and into the Solent, escorted by all her tugs. After being swung clear of the docks by the tugs, there was an explosion of water around her stern as the mighty steam driven engines burst into life. She headed slowly and majestically out to the open sea, a totally astonishing sight, the pinnacle of where Mike wanted to be in a few years' time.

Before he could give what he had just witnessed any more thought there was a shout of "Stand by fore and aft," and everybody seemed to be heading in different directions. Mike was sent aft to work with Paul and the Second Mate. They began together with four members of the crew to pay out a line to the tug, and to slacken the ropes and wire hawsers holding them alongside the dock wall. The dockworkers let go one of the stern lines and the wire spring, and they were winched aboard and stored away ready for the next port.

Mike heard for the first time the sound of the engine room telegraph as the Captain on the bridge gave the stand by order. Then as the tug took the strain the telegraph rang again slow astern. There was a huge whoosh as the compressed air used to start the engine escaped and a heavy vibration as the engine tried to start first time, but failed. The operation was repeated, and this time the engine burst into life. Slowly she began to move out of the dock, the last connection to the shore was let go, and they moved out into the Solent. The great adventure had begun and, according to the Second Mate, they were heading to where Mike had always wanted to go, the United States, and more precisely New Orleans.

CHAPTER 4

In what seemed to be very little time at all, they had stowed away everything that could move and turned out the deck lights, so that night arrived very quickly. The tugs had been let go as soon as they cleared the dock area, and now they were under their own power, with the 5 cylinder Doxford engine creating a huge vibrating rhythm throughout the ship as she moved out towards the open sea. Slightly astern and on the starboard side was a small vessel with its red and white light denoting a pilot launch, and from the bridge came the call to make ready the ladder for the Pilot to leave.

Mike and Paul made fast the ladder plus its extension. As the empty ship was riding extremely high in the water, they threw the bulk of it over the side, where it hung just above the water level. As they had come straight out of dry dock and had no cargo, and as yet very little ballast water in her tanks, it seemed a very long way down the ladder. Mike reflected that he was very glad that he would not be descending the ladder. Almost as soon as the ladder was ready there was a clang of the engine room telegraph, and the steady rhythm of the engine slowed dramatically.

The pilot launch caught up and moved alongside. The Pilot came down from the bridge and, with an exchange of good wishes, he was on the ladder watching for the movement of the launch as he descended towards it. Then with practised ease, the launch was manoeuvred towards the bottom of the ladder. The Pilot jumped aboard, and with a quick wave disappeared into the darkness. Once more the telegraph rang, this time for "Full ahead," as the last contact with the shore was lost and they were on their way to America.

Very quickly, they settled into the sea-going routine. Mike was given the 4-8 watch with the Chief Officer whilst Phil took the 12-4 with the Second Mate and Paul the 8-12 with the Third Mate. Tony, as something of a perk for his seniority, took the day work shift with the crew. On the face of it, the idea of working from 7am to 5pm did not seem much of a perk to Mike, and he did not envy Tony. However, nobody had yet explained to him that as an apprentice or cadet in this company 4-8 meant four in the morning until eight at night, a straight sixteen-hour day. He would be expected to be on the bridge at 0400 hrs, on lookout until 0700 hrs when he would join the rest of the crew for one hour's work before breakfast. He started work again at 0900 hrs and worked through until 1700 hrs, with a break for lunch. At 1700 hrs, he would be expected to have a quick dinner and then back onto the bridge as a lookout until the end of the watch at 2000 hrs, then to bed before being called again at 0330 hrs.

As there was still two hours of his watch left, Mike headed

for the bridge after first kitting himself out with sweaters and oilskins. The wheelhouse was occupied by the Chief Officer and a member of the crew at the wheel. The Mate told him to get a drink, and to make him one as well. The galley was closed at night, so this meant a journey with the teapot to the afterdeck where a large geyser was kept on the boil all night for the crew. Mike ladled dry tea into the pot, added the water and headed back up the two ladders to the wheelhouse. There he poured two steaming pint pots full of tea, and added sugar and condensed milk, in the absence of real milk. On the Mate's instructions, he headed out onto the bridge wing to peer into the darkness for any other shipping, and to nurse the hot pint pot of tea.

By now, the lights of Southampton were well astern and, with the exception of the odd lighthouse flashing its identifying signal, it was pitch black. His eyes tried to accustom themselves to the gloom. The crewmember had left the wheel and the Mate had set the Iron Mike. For Mike who, had not seen an autopilot before, it was slightly uncanny to realise that with the exception of course alterations, it would hardly be necessary for anyone to steer the ship until their arrival off New Orleans, as the Watch Officer would make the minor course adjustments.

His thoughts on this were interrupted by his sudden realisation that over on the port bow there were two masthead lights and a green starboard light that he had not noticed before. He rushed back into the wheelhouse to report to the Mate who had already picked up the other ship on the radar and watched as the ship altered course to starboard to pass astern of them. This was to be the most eventful thing to happen on his first watch at sea, and he walked out onto the bridge wing to continue the lookout. After a while, he started pacing the length of the bridge wing to warm himself up.

Although the bridge had a dodger to deflect the wind along the length of the wing there was still a very cold wind whipping around him, especially on his face as he peered over the dodger. It was difficult to see any new lights as his eyes started to water. The last forty-five minutes seemed to be interminable as he waited for the end of the watch, but eventually there was the welcome sight of Paul climbing up to the bridge to relieve him and he was able to head back down to the cabin and a night's sleep.

Apart from picking up his warm clothing, Mike had not been in the accommodation since leaving Southampton. Now what had been one of the quietest areas of the ship was vibrating constantly to the huge thuds of the ship's engine. He had been very cold on the bridge, but he was now sweltering from the heat generated in the accommodation by the huge 5 cylinder Doxford. In addition, the air was heavy with the smell of the gas oil and hot lubricating oil. He was too tired to worry as he stripped off his clothes and climbed, as quietly as possible, into his bunk. Phil was already having his first sleep session in preparation for his 12-4 watch, and very quickly, Mike headed the same way.

In what seemed an incredibly short time, Phil came to wake him at 0330 hrs in readiness for his watch, and he threw on his warm gear. Pausing only to make the tea in the crew's galley, he headed once again for the bridge and three hours as lookout. By now, there was no sight of any land. What had seemed an almost imperceptible movement the night before had, as a result of her having no cargo and only water ballast, developed into a very steady roll of ten degrees as she headed steadily on her course into the Gulf Stream.

The time on the bridge wing passed desperately slowly with little or nothing to report. He strained his eyes towards the horizon, looking for any lights that would indicate another ship. The Mate occasionally passed the odd comment, but spent most of his time moving between the chartroom and the wheelhouse, as he prepared to take the star sight that would give them their position. His regular calls for a pot of tea enabled Mike to stretch his legs and get out of the icy coldness of the bridge wing as he went down to the afterdeck for hot water. Once he had collected the hot water, he could take his time making the tea in the chartroom. This also provided some respite from the boredom, and the numbing cold of January in the North Atlantic.

As dawn slowly broke on the port quarter, the Mate armed with his sextant moved out onto the port wing. Mike moved into the warmth of the chartroom to watch the chronometer and note the time on the Mate's mark. All too soon he was back to start his sight calculations, and Mike headed back to the bridge wing to pass the time until he joined the rest of the apprentices and crew for day work.

At 0645 hrs, the Bosun arrived on the bridge to take his orders from the Mate for the day's work. Mike moved nearer to the wheelhouse door in the hope of hearing some news of what was going on. He was not disappointed. Up to this time all that was known about this voyage was that they were heading for New Orleans to take on cargo. The nature of the cargo, or cargoes, was a mystery to them. Not for much longer as the Mate explained to the Bosun that they would be loading bales of cotton in New Orleans and then sailing round to Galveston in Texas for a part cargo of grain. From Galveston, they would head back to Europe to discharge the cargo. But where in Europe was still a mystery.

To prepare the holds that would be carrying cotton, their steel decks had to be covered in dunnage. This was to be the work for the crew for the next few days. Dunnage, as Mike was to find out quite quickly, is the splintery lengths of wood that are the first cut from the log in a sawmill before a clean plank can be cut. To a sawmill this would be rubbish, but for cargo protection, a godsend. The dunnage was to be laid in two layers, the first layer laid athwartships to keep the bales off the steel deck, and to allow any sweating from the bales to run into the bilges on either side of the hold. Failure to follow this simple precaution would mean the cotton would soak in the sweat caused by the build-up of heat amongst the bales and be ruined. The second layer was laid fore and aft to keep the bales well above the first layer and to ensure the channels to the bilges were free of impediment.

Until this point Mike had harboured the thought that they may be treated as officer apprentices, and that like the cadets and apprentices in the major shipping lines such as Blue Funnel Line, P&O and Cunard they would remain in uniform during the daylight hours. This would leave time to study navigation, seamanship, mathematics and the Morse code in preparation for their Second Mates Certificate of Competency examinations in four years. Slowly the truth was dawning. He had excused all the long hours he had been working on readying the ship for sea, and the need to have all hands working as she left port. Now that excuse was no longer available, and yet the hours were still virtually the same, if not longer. He pondered once again on what he had done.

The Buries Markes theory on the education of cadets and apprentices was quite simple. If they worked them throughout the daylight hours with the crew, they would become first class seamen. When as officers they had to order the crew to carry out a job, most certainly they could do the job as well as, if not better than, any crewmember. During the hours of darkness, they were available for watch keeping, and should any other work be necessary they could also carry that out, so ensuring that the crew did not have to be called out, generating overtime payments. All apprentices were paid £9 3s 4d per month in their first year's apprenticeship rising to £12 in the second year and £20 in their fourth and final year. Their only other source of income was double pay for Sundays spent at sea, and the doubling of their wages if they were kept out of the UK for more than two years on any one voyage.

At 0700 hrs, Mike was despatched from the bridge to join Paul and Tony with the rest of the crew on day work. As Phil had been on the 12-4 watch, he was allowed to stay in his bunk until breakfast at 0800 hrs. They headed for the forecastle to collect lighting clusters to light the holds. They plugged them into the sockets on the mast house bulkhead, and lowered them down through the hold doorways into the tween decks.

The working party was split into two, and Mike together with the other two apprentices and four crewmembers descended the vertical steel ladder into the tween deck of No 1 hold. After rigging the clusters in the tween deck to illuminate the lower hold, they descended the remaining thirty feet on the open ladder to the bottom of the cavernous empty hold, which was lit by their eerie light.

Immediately upon reaching the steel deck, they started dragging large pieces of dunnage from the pile that had been deposited towards the forward end of the hold, and laying them neatly athwartships, as best they could with the steady roll of the ship. Within twenty minutes, the first splinter pierced the gloves he was wearing and imbedded itself in the palm of his hand, leaving four inches of wood exposed for him to drag it out of his hand. He let rip with a string of expletives as he shook his bloody hand in real pain, and pulled the splinter out. He eased his glove off to examine the damage, and was shaken by the amount of blood seeping into his glove.

The Bosun, on seeing this, pointed out that it was only a scratch, and he might as well wait until they stopped for breakfast before cleaning it up. His comments were somewhat stronger ten minutes later when he did exactly the same thing, when a piece of dunnage failed to move when he did, and it was decided to break for breakfast.

Mike cleaned up his hand as well as he could in the accommodation and went in search of the Chief Steward, the only qualified first-aider on board, for some antiseptic and an Elastoplast. He had been warned that the Chief Steward had a predilection for young apprentices and the like, and therefore took the antiseptic cream and plaster back to his cabin as quickly as possible, despite the Chief Steward's offer to apply them for him.

His next stop was the galley and a very welcome breakfast. As they were filthy from working in the hold, they were allowed to have their meal out on the No 4 hatch, instead of eating in the saloon in full uniform. The size of the meal surprised Mike, orange juice followed by curried eggs or kedgeree, cereal and then bacon, egg, tomatoes, flapjacks, toast, and tea or coffee. At home, he had cereal or toast and that was it, so he was not inclined to eat his way through the menu. But he had been working since 0400 hrs, so once he started he found it very easy to make the most of the meal.

The hour passed all too quickly. With difficulty, they motivated themselves to return to the hold and the dunnage spreading. Within half an hour all members of the working party had managed to damage their hands with the splinters from the rough wood, and the air was blue from strings of expletives. Mike had received a good grounding in expletives on his trawling trip, but he was learning by the minute. Tempers were becoming extremely short as everyone continued working with hands that were becoming sorer as the hours went by, but still they laid one plank after another until only the area on which the dunnage pile stood had not been covered.

Starting from the forward end again, they criss-crossed the dunnage with the second layer until they had exhausted the pile of timber. The whole hold had two complete layers, and was ready to take the planned cargo. Surprisingly by the time they had done this, they were ready for lunch.

This time they were not excused from eating in the saloon, so all four of them crowded into the bathroom for a quick wash before donning uniform and heading for the saloon. With the exception of the Second Mate who was on watch on the bridge, the Captain's table was full, with the Captain, Mate, Third Mate and Radio Officer at one end, and the four apprentices at the other. On the other side of the saloon the Chief Engineer's table was missing the Third Engineer and a junior engineer. Once again, the meal was substantial and not conducive to an afternoon's work, a first course of soup followed by a main course and a wonderful spotted dick pudding.

As soon as they finished their meal, they headed for their cabins. They changed into working gear, had time for a quick smoke, and then back to work. Mike had tried cigarettes before leaving school, and smiled to himself as he remembered attempting with four friends in Bridlington to gain access to the Lounge cinema to see Brigitte Bardot in the X certificated *Light Across the Street*. At this stage, X meant suitable for those aged 16 and over. Four of the group were under sixteen, so they bought a packet of ten Olivier and lit up as they entered the cinema. The eldest of the friends was the only one over sixteen, and the only one not smoking. He was the one rejected by the cinema staff.

Mike coughed and choked after inhaling his first cigarette.

This was far stronger than he was used to, but with opening of the Captain's bond, there was a choice only of Senior Service, John Player and Capstan Full Strength, at a cost of ten shillings for two hundred. As the choice was two hundred or nothing, his addiction was about to commence, and subsequently to last for eighteen years. Beside which smoking was one of the few pleasures available to them, and an opportunity for a break in the hectic work schedule. Nobody had mentioned at that time that smoking was dangerous to you, and the vast majority of officers and crew all smoked to the point that you almost had to cut your way into a cabin through the smoke. Mike didn't enjoy the cigarette particularly, but soon started looking forward to the shout of "Smoko," and the chance to sit down for a break.

Within the hour they were back on deck, this time into hold No 5 on the afterdeck, to do exactly the same spreading of dunnage as they had in hold No 1, and the remainder of the crew had in the No 3 hold. On the following day, they would start the huge task of rigging shifting boards in holds No 2 and No 4, and the preparation required for a grain cargo. For now, there were four more hours of splinter avoidance, with the added inconvenience of the propeller shaft tunnel running through the centre of the hold.

The tunnel stood some six to seven feet high, and therefore necessitated the throwing of fifty per cent of the dunnage over the top of it, which in turn produced an enormous cloud of choking dust, a relic from a previous cargo of anthracite or something similar. The dust then almost obscured the light from the clusters hanging in the tween deck, and in addition stuck to their sweating faces and bodies, giving them the appearance of the male cast of *The Black & White Minstrel Show*. Five o'clock could not come fast enough, and even the smoko halfway through the afternoon did not seem like much of a break from the awful conditions.

At five o'clock Mike raced for the shower, changed into uniform and headed for the dining saloon and another three-course meal. Unbelievably he was ready for the meal, and gobbled it down gratefully before returning to the cabin, grabbing his warm weather gear and making his way to the bridge for the remaining two hours of his watch.

The watch passed peacefully enough, and although they were only few days out from the UK the temperature was changing. He found that he didn't need as much clothing as he had before. The other major change was the spectacular sunsets as they sailed at a steady twelve or thirteen knots towards the Caribbean. There were wonderful golds, reds and indigo as the sun moved slowly below the horizon.

The sunset gave him his first opportunity to do something about his real reason for being there. The Mate sent him up onto the monkey island above the bridge to take a bearing on the setting Sun. At last, he felt he was moving towards the day when he would stand on his own bridge. With no protection against the wind on the monkey island, his eyes watered as he turned the screw knob that would allow him to lower the image of the sun in the prism onto the compass rose. He took a few minutes deciphering the black figures. Eventually he shouted "Stop," down the voice-pipe connecting the monkey island to the wheelhouse, and the Mate in the chartroom noted the time on the chronometer. After consulting the tables, he would be able to determine the compass error.

CHAPTER 5

On the following morning, the work that was hated by all started. It had been one of the sole topics of conversation since details of the cargo they were to load was announced. The rigging of the shifting boards in holds No 2 and No 4. The shifting boards would be rigged as a separator down the middle of the hold stretching from the tween deck at the top to half way between the tween deck and the deck of the hold. The boards themselves were twelve feet long, fifteen inches high and three and a half inches thick. They were extremely heavy and difficult to move around, particularly when it came to lowering them into their slots, down the hold and more especially if there were any movement of the ship.

The idea of using shifting boards was simply to help counteract any movement there may be of a grain cargo when the ship was rolling heavily. Prior to their invention, many ships were lost when the cargo shifted almost like liquid, and caused the ship to capsize. It was also necessary to build a feeder between the main deck and the tween deck by boxing in the area with heavy timber. When filled to the top with grain, it would feed the main hold and allow the cargo to settle down, so not dropping below the level of the bottom of the shifting boards.

At 0700 hrs the crew, together with the apprentices, assembled on deck and separated into the same teams as before. The majority of the crew headed for No 4 hold, and the remainder moved into No 2. Once again, they rigged clusters and descended into the tween deck. All the timber together with huge tie bars, cables and bottle screws were lashed to the bulkhead, where they had been stowed following the last occasion *La Cordillera* had carried a grain cargo.

As the required components were taken down, the air was filled once again with a huge dust cloud that reduced them to spluttering and coughing. The tie bars and bottle screws had been heavily caked with grease before being stowed away, and the grease had samples of the last three or four cargoes sticking to it. Mike had already worked out what their first job was going to be, and he was not disappointed. He was sent to get a container of paraffin and some rags to clean up the threads of the tie bars and bottle screws.

By the time they stopped for breakfast at 0800 hrs, he and Paul were covered in grease, dirty paraffin, anthracite and several other unspecified versions of gunge. The bottle screws, cables and tie bars had probably never looked better. Breakfast seemed to come and go with almost indecent haste. They were far too dirty to go into the saloon, so the four of them ate on the hatch cover outside the galley. Working from 0400 hrs certainly gave Mike an appetite, and he found no trouble going through the menu with seconds on the flapjacks and toast.

The weather was warming up, and sitting on the hatch was a pleasant way of relaxing and getting some fresh air before returning to the semi-darkness and dirt of the hold. In addition, a strong swell had built up and she was now rolling a steady fifteen degrees to each side. This was guaranteed to cause lots of amusement in the hold while they were trying to erect the heavy boards and steelwork for the shifting boards, and with this thought, they headed back to No 2 hold.

Alongside the ship were a large school of dolphins, the first Mike and Phil had ever seen. They watched as they swam ahead of the ship, criss-crossing from one side to the other, dropping back alongside one minute, then surging ahead the next. The sheer speed and grace of the fish kept them standing there, unable to take their eyes off them, until summoned by the Mate who had come to join and supervise the work party.

The work involved seemed to grow by the minute, first the hatch tarpaulins and wooden covers had to come off the hold, and then a single derrick rigged and lifted to act as a crane for the heavier steelwork. The first part of this was the lifting of a hatch cover beam in the tween deck, Mike and Paul fixed a hook on each end of the beam together with ropes to stop it swinging when lifted.

The winch started to lift, and pulled the beam clear of the

edge of the hatch and immediately the ship rolled and a half ton of steel was swinging crazily out of control, counteracted only by the apprentices hanging on the two ropes. For a few minutes, they were dragged around the tween deck, fighting to regain control and avoid the drop into the hold that would spell almost certain death. The other apprentices and crewmembers ran to help them, and after the beam had swung for several minutes over the chasm below, they were able to straighten it out and lower it into its slots across the hold.

As soon as they had time to get their breath, the Bosun took them aside and offered a piece of advice that Mike never forgot. "Remember lad, one hand for the company, and one hand for yourself." It was to prove useful on more than one occasion.

The huge steel upright that connected the beam they had just put into position to the hold deck came next. Once again, this had to be dragged out of the tween deck, and when lowered into the hold swung like a huge pendulum. Quickly they grabbed it and six of them held it whilst it was bolted to the flange on the deck, and the beam above. The cables and bottle screws that Mike and Paul had worked on early in the morning had then to be rigged to hold the upright in position after it had been bolted to both the hold deck and the beam.

The two-inch wire cable took a lot of lifting when

accompanied by its bottle screws and shackles. Slowly they took it in turns to climb a ladder and shackle the cable first to the upright and then to the hold bulkhead. After connecting the starboard side, they started on the port, until both sides were hanging like huge circus slack wires. Then taking a large marlinspike, they started to tighten the giant bottle screws, all the time clinging on as the ship rolled first one way and then the other. Eventually the cables were bar tight, and ready for the thousands of tons of grain they were going to have to withstand. The hatch was covered up and battened down, the derrick lowered and made secure. And all this before lunch.

When they returned from lunch, the actual shifting boards had to be fitted. The hold had returned to the gloom of the previous days with the eerie light from the clusters. Without a doubt, this was the most dangerous of the jobs involved in preparing the ship for a grain cargo. The huge boards had to be stacked at the side of the hold and then one by one dragged out to the centre and lowered into the slots in the upright and the central bulkheads.

This involved one person sitting on and sliding out along the metal beam that ran athwartships across the hold, gripping tightly with their knees and ankles and at the same time dragging the heavy board out into the centre of the hold. This had to be achieved without pulling their colleague at the other end into the hold. The board was cradled in two lengths of rope, one at either end, dragged to the middle of the hold and when it reached the centre point, lowered into its slots.

On the face of it, this seemed like a relatively simple job, but inevitably as they tried to withstand the movement of the ship the board was lowered at different rates, causing it to jam in the metal channel of the uprights. Considerable effort was needed to straighten it. Equally inevitable was the need occasionally to let go to avoid the huge drop into the hold. This could only be achieved if you first shouted to your colleague at the other end to let go quickly, so that they could also avoid being dragged down by the weight of the huge board.

This usually led to the use of a range of expletives, as one by one all the apprentices narrowly avoided the drop, either from the beam or the hold edge. Then came the equally difficult job of lifting the heavy board from the hold deck back into position. The ropes cut into hands already sore and calloused from dragging the boards, and the splinters previously received from the dunnage. The expletives continued to flow from everyone with the exception of Phil, who had never been heard to swear since joining the ship.

Slowly, board by board, the huge wooden wall started to take shape. Half the boards were eventually slotted into the forward end. Then they starting on the after section, repeating the same process until the halfway mark was reached, when the decision was taken to call it a day and they could drag themselves back to their cabins. They were cheered by the thought that the weekend was coming. They hoped for a break in the unremitting routine of working in the holds, and Sunday represented an extra day's pay.

If Mike had thought that the weekend would be a rest, he was about to be further disillusioned. As soon as it became light on Saturday, the Mate pointed out all the cleaning that was needed in the wheelhouse. The wooden deck had to be scrubbed, and the windows were caked in salt and had to be washed and polished. Much worse than this was the huge amount of brass that had to be polished. The compass binnacle, engine room telegraph, ship's bell and dozens of other small brass plates, handles etc.. He set to with the Brasso and a rough textured serge flag, which was perfect for the job. By the time he was relieved, all the brass was gleaming.

On Sunday, they had to start work on their cabins and bathroom, in readiness for the Captain's Sunday inspection. Once again, the decks needed scrubbing, the brass portholes required polishing together with all the woodwork, and in general it had to appear that the cabins were not lived in. When the cabins were completed, the bathroom was started on, mirrors, taps and showerhead polished, every nook and cranny of the lavatory scrubbed.

Similar activity was going on in every cabin and working

area of the ship, as the time for the start of the inspection drew near. In fact, the ritual was in all probability being observed on every British Merchant Navy vessel around the world. The seasoned sailors told stories about the Captains who carried out their inspections wearing white gloves, and woe betide anyone whose cabins caused him to dirty his gloves when running them along the tops of their lockers. The more fanciful knew of sailors who stuck razor blades on the edge of their lockers, with predictable results.

At 1115 hrs the Captain, together with Chief Officer and Chief Steward, entered the amidships accommodation and slowly made their way to the apprentices' cabins. Not a word was uttered by the Captain, as he inspected in far more detail than in previous cabins. The Mate nodded approvingly as he left. A great sigh of relief was breathed by all.

Shortly after the inspection, they donned their uniforms and headed for the saloon. Whilst the food on board was reasonably good, Sunday was always special at sea with roast chicken followed by tinned fruit. Preceding these delights was the first variation of the new soup of the week, extremely thin chicken soup. The cook prepared one large stockpot of soup on Sunday and this was then the base of all soup throughout the week. Chicken Noodle on Monday, followed by Vegetable on Tuesday, Tomato on Wednesday and so on until Friday's Brown Windsor and then, only for the bravest souls, a thick throat burning, sweat producing

Mulligatawny on Saturday.

For the first time since leaving Southampton, they had an afternoon to themselves, or what remained of it if not on watch. Officially this was supposed to be for studying, but as they had not had chance to wash or iron any clothes since leaving, this became laundry time, a completely new experience for Mike who had never washed or ironed any clothes in his life before then. He considered whether rigging shifting boards was preferable to this, and found the choice very hard.

Before starting his watch and whilst waiting for the hot water geyser to boil Mike stood by the rail on the afterdeck and reflected on his first Sunday at sea. The morning had dawned much warmer still and the sea had calmed dramatically. On its surface were large clumps of Sargasso weed. Centuries ago, this was supposed to hold unwary mariners in the Sargasso Sea, growing over their ships and causing the slow lingering death of all on board. On the crest of the waves caused by the ship's movement through the water, was an incredible spectacle. Flying fish glided along for many feet before landing back in the sea, the sun glistening off their iridescent bodies. Mike had previously doubted their existence, but there was no doubting the performance unfolding before him, and he regretted leaving the scene.

Overall, the Sunday at sea had been the most pleasant day

that he had experienced since leaving home. Even the watch was more relaxed. The Mate came out on the bridge wing and chatted about Mike's ambitions. He asked him lots of questions about his home and past experiences. In return, he told him far more about Buries Markes than he had heard before. The different ships he was likely to be appointed to, bulk ore carriers, Lakes cargo liners, ships specialising in carrying Volkswagen cars to the USA, and lots more of the type of ship he was on. The point of the conversation being that if he signed indentures and served his time with the company, he could expect a fast track to his own command. The average age for Captains, having served their time with the company, was in the region of 28 or 29 years.

After their conversation Mike reverted to his normal lookout at the far end of the wing, the sun was setting on the starboard quarter in an ever more stunning sequence of colours, and Mike watched with astonishment until it finally dropped below the horizon as a huge fiery ruby ball. The whole 360 degree horizon started to take on the most incredible colours from all sections of the spectrum, which gradually deepened in their intensity until night finally took over.

For the first time since leaving home, his mind was filled with thoughts of his family and friends back in Bridlington and the wish that they could be here to see this spectacle. He calculated the time back in the UK and where he would have been if he had been there. Sunday evening usually meant church followed by the youth club and a walk to one of two cafes in the town.

They virtually always moved around as a group, two to three boys and five or six girls, which seemed to Mike to be the most enjoyable ratio possible. They would spend a boisterous hour drinking expresso coffees before moving off in the direction of their homes. They had been a group for some two years, and spent each weekend together, along with holidays and free time. Up until now they had resisted any urge there may have been to pair off and so ruin the benefits of the large group. But with Mike's departure, this would not last. Already Jono, his best friend, had started spending a large amount of his time with Alison. If he was totally honest, Mike was hoping to start a more personal relationship with Jacqui. This however would have to wait until his return, assuming that someone else did not beat him to it. That thought upset him, and caused him to re-examine his love life to date. To refer to Mike's experience as his love life, was something of a gross exaggeration, there had only been three girls in his life so far, and each had been a relatively chaste relationship.

Mike was brought back to reality when Paul tapped him on the shoulder as he came to relieve him for his watch. He looked around the now totally black horizon, and was grateful that no ships had appeared whilst his mind was so far away.

The temperature on the next day had continued its rise as they approached The Bahamas and The Florida Strait. The fact that they were now in the lee of the mainland was the reason for the almost glassy sea. The sea state was particularly welcome whilst they continued rigging the shifting boards, but the temperature was causing them to sweat prolifically, certainly a change from the UK in January.

The practice they had already, together with the flat calm, made the completion of the wall much easier than previously, and by lunch time that part of the work was finished. Next came the construction of the feeder. Similar sized boards had to be placed in slots to form a vertical wall stretching from the edge of the hold in the tween deck, to the deck head above, and extending right around the hold on all four sides. When all sides were complete, an enormous tie bar was run through the middle and long flat steel bars holding the boards together were slotted onto the tie bar before two huge nuts were fitted onto the threads, and tightened with an equally large shifting spanner. With a great sigh of relief, and an extra long smoking break, they celebrated that at long last she was almost ready to receive the planned cargo.

All that was left to do in the holds where the grain would be carried was to cover the bilge boards to ensure that grain could not seep down into the bilges. Failure to do this would mean tons of wet stinking grain to be cleared out by hand on the next voyage. According to Tony, who had experienced the problem on *M/V La Orilla*, it was not a job to be recommended. A huge roll of heavy brown paper was lowered into the hold together with wooden battens to fix the paper to the wooden boards and the rest of the day was spent nailing the battens over the paper, into the boards.

During his watch that evening, Mike was able to see the lights of Miami on the starboard side as they neared the Florida Keys and the entrance to the Caribbean. The excitement was mounting as they were now within two days of their destination: New Orleans.

Mike had hoped there may be some respite after the sixteen-hour days they had worked since leaving Southampton. As always, an eternal optimist, he was brought back to reality when on the following morning they were issued with buckets, cloths and a measure of Teepol. The instructions was to start on the forward accommodation block, and wash all the paintwork in preparation for painting.

They started on the bridge deck washing all the salt off the white paint. He had not really noticed how much white paint there was until then, but there appeared to be acres of it. The next deck down had an even larger expanse of white paint, and below that, the main deck had more still. They spent the whole day washing the paintwork, in the knowledge that on the next day they would have to paint all the area they had washed. When that was done the amidships accommodation would need to be tackled. By comparison, the time they had spent in the holds preparing for the cargo seemed enjoyable.

The following day, as promised, they were each issued with large paint kettles, a range of brushes, rollers, trays and a five-gallon drum of white gloss. The numbingly boring job was made bearable by the glorious Caribbean sunshine. They set to with a will to complete at least the forward accommodation block before arriving at their first port of call. By lunch time, they were covered in paint. Their faces, hair and clothes all bore testimony to the speed at which they were working.

After lunching on the hatch top, they made their way to their bathroom to attempt to move some of the paint from their hair and faces. As a last resort, they filled a washbasin with paraffin and washed their hair in it to shift the paint. The burning on their scalps was a warning that this was possibly not the best way of washing their hair. They washed off the paraffin with a bar of Lifebuoy, and returned to the painting confident that they had found a solution to the problem.

Following a Herculean effort from the apprentices, the end of the day's work saw the sides and rear of the forward block finished. Either in port, or after leaving Galveston, the front of the bridge and the accommodation would have to be painted. This would involve rigging stages, which could be lowered from the wheelhouse level. But before that, the Mate had already decided that the time in port would be spent painting the ship's side, rather than the superstructure. The only difference this meant to the apprentices was that their hair and faces would be black rather than white.

When Mike was called for his watch the following morning, he was aware that something was different, but couldn't put his finger on what it was. He was dressed and on his way to make the tea before realising that the vibration was non-existent and the huge engine was moving very slowly, meaning one thing. They must be near their destination.

He rushed out onto deck in time to see the Pilot board and ahead of them the lights marking the start of the mighty Mississippi. With the Pilot on the bridge, they moved slowly between the lights and began a steady journey up river. Mike was lost for words for a moment, his mind racing through everything he had heard and read about this famous river. Only gradually it registered with him that he was indeed sailing up the Mississippi. Through the gloom that was gradually manifesting itself into a new dawn, he could see the incredible wetlands of the Mississippi delta, stretching as far as the eye could see on either side. They were just one hundred miles from his first real experience of the United States, the port of New Orleans.

CHAPTER 6

Mike only had a short time to get used to the idea that he was indeed about to enter the United States. "All Hands on Deck" was called, and the crew together with apprentices dragged themselves forward in the early morning light to ready the ship for its arrival in port. The huge manila mooring ropes had to be dragged from the rope locker to the windlass and thence using the electric winch to the forward end of the forecastle.

The combination ropes following these were a mixture of rope and wire. Because of the tendency for the thin individual strands of wire to part, they were the worst to handle. When running through your hands, the jags would embed themselves in the skin penetrating to a considerable depth and causing severe damage. Wearing working gloves with these ropes could be even more lethal, as they would catch in the glove and drag the wearer into a winch or other dangerous situation. The effects on a ring wearer didn't even bear contemplation.

After the combinations came the springs, hundred percent wire ropes with a will of their own. They were less than a third of the thickness of the manilas, with similar strength, but they did not have the elasticity of the rope. They were the first to break in a crisis where the ship's movement could not be halted and the full weight of the ship moved against the ropes. When they parted, it was very quick and the whipping this caused could easily cut a person in half. In addition, because of their composition of wires all running in the same direction, they were difficult to coil down on the deck and much energy had to be expelled in taking the turns out of the coils.

Once the ropes were prepared and fenders brought out onto the deck, it was time to rig the derricks for all of the five holds. The derricks were long steel booms, two to each hold, that were connected by blocks and heavy wires to the electric winches. In port, they acted as cranes to load and unload cargoes, with one derrick directly over the hold and the other over the dockside. The cargo was lifted off the dockside by one winch, and pulled over the hold by the winch on the other derrick, then lowered into the hold.

Before the derricks could be used, they had to be raised from their clamped horizontal sea-going position, to one of forty-five degrees, or less. This was a hazardous operation, as the derricks were very heavy and had to be lifted by attaching the wire that ran all the way up to the Samson posts or the crosstrees on the mast, to the end of the derrick, to the winch drum. After putting three or four turns on the drum, the derrick started to lift.

When it reached the right height, a short chain stopper was wound around the wire effectively taking all the weight, whilst the wire was taken off the winch and fastened onto a cleat on the Samson post. Dependent upon the way they were rigged, with blocks and tackle they could lift loads between two and five tons, and on ships with heavy lifting gear fifty tons and more.

Due to the amount of work and the speed with which it was being performed, there was no time to reflect on the size and majesty of the river they were moving along. They were still passing through the wetlands with small hamlets on either side with unusual French names, reflecting the original ownership of Louisiana. On one side in the distance, he could see the open water of Lake Borgne and on the other Lake Salvador.

However it was not until he saw, tied up alongside a jetty, the *Natchez*, a riverboat with its huge stern paddle wheel that the whole scene meant something to him. He thought back to all the Mark Twain stories of life on the Mississippi. The Showboats, the gamblers, the leadsman singing out the depth of water and the cotton bales making their way down river to New Orleans. There for decades the bales had been loaded onto ships bound for all parts of the world, as in a few hours' time they would be loaded into the holds they had been preparing over the past ten days. Somehow, the huge skyscrapers and modern warehouses they were approaching did not seem to fit the same picture.

In a very short time a tug had approached them, been made

fast and was helping them towards the kind of dock that anyone living near docks in the UK could only dream of. Clean, modern, spacious and on one level. Forklift trucks, virtually unknown on UK quaysides, were hurtling everywhere stacking cotton bales as they prepared for *La Cordillera*. The tug edged the ship towards the dock, and the crew and apprentices took up the positions they had held when leaving Southampton, fore and aft. Mike collected a heaving line from the locker, and coiled it neatly into his left hand as he had been shown. He split the coils into two even coils, making one end fast to the heavy manila stern line.

The coil that had been finished with a large monkey's fist knot he placed in his right hand and the other coil in his left. As soon as he felt he could reach the quayside he hurled the coil in his right hand towards a dockworker who caught it first time and started to drag the stern line towards the quay, with the help of his colleagues. Within minutes, the same operation had been performed with two more stern lines and a spring, and in the same way on the forecastle with the bow lines. *La Cordillera* was securely moored fore and aft. Within seconds of all the lines being made fast, there was a clanging of the engine room telegraph as "Finished with engines" was rung. They had arrived in the United States.

The accommodation ladder was swung out from its storage area on the ship's side, rigged with stanchions and ropes until it resembled a gangway. Only then was it lowered onto the quayside and a long procession of officials began to board the ship: customs, immigration, health, security and the ship's agent bearing the most important documents of all, the mail. Mike was amazed to see how many people found it necessary to carry guns as part of their official uniform.

He was even more startled when the health authorities sealed all the refrigerated areas of the ship to ensure that no unhealthy British food was consumed whilst in the United States or its waters. On the plus side, this meant a return to fresh milk, instead of the evaporated and condensed versions they been drinking since leaving home.

Presently the whole crew was called into the dining saloon for inspection by the health authorities. A variety of stories were recalled as to what form the inspection would take, varying from an inspection of a very personal nature, jokingly referred to as a "short arm inspection" to a simple verbal questioning. In the end, it was the latter. Moving from table to table they slowly completed all the formalities and were eventually awarded their Alien Crewmen Landing Permits.

The Chief Officer had completely lost his patience with the different authorities over the time they were taking to complete the formalities and the holding up of the crew. He announced to all present "America is built on bullshit surrounded by water and that is why it is sinking fast". Needless to say, he was not given his landing permit and an armed guard was put on the gangway to ensure he could not go ashore. As a regular visitor to the United States, he was not at all worried by this.

By the time the formalities had been completed, the ship looked as if it had been invaded. Teams of stevedores had come aboard and stripped the hatches of their covers and hatch boards, and were in the process of lifting out the beams prior to loading. In addition, something that Mike had completely forgotten about was very much in operation. A colour bar. The holds on the fore deck were all being worked by totally white crews of stevedores, whereas the afterdeck had black crews.

Mike was of the opinion that this kind of thing did not happen anymore. But quite clearly, these teams were not going to mix in any way. He had never experienced anything like this before and in reality had never met any Afro-Americans before. His own home town was limited to one half Asian/half English family and even in Hull he had not noticed any coloured people.

Together with Paul, he ventured onto the afterdeck and was greeted warmly by two huge black stevedores who were directing the winch men loading the first of the thousands of cotton bales into the cavernous holds. They wanted to know where in England they came from and about life there in general. They, along with most other Americans they were to meet, were genuinely interested in England and anything connected with it. Many had served in the US forces during the war and spoke very warmly of their time there. They were a bit shaken by the language of the stevedores. After his experience on the trawler, and having been in the Merchant Navy for all of three weeks, Mike thought he was familiar with most types of swearing, but the constant addition of mother fucking to the description of everything and everybody came as a shock even to him.

They spent as much time as possible away from the eyes of the Mate and the Bosun, wandering through the tween decks, watching the cotton being swung aboard and lowered into the depths of the holds, onto the dunnage which had been prepared for them. The bales were manhandled to the hold extremities until they met in the centre and the second layer was started. After about five days, the whole of three of the holds plus the tween decks in the other two holds would be filled with cotton and they would leave for Galveston. In the meantime, he had to enjoy the delights of New Orleans with the princely sum of $12. This was the maximum that the cadets were allowed to draw from their wages. At £9 3s 4d a month they had only earned around £6 for their work to date, with stoppages and an exchange rate of $2.72 to the pound that was the best they could hope for. But before they could hit New

Orleans, they had a day's work to do and the most enjoyable experience of all, the distribution of the mail.

The ship's agent delivered the mail to the Captain, and it was sorted and distributed by the Chief Steward, who enjoyed his few minutes of extreme popularity. All work amongst the ship's officers and crew had effectively stopped as soon as the mail left the Captain's cabin, and they waited impatiently for their names to be called by the Chief Steward. Due to them only having left the UK a couple of weeks ago, there was not the usual amount of Mail. There were many disappointed faces around as the pile shrunk and finally there were no more letters remaining.

Mike had received one letter from his Mother updating him with the goings-on in Bridlington and containing pieces written under duress from his brothers and sister. Although he would love to be home, the thought of Bridlington in January with the snow his Mother had written about did not compare with the Louisiana sunshine he was currently enjoying.

They were not given much time to think about their contact with home, as they could hear the distinctive walk of the Bosun with his artificial leg coming down the alleyway towards them. They had never been able to hear this when the engine was running. Despite the excitement of being in America, the painting of the superstructure and areas where they would not be in the way of the stevedoring gangs still had to be carried out. They headed for the forecastle and collected paint kettle and brushes. They set to work with a will buoyed by the fact that with the exception of Tony, who was on night watch, they were now on day work and would finish at five o'clock, with no work until seven in the morning. New Orleans beckoned.

By five o'clock, they had cleared away the painting tackle, cleaned themselves up with white spirit and quickly headed for the shower. They dressed casually but smartly and made their way to the gangway. As they approached the gangway, the Mate passed them, heading for his dinner and an evening in his cabin.

"Don't go near any cat houses," he shouted, with a cheerful wave as the three of them made their descent. Mike gave this remark some thought as they walked off the dock. He had never really been a cat lover, more a dog sort of person, and wondered why the Mate had thought otherwise.

They were impressed with the cleanliness of the dock area by comparison with the UK, and the openness. No Police, no barbed wire, in fact very little to stop anyone coming onto the dock. At the end of the dock was a bus stop where they could catch a bus to the city centre. The bus arrived within a few minutes; a single decker with a driver operated door on the right hand side. This was new to them. Next, they faced the question of where did they want to go, and the three of them looked at each other and brashly asked for the main drag.

"Canal Street?" asked the driver. Not wishing to show their ignorance, they nodded.

The skyscrapers became ever more imposing as they neared the city itself, the neon lights became more numerous and the number of huge cars grew by the second. They were almost open-mouthed as the driver announced Canal Street. They stood for a second, motionless on the sidewalk as the bus pulled away, surveying the scene around them, their senses assaulted by all the colour, noise and light. This was everything Mike had seen in the movies, but somehow much, much more.

They walked from one end of the street to the other, stopping like small children at every shop, diner, bar and building, looking through the windows and calculating their prices in Sterling. Despite their age, all three of them had been in pubs in the UK. Here there was no chance. The bars looked very unwelcoming, with few if any women and no coloured customers. To gain access you would be required to produce evidence that you were at least twenty-one and even then the chances of enjoying the chemical beer, such as Schlitz and Budweiser were unlikely, after being used to the heavy British beers.

Mike decided to invest in a Zippo lighter, as seen in all

good American movies. Its large flame suitable for lighting on the bridge wing and lifetime guarantee particularly appealed to him. After looking at all the stock, he selected a plain brushed stainless steel model, which also happened to be the cheapest in the store. They picked their way through a large selection of postcards, selected a few and then purchased a few souvenirs before heading for a diner. As they sat down in the chrome, plastic and Formica surroundings, they were served with iced water, and pretty soon their orders for Coke and indescribably luxurious strawberry shortcake covered in fresh strawberries were in front of them. Buddy Holly's new release *That'll be the day* blared from the jukebox, and they considered whether the hard work had been worth it. After several Cokes and even more shortcake, they decided it was.

Presently they had stuffed themselves fully with Cokes, shortcake and milk shakes, the like of which they had never seen before. They were made with large quantities of ice cream and so thick that it left you breathless attempting to suck it up a straw. The time had come to return to the ship. They decided they would like to save money for a second night ashore, and work off what they had eaten, by walking back to the docks. Mike had always been convinced that he had an in-built navigation system, and had never been known to get lost, so he volunteered to lead the way.

They had walked for almost an hour when Mike recognised

a building they had passed on the bus. This gave him renewed confidence in his ability to return them to the ship. Shortly afterwards they saw pallet loads of cargo, forklift trucks and some familiar warehouses. A few minutes later, there was the dock exactly as he had pictured when memorising the return route. Only one thing spoilt the picture of the dock that he held in his memory, no *La Cordillera*.

The shock hit all three of them at the same time. What had happened to cause the ship to move? What was going to happen to them? How would they ever return to England? They stood and looked in disbelief for a minute or two, and then it slowly dawned on them. The dock was an absolute mirror image of the one *La Cordillera* was berthed in. Even the sheds bore the same numbers. But where was the correct dock? After talking to several natives, they found the answer. It was a further two miles down the road.

Cheered by this news and the lifting from their shoulders of the worry of how to get home, they set out to cover the two miles as quickly as possible. Forty minutes later, they were back on board ship relating their adventures to Tony, who would be able to go to the city as soon as he finished night watch at seven o'clock, or after he had slept.

Refreshed by their evening ashore they painted with even more vigour than before as the Mate had given them a job and finish on the painting of the port side of the forward accommodation. They completed the work by 3 o'clock and were showered, dressed and ashore by 4 o'clock. Once again, they travelled on the bus into the centre, with the intention of walking back and once again they made the most of the different diners they found. Eventually they had eaten and drunk as much as possible, purchased as many souvenirs and presents as they could afford and started the walk back to the ship. They took a slightly different route on this occasion, through a less populated and seedier area. They didn't recognise it, but they were convinced they would get back to the docks.

Ahead of them two young and quite attractive girls blocked the sidewalk. If one was to be cruel, they were a bit underdressed for where they were, and their make-up was rather heavy. The three excused themselves as they moved between the two girls, who picked up immediately on the English accent and responded by asking if they wanted a good time. Phil and Mike considered the offer for a second, oblivious to its significance. Fortunately, Paul had been abroad with the company before and whispered, "They're whores," and kept moving down the road. Mike and Phil followed him after politely declining the girls' offer. They were fascinated by this addition to their education. Subsequently they met several more girls during their walk, all offering the same good time.

The following day they related their experiences to one of the foreman stevedores, who laughingly pointed out that they had walked through the cat house region of New Orleans. Only then did the Mate's warning about cat houses mean something to Mike.

On the third day in port, the holds were reaching capacity. Thousands of bales had been loaded and neatly stacked in the lower holds. It was now time for the tween decks, as each of the three lower holds were covered up with hatch boards to form a platform for the bales. The bales were manhandled through into the tween decks of the holds that had been prepared for the grain cargo to more evenly spread the weight around the ship. Although the air temperature on deck was quite pleasant, the heat in the hold was almost unbearable, and the reason for the laying of the dunnage athwartships became obvious. The temperature in the centre of the lower holds must have been something akin to a very hot sauna. Although the cotton would absorb the sweating from the bales, the bulkheads would be running with sweat, which had to be channelled into the bilges and pumped out, via the engine room.

On the following day, they would complete the loading of the cotton and begin their journey round the coast to Galveston. Already the ship was very noticeably lower in the water.

Mike was fascinated by the need to transport cargoes from one part of the world to another. He took every opportunity he had to visit his Father's ship in dock in Hull. Every year the school Geographical Society had a visit to Hull docks, and each year the first name on the list would be Mike's. He would watch, enthralled, the unloading of wool from Australia in King George Dock, together with timber from Canada and Scandinavia, grain from America and the revolting smelling wet hides from Africa. Without fail, he would be the last boy to board the bus home.

By the time they had finished lunch, the last of the bales were being loaded. The No 3 hold was being battened down and No 1 and No 5 were not far behind. The bales of cotton were crammed in to the point where the beams on which the hatch boards rested were virtually touching the bales. This made the replacing of the hatch boards much easier than normal. As soon as the hatches were covered, the stevedores left to board the ship moored ahead of them and the crew was left to make the ship ready for sea. The derricks were lowered back into their clamps and all the blocks and tackle connected to them tightened along the length of them and neatly coiled down.

Promptly at three o'clock, a tug arrived alongside and the Pilot boarded. The crew went to their stations for leaving port, the telegraph rang "Stand by," and within minutes they had singled up to a single head and stern line and springs. The tug took the strain on the port bow and the forward lines were let go, as she moved very slowly astern on the spring, which helped to pull the bow to port. The stern line was let go and as she started to move out into the dock. Finally the spring line taken in. Within a short time, they were heading back down the Mississippi bound for Texas.

The Pilot left during Mike's watch. They had needed to rig an extension when leaving Southampton, but now they required only a few rungs to leave the ladder clear of the water. Once again, the whole operation was very quick. The pilot launch approached at speed and timed its run to coincide with Mike escorting the Pilot onto the deck. With a cheerful "Have a good voyage," he was on his way. As the telegraph rang "Full ahead", Mike stowed the ladder away and returned to his watch on the bridge via the hot water geyser in the after mast house.

The rest of his watch was far more interesting than normal. They were close to the land and would not be out of sight of the land all the way to Galveston. He took bearings every half-hour on the different lighthouses from the monkey island. The Mate plotted their position and confirmed it with the radar. At the least, it made Mike think he was getting nearer to being a Deck Officer.

Where New Orleans had been colourful and vibrant, Galveston gave the impression of being a very drab place. They moored alongside a huge grain silo that appeared to be miles away from the nearest habitation and went through some of the same procedures they had undergone in New Orleans, although most of them were a formality. The derricks on holds No 2 and 4 were raised and swung over to one side to allow the grain elevators to position themselves over the centre of the holds on the following morning. As Phil, Paul and Mike had a small amount of money left in dollars, they headed to a roadside diner and made the most of what they had. Milk shakes, hamburgers and great coffee were first in line, and the remainder was loaded into the jukebox. They didn't know when their next night ashore would be, so they made the most of their limited resources.

The two hatches were stripped first thing in the morning, and the stevedore gangs came aboard. This time there were only three men per hold, and they were armed with what looked to Mike like surfboards made of very highly polished wood. These were trimming boards. The huge elevator pipes were lowered into the holds, and almost immediately began to spew grain at an enormous rate. Within a very short space of time, the hold floor was covered as the gang moved the flexible pipe from one side to the other, and then the wooden boards came into play.

Mike and Phil headed down into the holds to watch the amazing scene as the men held the board under the constant heavy stream of grain causing it to shoot into the furthest points of the hold. The precision with which they could control where the grain went was incredible, and they marvelled at how they were able to keep the level constant throughout the hold. The dust cloud in the hold was almost obscuring everything. They had no masks, so they were finding breathing difficult and headed up the ladder onto the main deck.

By late afternoon, both holds were full and the feeders had been topped up to ensure that the grain would not settle below the shifting boards, the hatches were covered and they made ready for sea. Mike went with the Third Mate to check the draught fore and aft. The figures in roman numerals were painted on the bow and stern six inches high to aid calculations. They calculated that she was drawing twenty-three feet forward and twenty-three foot six inches aft, an almost perfect trim. Amidships she was virtually sitting on her marks, a triumph for the Mate's original calculations, which would need no adjustments with ballast.

They cleared Galveston quickly and headed out into the Gulf of Mexico bound for where, they did not know. Rumours again had abounded as to what their next port of call would be. The consensus was that it would be a European port, probably Rotterdam or Antwerp, but all they could learn for certain were the three letters LEO, translated as Land's End for orders. When they reached Land's End, the Captain would speak to the London office and receive his instructions as to where they should proceed and where their next voyage would take them. All this would depend on the cargo being sold, possibly several times over before they reached that point.

CHAPTER 7

The weather remained sunny and warm during their passage across the Gulf and life had returned to normal after the excitement of New Orleans and Galveston. The only major change was the motion of the ship. Instead of rolling or pitching in the smallest of seas, she seemed to be driving straight through the waves with virtually no movement at all. The huge cargo was ensuring that she was very heavy in the water and that the sea was in very close proximity to the deck. Mike remembered the last occasion he had been so close to the sea on the *Rossallian*, and hoped that they would not be meeting similar sea conditions when they emerged into the Atlantic.

As soon as they had cleared Galveston, the pattern for the work on deck became apparent. The crew would be completing the painting of the exterior of the accommodation and the deckhouses, whilst the apprentices would be chipping the foredeck. Both jobs should last for the duration of the passage to Europe, assuming that they had good weather. Mike had wondered about the strange shaped hammers he had seen in the forecastle. He did not realise what an enormous part they were to have in his life as a cadet and apprentice. The ends of the hammers were shaped like a cold chisel, on one end vertical, on the other horizontal and quite simply you hit the deck with either end causing the rust to break up on the steel deck and flake off. When the rust was displaced, the area that had been chipped was scrubbed with a wire brush and then coated with boiled linseed oil until a sufficiently large area had been cleared, when it would be painted first with red lead, then primer, then a deep red deck paint.

Mike looked at the chipping hammers, and then at the enormous expanse of the foredeck. He calculated the job would last for years, rather than the ten days that the crossing should take. Once again, he was in for a surprise. The hammers were only to chip areas where the machine he was about to be introduced to could not reach.

The Bosun had dragged three large machines from the forecastle. These consisted of a large electric motor, a heavy duty six foot flexible shaft, and on the end the chipping head, a circular collection of four two inch flails mounted in blocks of three. The flail head rotated at high speed chipping the rust off the deck in a black cloud of dirty rusted steel, old paint, and primer, showering everyone and everything in the vicinity. The noise as the flails hit the deck was indescribable, and with no ear defenders to wear, they wondered if they had gone deaf when all the machines were switched off at the same time.

If they had thought working in the holds was dirty, this was worse than ever. Even with goggles on and scarves around their mouths and noses, the black filth penetrated everything. All they could taste and smell day after day was the rust; it was in their eyes, ears, noses, mouths, hair and clothes.

Even when they came out of the shower, clean at last, their hands and arms were still vibrating from the day on the machines, and they had lost most of the feeling in their fingers. No wonder the Mate and Bosun had not asked the crew to do the chipping. The four of them considered the words of the Bosun that "This experience would make them better officers one day". They were not convinced, and still believed they were being used purely as cheap labour for jobs that normal seamen would moan about.

By the time they had cleared the Gulf and set course for Europe, a large expanse of the foredeck had been chipped, oiled, red-leaded, primed and lay resplendent in its new coat of deck paint. Day after day, the noise and filth were the same. They longed for Sunday when they could have a break from the chipping, and do something mundane like cleaning the cabins and only work normal watch hours. Or even Saturday when they would clean the bridge and polish all the brass. Either were preferable as a break from chipping. They almost hoped for some bad weather that would keep them off the deck, but considered that this was going too far. But whether they hoped for it or not, it was out there in the Atlantic waiting for them.

Mike noticed the change at 0330 hrs when he was called for

his watch. She had started to pitch slightly, and there was a strange shuddering every time the bow went down. The change in the weather became very evident as soon as he ventured out onto the afterdeck to make the tea. Water was running alongside the accommodation and the afterdeck, still frothing. He dived for the mast house and made it before the next water flushed down the deck. He waited for a few minutes for the geyser to boil and then made the tea.

Until the tea was made, he had not considered how he was going to get it up to the bridge. The water was pouring down both alleyways and it was hard to tell which was the lee side. He elected to take the starboard side and darted back into the accommodation, walking the length of it until he reached the forward end. He opened the door into the starboard alleyway and went to step over the deep sill, but then jumped back quickly as a large amount of water shot past him.

After standing for a few minutes, he thought he had timed it to perfection and he stepped out onto the deck only to be nearly washed the length of the starboard alleyway. Eventually after several very wet attempts, he worked out the way the water was moving and shot out of the door like a sprinter out of his blocks. He ran the length of the No 3 hold, and dived just in time for the ladder leading to the bridge. The water passed under him as he headed up the next ladder to the safety of the wheelhouse. He poured two pint mugs of tea, added the condensed milk and sugar and handed one to the Mate. "This tea's a bit cold," said the Mate.

As he took his place out on the bridge wing, he was greeted by a wall of spray and tried in vain to protect his mug of tea. The reason for all the water became immediately apparent. As they had moved out into the Atlantic, the sea state had changed from a gentle swell to fairly large waves. She was pitching into each wave, and every time the bow went down tons of water broke over the forecastle and ran down the decks. With each wave, a huge wall of spray covered the foredeck and the bridge accommodation. Mike, despite the water running off his face, thought only of the fact that they would not be chipping the deck today.

The watch passed slowly as he waited for dawn to break. He had been immersed in the continuous spray for two hours when it did. The water was running down his neck and soaking into his clothes, but this was a small price to pay for a day off day work. He had worked out that they could not carry on chipping with the water breaking over the deck, and they would not be able to reach the forecastle to collect paint, cleaning gear or tools for the same reason. Probably he should have known better, but he spent the remaining time thinking how he was going to spend his day. The Mate telling him to call his colleagues so that they could spend the day cleaning all the brass work on the bridge and scrubbing out the wheelhouse brought him down to Earth.

On the face of it there did not appear to be an enormous amount of brass on the bridge. Two engine room telegraphs, the ship's bell, rudder indicator, compass binnacle, and surrounds to all of the windows. In reality, this was major work. The internal telegraph stood over four feet high, and was solid brass with the exception of the two faces repeating the engine speeds. The internal one had been cleaned on a weekly basis along with much of the other brass, but outside the wheelhouse on the bridge wing was the second telegraph that had not been cleaned in years. It was green, salt caked, and in all probability when it was last cleaned it had been varnished to protect it from the salt air. This would now entail polishing off the varnish film with wire wool before tackling the brass with Brasso.

They set to work with a will in the wheelhouse and the chart room until every piece of brass gleamed like newly smelted gold. Even the brass inlays within the ship's wheel and the chart table gleamed. But the harder they worked, the nearer they got to the inevitable time when the outside telegraph would have to be tackled.

After lunch, the inevitable could not be put off any longer. Phil and Mike, their fingers still aching from the morning's polishing, collected some wire wool from the store together with a further tin of Brasso and headed for the port wing of the bridge. They soaked wads of wire wool with the Brasso and started scrubbing the brass, for what seemed like ages there was no change to the horribly discoloured surface.

After a considerable time rubbing the same area, a small light coloured patch started to appear. After applying further pressure on the wire wool, the area almost imperceptibly started to grow until an hour or so later they had completed everything except the telegraph top, handles and faces.

By five o'clock, the telegraph was finished and stood gleaming. They debated what to do with it now it was clean, as it was obvious that with the spray from the pitching of the ship it would not stay gleaming for very long. One solution would be to varnish it, but this seemed to defeat everything they had spent the afternoon doing. So they applied a light film of grease to protect it in the hopes that this would come off with white spirit each week to enable them to keep it polished. They headed for the shower, determined to shift some of the ingrained filth from their hands and faces, before presenting themselves in the saloon for dinner.

Within three quarters of an hour, Mike was back on the bridge for his evening watch. His fingers were so sore that he had trouble spinning the wheel on his newly acquired Zippo to light his cigarette. For a moment, he considered what it would be like to be on a ship owned by a company who looked upon apprentices as embryonic Deck Officers, and treated them accordingly. Being schooled in navigation, mathematics, signalling and seamanship seemed like a good idea, with maybe a bit of fraternisation with passengers thrown in for good measure. Mike had heard stories about fraternisation with passengers on the long crossings to Australia and New Zealand from a Radio Officer friend in Bridlington. It seemed like a very good life to him.

His friend had told him of how he had brought a lady passenger back to his cabin late at night only to find the lady whom he had escorted on the previous evening in bed waiting for him. It seemed to beat chipping decks, rigging shifting boards and polishing brass. But if he were clairvoyant and able to see what was in store for them on *La Cordillera*, he would have settled for his lot without hesitation.

The sea had calmed slightly during the day and she was no longer pounding into the waves, just pitching gently. The sun was setting in another fabulous display of all the colours of the rainbow, the evening was warm and he had a further two hours to kill on lookout before the end of his watch. He considered his career to date and his mind went back to the school he had left only seven weeks before.

Mike probably would never be able to say that his school days were the happiest of his life, but from what he had seen so far of working life they were the easiest. Although he was proud of the wonderful grammar school he had been to, he was by no means proud of the time he had spent there. He had taken his eleven plus exam very late, after being ill on the day of the original exams. The illness was probably caused by severe fright at the thought of the exams. He was ill on the day that he subsequently took the exams, and spent the lunch break doubled-up in pain.

Although his parents had only ever considered a place at the grammar school, Mike had never believed he would get there. It was no surprise when he saw on his teacher's desk the list of boys who would be attending the secondary modern school from September. It included his name. He did not have the heart to tell his Mother what he had accidentally seen. He hoped that it would go away, or that at least he could enjoy the holidays before the news broke officially. He was therefore totally amazed when returning from the harbour one day, his visiting older cousin ran down the road towards him shouting, "You've passed, you've passed!"

Sure enough, there was a letter congratulating him on passing his scholarship and advising him that he would be starting at Bridlington School in September. The best part about the news was that he had been promised a new bike, and without delay they set out to purchase the new machine. A Rudge, resplendent in black with gold lining was selected and paid for. Mike promptly tried to forget about the new school and everything connected with it. He set about enjoying his new prized possession. He succeeded totally in both.

Eventually September arrived, and together with several of his friends, he set off to grammar school. Mike was extremely single minded in what he wanted from school. He needed the qualifications to secure himself an apprenticeship in the Merchant Navy. He had never considered a career other than going to sea like his Father, and would under no circumstances be detracted from his ambition. So the thought of having to learn Latin, which he considered to be of no use to anyone other than a Doctor or Chemist, filled him with a sense of "Why am I wasting my time doing this?" This attitude was unlikely to endear him to the teachers at Bridlington School.

His first year studying Latin was fairly disastrous, but came nowhere near the results he would achieve in the second year. In the first year, his form master, a pleasant amiable man, tried hard to interest Mike in the subject, but with little success.

In the second year, he was faced with the school's teaching bully, Mr Greenhay, a tall cadaverous man with thick glasses that looked like the bottom of two bottles. In order to try to prove that he did not pick on any boy in particular, at the start of the year each boy was given the name of a playing card to memorise. The teacher then shuffled a pack of cards before asking any questions. The boy with the card taken from the pack would then have to answer the question. Mike was the four of spades, a card that would haunt him for years afterwards.

His life was a misery as the year progressed. The four of spades was pulled out with monotonous regularity. He would try to find any reason for missing the days on which he had Latin lessons. In the first exam of the year, he scored five marks out of a hundred, and his report stated that he had almost lost touch with the subject. He was still not bottom of the class. A farmer's son, who was similarly single-minded, held this distinction. The bullying became worse and worse. He was hit round the head every time he could not answer the questions. Eventually in desperation, he took a large sheath knife to school believing that he would stick it into Greenhay if he hit him again.

By the end of the year, his report said he had completely lost touch with Latin. He had dropped to scoring four marks out of a hundred, but once again, the farmer's son was below him. The day at the end of the second year when he could drop Latin forever was one of the most enjoyable of his school career.

During the second year, he had started to learn French. This seemed to him to be an eminently sensible language to learn if he was to spend most of his life travelling. It was helped by the fact that the French teacher, Mr Bowen was also the head of the Royal Naval section of the schools Combined Cadet Force, which featured heavily in Mike's plans for his time at school. The teacher had the nickname of Snorker, which sometime later Mike realised was probably in honour of the unpleasant First Lieutenant of

HMS Compass Rose played by Stanley Baker in *The Cruel Sea*, one of Mike's favourite films.

The CCF formed a very important part of life at Bridlington School. All boys were encouraged to join as soon as they reached the age of thirteen. Nine years after the end of the war, rather than being viewed as pacifists or worse, effeminate, the majority of the boys joined up. The school timetable was organised to ensure that the CCF was given full prominence. Wednesday afternoon was designated for the Cadet Force, and the school made up the time by holding normal lessons on Saturday morning. Saturday afternoon was detention time.

The first year was spent in the Army section where basic drill, rifle handling, shooting and similar disciplines were taught and the first camp experienced. This was usually the first time away from home for all the boys, with the exception of the boarders who came from all over the world. It was made more traumatic than usual by being held at an Army establishment, where drill and the usual discipline was all important. At the end of the year all boys were allowed to choose between the Army, Air Force and Naval sections, for more specialised training.

The Army section split into three sections, signals, infantry and band. The signals section had their own radio shack where they could communicate with similar sections and radio hams throughout the world. The infantry their own twenty-five pound Howitzer to practise gunnery drill on. The band was composed of drums and bugles, and led the whole Cadet Force wherever they paraded.

The Air Force section had their glider. This very basic craft was launched by dozens of boys pulling on an elasticated rope. When the rope had been stretched as far as possible, the glider was catapulted into the air for a hundred yards or so. The would-be pilot fought to stop it diving nose first into the field. The section visited local RAF stations for added flight training.

One of the highlights of Mike's time at school was the crashing of the glider on the hallowed cricket square. The square was roped off at all times except when the first eleven were playing, and was the Headmasters pride and joy, where no mere boy was allowed to tread. The sight of the glider's nose ploughing into this wonderful piece of turf had the boys in fits of silent laughter.

The Naval section had a very old cutter kept in the harbour, and an even older Whaler at the school, where rigging and correct oar work could be practised. In the same way as the other sections, they went to camp during every summer holiday. Mike was able to camp at *HMS Dolphin,* the Royal Navy's submarine base in Gosport, Portsmouth where he experienced his first flight from the local Fleet Air Arm base. Eventually he camped at *HMS Blackcap*, a Fleet Air Arm base near Warrington, where he was able to fly several more times, diving on the mud flats of the Mersey, whilst being flown by a naval officer who was probably a would-be Kamikaze pilot.

Mike realised that not every school had two rifle ranges, one indoor and one outdoor and an armoury consisting of several hundred rifles, sten and bren guns and its own Howitzer. He never gave it much thought until much later in life. He regularly spent his lunch times in the indoor range practicing for his Marksman's badge. He lived for Wednesday afternoons and, eventually, the day he would be able to go to sea.

Now he had fulfilled the ambition. He finally stood on the bridge of a large merchant ship, albeit a long way from it being his bridge. He regretted his single mindedness and the wasted time at school, and hoped that it would not affect his life in the future. With the exception of Geography, History, and the CCF he had not enjoyed his time there. He headed back to the cabin, at the end of the watch with the thought that tomorrow they would be back on the chipping machines.

Sure enough, at 0645 hrs the Bosun arrived on the bridge and discussed the day's work with the Mate. The first item on the agenda was the resumption of chipping on the foredeck. At 0700 hrs they headed for the forecastle and collected their machines. By 0800 hrs when they stopped for breakfast they were already black from the rust and old paint, and so ate their breakfasts sitting on the hatch cover outside the galley.

Their hands were trembling from the vibration of the flails, and they found it difficult to hold their mugs of coffee. The thought of returning to the machines at 0900 hrs did not appeal. The day passed very slowly and dirtily, but they were cheered by the news that as it was Saturday on the next day, they would be on a "job and finish" cleaning the wheelhouse and chartroom, and then be free until their normal watches.

On Sunday, they would clean their accommodation for the Captain's inspection and only work their normal watch hours as lookout or practise calculating azimuths from the stars and the rising sun. The meals on Sunday were also special, which when added to double pay for Sunday at sea made the day something to look forward to.

Mike had noticed as he walked around the decks a sudden appearance of thin wires emanating from portholes in many of the cabins around the ship. Each of these wires travelled to the highest point possible on the boat deck, the lifeboat davits, funnel or Samson posts, and were connected to the very latest in marine radios in the cabins. The significance of these wires was not apparent until after he was ordered by the Mate to cut them down because they were an eyesore.

Almost as soon as he tried to take the wires down, their

owners accosted him. Only then did he find why the aerials had been put up. The crew was expecting the Captain to talk to the owners as soon as they were close enough to Land's End to use the radiotelephone. He would receive his orders to proceed to the designated port in Europe where the cargo was required, and everyone wanted to know first. In fact, a substantial book was running on which port would be their destination. The wires were extending the normal range of the radios to allow any conversations from the ship to be heard.

The sweepstake had the favourite ports as Rotterdam followed by Antwerp and Hamburg. If he were not too diligent in his work taking down the aerials, he would be invited to join in. Although the whole crew wanted to return to the UK, they thought it unlikely. It would mean paying off and starting again for the next voyage. As Mike had not visited The Netherlands, Belgium or Germany, he was excited at any possibility, but would settle happily for an opportunity to go home.

By Tuesday, excitement was at fever pitch. Every spare minute was spent trawling up and down the short wave bands listening for any traffic from the ship's wireless room. Another attempt was made to remove the aerials on the Captain's orders to try to ensure privacy. But it was a losing battle. The wires went up again almost as soon as they were cleared. Every time the ship's "Sparks" went on air, a cry went up from the accommodation, and the majority of the ship's company headed for the cabins.

On Wednesday, they were well in range for a radiotelephone conversation through Portishead. At lunchtime, the listeners were rewarded at last by hearing the Captain in discussion with the Buries Markes Head Office in London. The conversation lasted for some time, discussing a variety of subjects, until at last came the news they wanted. The port for discharging the cargo was to be Liverpool.

CHAPTER 8

The excitement spread like wildfire around the ship's company. Nobody had really believed that they would be returning to the UK. The news seemed to put a spring into everybody's step. For Tony, Paul, Phil and Mike as apprentices and cadets there would be the pay off, and then the added uncertainty of whether they would have any shore leave after such a short voyage. More importantly, would they remain on *La Cordillera,* or be transferred to another of the company's ships?

For the remainder of the contracted officers there was certainly a chance to go home and return to the ship for the next voyage. For the rest of the ship's crew, the pay off was the opportunity to go on leave and find another ship when the money ran out. From talking to them, it became apparent that many of them would choose this route.

The time spent on the chipping machines seemed to pass faster as each of them thought of what Liverpool would bring them. At times, it was difficult to concentrate on the square of deck that was being chipped. But the damage that a moment's lack of concentration could do to ones legs or face did not bear thinking about. Without a doubt, the flail head would cut straight down to the bone. A hit in the face would be far worse. By the time they finished day work at

1700 hrs the majority of the foredeck had been chipped, oiled and painted and certainly one more day of good weather would ensure that it looked good and clean for arrival in port.

Mike headed for the bridge after dinner, complete with his oilskin and a sweater. The temperature had dropped considerably as they travelled ever further north. In two days' time, they would be in England enjoying the usual February ice and snow, and the bone chilling cold that came with it. He would miss standing on the bridge in shirt and shorts watching the wonderful sunsets, but there may be other benefits to persuade him that England was best.

If he were to have an opportunity to go home, he would have to make an effort to find a regular girlfriend. He had left home shortly after parting company with Marcia, a lovely girl from the secondary modern school and member of the same church choir as Mike. The thought of having a boyfriend who only put in appearances once or twice a year did not really appeal to someone who had to fight off predatory males on a regular basis. He had hoped that they would remain friends, but in reality knew this would not be the case.

Whilst Mike had seen the romance of the sea and the uniform as a positive aid to romance, the girls had not exactly lined up to be a replacement for the much lamented Marcia. In the short time that he was likely to be home, his best hope was to talk to Julia, who despite everything that had gone before was still his closest female friend. They had grown up quite a lot since their original courting days as innocent fourteen-year-olds.

Julia and he were now probably as close as any friends could be without sex coming into the equation. He had felt able to talk to Julia about most subjects without the conversation becoming general knowledge. In all probability the relationship could turn into something far more, were it not for the type of terminal illness that Julia and most of her friends suffered. The illness manifested itself in the inability to pass a jeweller's shop without stopping to look at engagement rings. The last thing on Mike's mind was engagement or marriage. He had just started his new career and did not see marriage on the horizon for at least another ten years.

Julia had many suitors and she was never short of someone to escort her on a casual basis. Mike sensed that she had a soft spot for him, as her very first boyfriend, and this suited both of them. If he were able to go home, and at this point it was a very big if, he would call her as soon as possible to organise a date or a homecoming party. He would enjoy her company immensely, especially after the company of forty men for the past six weeks. Rather selfishly, he hoped that she had not started any long-term relationship that would stop her accompanying him.

He had not heard anything from his best friend Jono whilst he had been away. Mike was worried that he may have formed a relationship with Alison that would preclude him from spending most of his spare time with Mike. This would be a total tragedy, as they had been mostly inseparable since the age of thirteen. Virtually all the trouble that Mike had been in during his schooldays he had shared with Jono. If one of them were caught at school, the masters or prefects would come looking for the other one. Sometimes with reason, sometimes not.

Jono shared Mike's sense of humour and could usually find something funny in most situations. The only time this failed badly was when they were both to be found outside the Headmaster's study waiting to be caned for some high-spirited performance in a coffee bar during the weekend. His humour also extended to the constabulary, and on one occasion after having several illegal drinks they found themselves riding their bikes home. A voice from the pavement said, "Where's your lights?"

"Next to me liver," shouted Jono to the policeman who had asked the question. For the next ten minutes, they pedalled as if their life depended upon it and arrived at his house totally exhausted.

In the later years, Mike had spent most of his time at Jono's house and his parents accepted him as part of the family. His Father, a former Royal Marines officer, was someone who Mike could look up to while his own Father was away at sea. His Mother was the producer of all the local amateur operatic shows and was largely responsible for Mike's abiding love of all things Gilbert and Sullivan, together with Franz Lehar.

Mike's original interest in G&S had started some years ago. The Girls' High School senior boarders were being taken to see the production of *Iolanthe*. His reason for attending then had very little to do with the works of Gilbert and Sullivan, rather his chance to see a girl who every Sunday morning smiled at him from the front pew at Church. He and his fellow head choirboy Neville had managed to meet two of the girls and talk to them through the fence at their concentration camp like boarding residence. The Mistresses frowned upon all contact with boys at the school and so the relationship was conducted at a very long distance. As a result, if it meant sitting through a whole operetta to have a chance of seeing his would-be girlfriend, so be it.

To his surprise, Mike found the music entirely to his taste. He volunteered with Jono to be ushers at all subsequent performances for the next three years. *HMS Pinafore* followed *Iolanthe*, Lehar's *Land of Smiles*, and *The Arcadians* followed that. He never tired of watching the performances, and longed for the time when his voice would be stabilised again and he could join the Company. This, together with his interest in sacred choral works such as *Messiah*, which he had sung from the age of seven, gave him the basis of an interest in music that would never fade.

Prior to joining *La Cordillera,* he had undergone a voice test with the organist and choirmaster of Christ Church Bridlington. The test pieces had been the opening Tenor solos from *Messiah*, "Comfort ye my people" and "Every valley shall be exalted" which he had found very difficult. The top of the tenor range was beyond him, and when attempted in a baritone key he could not reach the depths of the baritone range. He had decided that he was probably not going to be confident in either range, and so turned down a chance to be in the choir, for the time being. At school, both he and Jono were mercilessly teased about their taste in music. It was the same at sea when Mike had mentioned it in conversation.

Alison had joined the Amateurs for *The Arcadians*, and this looked to Mike like the beginning of the end of the relationship, which in reality had probably started to founder when he joined *La Cordillera*. Jono certainly would not be allowed to join Mike for the kind of days and evenings they had previously enjoyed. Although she was by far the quietest of the girls in the group that Mike and Jono hung around with, she along with Jacqui was the most attractive. She was a brilliant pianist and musician and very, very, single-minded when it came to Jono. Mike had harboured visions at one time of taking Alison out himself, but she had set her mind on Jono and so Mike had given up any similar thoughts.

Over a cup of cocoa, the Mate came out to talk to Mike for the first time on the homeward voyage. They started like all good Englishmen with the weather, the sun they had been enjoying and the cold they were heading into. He gave the impression of being totally relaxed now the ship was looking good, the cargo was not giving any problems and they would soon be in the UK. Pretty soon, the conversation changed to what came next. He asked Mike if he was happy and ready to sign indentures, to which Mike replied that he was. Why he had said that, Mike could not remember when asked later. Mike broached the subject of the next voyage, but the Mate did not know where they would be going. He believed the company had not yet taken a charter. But he then dropped a real bombshell. He would not be there regardless of where she went.

Mike was quite taken aback. Although he had worked them hard throughout the voyage, he had always seemed to be a decent sort of man and in any case, better the devil you know than the one you don't. If Mike had known how true that was, there would have been at least two of them leaving in Liverpool. The Mate was going to join the new addition to the Buries Markes fleet, *M/V La Pradera*. She had just completed her maiden voyage and would be coming into Liverpool at about the same time as *La Cordillera*. He was highly thought of by the company and was being put under the spotlight on the flagship prior to gaining his own command in the next year or two.

At 2000 hours when Paul relieved him, he told him the news and then set off for the accommodation to tell Phil and Tony, who were similarly surprised. Tony having sailed with several other Mates was not particularly worried, but Phil shared Mike's concern. After being with the company for the past two months, and having an inkling of the way the company worked its cadets and apprentices, they realised life could be a lot worse under a less affable Mate. He had not been too bad, had he? Already they were starting to sound like old hands who, no matter how bad the previous ship was, it was always the best ship they had ever been on. They could have experienced plague, starvation and mutiny and yet they could only conjure up the good times.

By next morning, they were only a day away from England and the rumourmongers were busy again. In general, the majority of the crew could not care less where she was bound for on her next voyage, as they were leaving and not coming back. But the deck officers and apprentices, the engineer officers and juniors were spending every available minute discussing it. Because the Mate had told him that it had not been decided yet, Mike just listened to the speculation that varied enormously.

One of the favourites was to repeat the same voyage. This certainly would be highly desirable, as the shifting boards could remain in place and the dunnage in the other holds would not require too much work either. In fact, all the hard work that they had done on the way out last time would be already done for them. All that would be required was the holds to be swept, the paper to be renewed on the bilge covers and the bilges emptied of any grain that had permeated. In addition, they would be very happy to renew their acquaintanceship with New Orleans. It would also mean another pay off in around two months' time, which would be very acceptable.

There were three other favourites. The first was collecting a cargo of wood pulp or pulpwood from Quebec or Newfoundland and returning to the UK or Europe. Then there was loading Volkswagen spares, or cars, in Germany for the USA or Australia. This one had a lot of takers as the company had three new ships specifically built for carrying cars and on long term charters to Volkswagen. Finally, there was sailing to north Africa for a cargo of iron ore for UK steelworks. Once again, as the company had a fifteen year charter for one of its ships with the British Iron & Steel Company, this was a reasonable possibility as well.

One option that received a lot of votes was any port in the world providing that they loaded a cargo in the UK first, keeping them in Liverpool for three to four weeks. The other alternatives were many and varied, and some quite fanciful. No one was anywhere near correct with his guess.

With only twenty fours to go, they spent the whole day cleaning throughout. Starting at the forecastle, they stowed away all paint, brushes, chipping machines and anything that had been left on the deck. They cleaned all the paintbrushes and kettles, and stowed away all rope that would not be required for mooring. Next came the bridge and wheelhouse. The wooden deck was scrubbed and all the brass and woodwork polished. By the afternoon, they had reached the accommodation and this too was scrubbed and polished, until you could see your face reflected in any surface.

By the time Mike started his last evening watch, the temperature had dropped dramatically and the wind chill factor put it below zero. Mike huddled into the corner of the bridge wing as he tried to keep track of the shipping coming out of the Irish Sea. He reported each new set of lights in turn to the Mate. Eventually he saw the Tuskar Rock light on the Irish coast, followed by the lights of the Welsh coast. The excitement started to mount. By this time tomorrow, they would be tied up in Liverpool, and would know more about their futures. Would he or any of his colleagues be switched to *La Pradera*? What would life be like on the company's flagship? Would he be required for a further voyage? All these and many other questions were running through his mind as he headed below for his bunk.

Eight hours later, he headed back to the bridge. The lights of Llandudno, Colwyn Bay, Rhyl and Prestatyn were twinkling on the starboard side. Ahead of them as he climbed up to the bridge was the lume of the lights of

Birkenhead and Liverpool itself. This time the Captain was on the bridge as well as the Mate, both of them taking it in turns to study the lights ahead and the radar screen that would indicate the whereabouts of the pilot boat. The sea ahead was a clutter of lights, fishing boats, coasters, Isle of Man ferries, and large ships leaving Liverpool. No sooner had he arrived on the bridge than he was sent down to the deck to rig the ladder for the Pilot. That done he was back on the bridge making tea for all three of them.

When the pilot boat was located, he was back down on deck to throw the ladder over the starboard side. The engine room telegraph clanged and the engine that had been running flat out since leaving Galveston slowed dramatically. By the time the way had dropped off the ship the pilot launch was alongside. The Pilot in the bow timed his jump for the ladder, which was accomplished first time with no problems. Mike helped him aboard, pulled up the ladder and escorted him to the bridge.

"Call Eames for the wheel," said the Captain, and Mike headed down yet again to the accommodation to call Tony, who was naturally delighted to be called out at 0500 hrs to act as coxswain for the length of the pilotage.

Upon returning to the bridge, Mike was ordered to take the wheel himself until Tony arrived. He considered whether he should tell them he had never done this before in his life, but decided against it.

"How's your head?" asked the Pilot. Mike resisted the obvious comment of the type that had him in trouble so many times before, and replied "050, Sir."

"Steer 080," said the Pilot.

"080, Sir," replied Mike as he turned the wheel gently to starboard. He saw the bow start to swing to starboard and checked the swing almost immediately.

"080 it is, Sir." He had never known such power before. He could get used to this, but before he did, Tony arrived and took over. Mike was given the job of recording the engine movements and the timing of them. It was later explained to him that these would form the basis of any claim, or inquiry should there be a collision or grounding.

This was the biggest thrill he had experienced since joining the ship. A grandstand view of everything that happened when a large ship entered port. He watched in fascination as they made their progress up the Mersey, their destination coming ever nearer. Shortly after it became daylight, he could make out and recognise the Liver Building with its famous birds, despite the fact that he had never been to Liverpool before. Eventually he was sent to wake up the crew, in order that they could have some breakfast before they raised the derricks and went to their stations for entering port. On this one occasion he did not have abuse hurled at him for waking them early, such was the enthusiasm for the coming day's work.

By the time the derricks had been raised, the mooring lines dragged out from the rope locker, and everybody breakfasted they were ready to stand by fore and aft. Two tugs were heading towards them, and in a matter of minutes were made fast prior to swinging towards the locks that would take them into Sandon dock where the cargo would be discharged. Slowly the tugs edged her into the lock, and the heaving lines were thrown prior to paying out the head and stern lines that would hold her while the lock filled.

As there was little difference between the height of the river and the dock level, they were on their way again very shortly. The tugs held her steady as they past Wellington Dock, full to capacity with ships loading and discharging their cargoes from all over the world. Next came Sandon, and the tugs set to work to turn her ninety degrees to starboard and line her up for the dock entrance, which she passed through without need for the fenders which they had hastily thrown over both sides in case they scraped the dock entrance.

Where New Orleans had been clean and modern, Sandon Dock was exactly the opposite. Graffiti covered the dock walls, puddles of oily water gathered on the quay, the warehouses were black from all the years of the industrial revolution, the cranes were rusty with large areas thick with black grease and the general impression was one of grime and neglect. But never the less this represented home for now, and they watched fascinated as the ship was pushed towards the dockside by the tugs and they readied the lines which when made fast would signal the end of the voyage.

Within minutes two head lines and stern lines plus fore and aft springs were run out and made fast. Once she was in position the tugs were let go, the telegraph rang "Finished with engines," the accommodation ladder was lowered and the usual crowd of customs, immigration, agents and head office personnel came aboard.

Everyone appeared to be at a loss as to what happened next. The crew and stewards stood around in groups waiting for news of the pay off. The apprentices decided to make themselves scarce and headed to their cabins with mugs of tea. If anyone wanted them, they would have to come and find them. It was the first time in weeks that they had been able to sit together in the cabin, and it felt like a luxury to be able to talk without someone giving them another job to do.

The main topic of conversation was their chances of going home before the next voyage. Tony and Paul, the only ones with experience in the matter, were divided on the subject, but both were certain that they would not all be allowed to go at the same time, as there would be no crew available. The apprentices would have to carry out any deck work that was necessary during their stay in Liverpool, take on board stores if they arrived before the crew and if necessary move the ship along the quayside if required for the grain elevators. In addition to there being no crew, they would be short on officers as well. The Mate was moving to *La Pradera*, the Second Mate had announced that he would be going on leave as soon as they docked, or he would not be sailing on the next voyage. That left the Captain, Third Mate and the apprentices. It was starting to look bleak.

Presently they heard footsteps in the alleyway, and resigned themselves to having to start work. Instead of the Mate or the Bosun, it was the customs rummagers searching the accommodation for contraband, primarily cigarettes and spirits. Mike knew from the amount of cigarettes that had been purchased on the last occasion that the Captain's bond was open that there must be thousands and thousands of cigarettes hidden around the ship, but he only had an inkling of where. The apprentices each had around 380 cigarettes, although Phil did not smoke. The rummagers were not interested in these, only the large numbers plus anything more sinister.

Mike had heard two of the Engineers talking about their perfect hiding place in the engine room, but had not thought much about it at the time. Now the thought intrigued him as he recalled the conversation. The huge Doxford engine required an enormous amount of compressed air to start it, and this was kept in two large tanks big enough for a person to climb in through the inspection lids. The tanks were sealed and the pressure built up until there was sufficient in both tanks to start the engine, should there be any manoeuvres requiring the engine to be stopped. It was their intention to store several thousand cigarettes in one of the tanks and then pressurise it, so that it could not be opened. Certainly the rummagers didn't look in there, although they did lift many of the engine room deck plates. They moved on to inspect what space there was in the holds and left apparently empty handed, some two hours later.

They were disturbed again from their conversation by the sound of running feet in the alleyway. The crew had heard that the pay off had started, and were heading en masse towards the saloon. The boys reasoned that if the crew, stewards and greasers got there first they might as well hang on for the next hour, and so settled down again.

The Mate was the next one to enter the cabin, bringing the news that they were waiting for. He started by thanking them for all their hard work during the voyage, and hoped that he would meet up with them within the company in the near future. Then came the bit they were really waiting for. They were expecting the ship to be in Liverpool for ten days, so two of them could go home as soon as they completed their pay off, and the other two would go home in five days' time when the first two returned.

The news took a few minutes to sink in. They were really

going home for some leave, which was more than they had dared hope. The decision was taken that Tony and Phil would go immediately, and Paul and Mike would go upon their return. With a few half-hearted threats as to what would happen if they did not return on time, Tony and Phil were showered, dressed and into the pay off queue. Within the hour were heading down the gangway to a waiting taxi. Paul and Mike headed for the saloon and a very sparsely attended and subdued lunch.

CHAPTER 9

The next five days passed pleasantly enough. The Mate had moved his personal effects to *La Pradera,* which had berthed the next day in Huskisson No 3 dock only a few hundred yards from where *La Cordillera* lay. As a result of that and the Bosun going home for some leave, there was no one to chase Paul and Mike. The Third Mate spent most of his time in his cabin when not patrolling the decks whilst the cargo was being discharged. Apart from checking the mooring lines and fitting rat guards to them, Paul and Mike made the most of their time in dock.

They had paid off at the same time as the rest of the ship's company, and Mike had untold riches in his pocket from the two months at sea, together with a rail warrant to take him home and back. What more could anyone want? After subtracting his sub in New Orleans and his bond bill, he had the grand total of £8 0s 4d to spend. Paul had slightly more, as he was on second year wages of £12 per month. Together they had one wild night out in Liverpool, with Mike experiencing his first ever Chinese meal at the Empress on Lime Street, and a pint of Tennents at a nearby pub. After this night of excess, they decided they would save their money for when they arrived home in three days' time.

On the third day, he was called up to the Captain's cabin, and given a package to take to the Mate on *La Pradera*. This was an opportunity he had really been looking forward to. A chance to look around the current flagship and compare it with his present ship. He dressed in his battle dress uniform and headed round to Huskisson No 3 dock. He saw the ship immediately he rounded Huskisson No 1. She lay on the far side of the dock, gleaming in the winter sun, her paintwork virtually immaculate from bridge to waterline and from stem to stern.

She impressed him like the *Lammermuir* had several years before, totally different from anything he had seen. Instead of having accommodation amidships, everything was at the stern with a huge foredeck comprising five holds. This was the way Buries Markes saw the future, and they were currently building three similar motor ships, *La Marea, La Selva* and *La Primavera*, with *La Colina* due to start her maiden voyage any day. In turn, the older ships were being sold off and *La Cordillera* was the fourth oldest ship in the fleet at eleven years old. Before long, they would have the most modern fleet in the UK. Mike was well aware that if he remained with them and passed all his exams he could expect his own command by the age of twenty-eight. That seemed several lifetimes away.

He made his way up the gangway and onto the foredeck to look at the cargo. She was loaded with 14,000 tons of grain and they had started work on discharging two of the holds.

He noticed immediately that the bulkheads of the holds were painted and looked clean. It would probably be the only time they would look like that. But the most impressive thing he noticed was that she was fitted with steel hatch covers. No more taking out the heavy beams and fitting the wooden hatch boards into their slots, and above all no canvas cover to fit and wedges to hammer in. At a stroke four of the worst jobs they had to do on deck when entering or leaving port had been replaced.

Next stop was the accommodation and the Mate's cabin three decks up. Instead of the small cabin he had on *La Cordillera* he now had a large day room/office and separate bedroom. He saw Mike's face and laughed, pointing out that this was the face of the future, and invited him to look around the ship. The Mate thanked him again and wished him all the best in his career, and Mike headed for his favourite spot on a ship, the bridge.

The bridge bristled with the latest in technology. Telephones between the Captain and engine room where previously they had used a tube and whistle system, and to the forecastle head and stern for entering and leaving port. A far more modern radar and autopilot system meant a substantial reduction in the amount of brass work. The impressive view of the huge foredeck was really spectacular, and Mike stood behind the wheel reflecting on how she would handle. He didn't know then that in thirty-four months' time he would stand in exactly the same position as Senior Apprentice, as he took the ship into Cape Town at daybreak with the spectacular view of Table Mountain ahead of him.

He returned to *La Cordillera* and told Paul of what he had seen. They both hoped that their next appointment would be to one of these new ships, with their many labour saving devices. In the meantime their one interest was in getting through the next two days so that they could head for home, Paul to Newcastle and Mike to Bridlington.

The Third Mate, who had come to tell them to take the Captains baggage down to the taxi waiting on the quayside, jerked them out of their thoughts. They assumed, wrongly, that he was going on leave and would be back at the same time as they returned. Upon reaching his cabin they saw a large number of suitcases and boxes, and realised that he was leaving the ship. Beside the cases stood a tall immaculately dressed man with a well-groomed moustache and goatee beard. This was Captain Ralph Eyre-Walker, self-appointed Commodore of the Buries Markes fleet and the new Captain of *La Cordillera*. Captain Pearson briefly introduced them, and they received a nod in their direction from his replacement. They carried the bags to the taxi, and received a thank you from the Captain who disappeared into obscurity as far as Buries Markes were concerned, taking a command with an associate company.

The subject of the new Captain was a source of endless

conversation and speculation between the two apprentices, the Chief Steward and the engineers left on board. Why would the Captain of the company's flagship be switched to *La Cordillera* and would it affect them in any way? He gave the impression of not being particularly thrilled with the move to a ship that was totally beneath him and his capabilities. In fact, as he strode around the ship, one could be forgiven for thinking that he smelled something rather unpleasant. If the Captain was something to worry about and the subject of endless gossip, then far worse was to come. On the next day, the Mate arrived.

Chief Officer Barry Kirton was built like a huge gorilla. The suit and raincoat he was wearing did nothing to disguise it. He was muscle bound to the point that his arms were at a perpetual angle, unable to hang down at his side. He stood on the dockside after paying his taxi and shouted at Paul and Mike, who were walking on deck, to come and carry his baggage aboard. There was no please or thank you, just a series of grunts and nods, as he directed them.

One box was particularly heavy, and Mike struggled to lift it. Kirton picked it up with little or no effort. The box apparently contained his weights which he would use at every opportunity to acquire what he thought was the body beautiful. He made a comment to the effect that Mike would be able to lift it with ease by the time they arrived home again. Mike reflected that the coming voyage was going to be an awfully long one

With Kirton safely ensconced in his cabin, Paul and Mike made themselves scarce. They wanted to stay well out of his way until they could safely leave the ship on the next day. Each of them prayed for the return of the previous Mate, but knew that it would never happen. They packed their cases and hoped that Tony and Phil would be back on time the following morning and that nothing would happen before then to spoil their chances of going home. A vision haunted them of Kirton deciding that he required them on board whilst the ship was in Liverpool and cancelling their leave.

No sooner had they finished breakfast on the next morning, than the vision started to become a reality. A white boiler-suited Kirton collared them and took them around the decks. They started on the forecastle head with a continual flow of orders, "Fasten the rat guards together properly," "Tidy up all the ropes," "Take up the slack on the forward spring," "Coil up the ropes on all the derrick guys," and they were only level with the No 1 hold. The derricks were not being used on the No 2 hold because of the grain elevator, so he wanted all the wires running off the winch drum greasing thoroughly and running back onto the drums tidily. This was a major job, as well as being a filthy one, which would take them half a day alone. Their leave prospects seemed to be receding fast.

They worked at a cracking pace for the whole of the morning, stopping for neither coffee nor cigarettes, and by lunch time they were nearly totally exhausted. Only the sight of Tony and Phil, who had travelled back from the south together, dispelled this. They were given a rapturous welcome, which was tempered by the news of the new Mate, and given the list of outstanding jobs from the morning's inspection.

At this point Paul and Mike made the decision that come hell or high water, they were going home and would live with any problems this caused later. They hid their suitcases in the storage area under the settees and headed for the shower. Within minutes, they were showered, dressed and ready to head down the gangway. Tony had called a taxi and they now had to wait for fifteen minutes until it arrived. At the same time, they had to keep out of sight in case Kirton saw them and decided that they were not going on leave because he wanted them working on board.

The fifteen minutes seemed interminable, as every second dragged by. They did not want to consider the possibility of having to stay in Liverpool, but the sadistic streak that Kirton appeared to possess where apprentices were concerned made it distinctly possible. They joked weakly together as they took it in turns to keep an eye on the dockside for a sign of the taxi and their chance of freedom for a few days.

Almost dead on time an empty taxi appeared at the end of

the warehouse. Paul and Mike dragged their cases from their hiding place and just as they did they heard heavy footsteps in the alleyway. They froze immediately, and all their negative thoughts swept back. Was this Kirton looking for them? Was he about to order them back on deck? Were they doomed to stay on the ship until the end of the next voyage? The Chief Steward put his head around the cabin door, and wished them a good leave.

They checked up and down the starboard side before stepping out of the accommodation and then, cases in hand, sprinted for the gangway. They did not stop, look back or anything else until they were safely in the taxi. Only then did they see Kirton heading towards the apprentices cabins, but it was too late. They were on their way. They laughed about their escapade all the way to Lime Street Station, however they knew there could be a price to be paid upon their return in five days' time. But that was five days away, and before then they were going home to see their family and friends.

Upon arrival at Lime Street, they took a train to Manchester before splitting up, Paul taking a train to Newcastle, Mike to Bridlington via Hull. They had arranged to meet on the following Tuesday at the station before travelling back to the ship, and to whatever problem lay in wait for them. Mike settled back into his seat on the Trans-Pennine diesel. His mind focused solely on Bridlington and the next four and a half days.

For the first time in seven weeks he was on his own. No cabin mate, no Mate or Bosun pushing him to new limits, no watch look out. Just the beauty of the wild Pennines and the grime of the mill towns along the route to Hull. After a short wait on Paragon Station in Hull, he caught the train to Bridlington. Then it was along the familiar route through Cottingham, Beverley, Driffield and all the small stations in between. As they pulled into Bridlington station, the light was fading in the west behind his old school. Mr Bampton was on the taxi rank, and his eyes light up when he saw Mike. Within seconds, he was back in the black Austin that began his adventure.

As they pulled up outside the house, his sister and two brothers ran out to welcome him home. On the doorstep his Mother stood waiting. A cup of tea was thrust into his hand and he settled into a comfortable chair to recount the events of the past seven weeks.

CHAPTER 10

Mike had expected the remaining four days would pass very quickly. He spent time with his family, time with his friend Jono and time with Julia. But all too soon, it was time to return to Liverpool. In one way he was looking forward to the next voyage, as he believed that they were about to repeat the first voyage. But the thought of a voyage with Kirton as Chief Officer filled him with a strange dread.

He was tempted to stay at home and find another company to serve his apprenticeship with, but the chance of doing so was nil. If they were to repeat the voyage he could always find a way out at the end of it. In any case it would only be seven weeks. Surely he could put with Kirton for seven weeks, couldn't he?

He had really enjoyed the short time at home, not just for the rest and the wonderful home cooking. He had been in demand everywhere. Nobody he knew except his Father had been to the USA and they all envied him. Everybody he met wanted to hear about New Orleans and the voyage in general. The stories he told and the uniform were guaranteed girl-pullers, and he made a note of the most interested ones for when he returned.

Now he was back in uniform and heading to the railway station in Mr Bampton's black Austin. He was nowhere near as nervous as last time, but still did not exude the confidence that he was known for back home. The time on the trains to Manchester gave him some time to think about what he was doing.

He was still convinced that he was doing the right thing, but it was different from his original expectations. Everyone he had told of the treatment of the apprentices said the same thing. "Four years will soon pass." At the age of sixteen it represented a quarter of his life.

Still he had completed two of the forty-eight months and with the average leave that would accrue, he thought he would be able to manage forty months. Hopefully they would not feel as long as the next two might.

He met up with Paul in Manchester, and together they made the connection to Liverpool with plenty of time to spare. They settled down in their compartment with a cigarette to enjoy what would be the last few hours of real freedom for nine months.

In no time at all they reached Lime Street and were transported by taxi back to Sandon Dock and *La Cordillera*. They dropped their cases in the cabins and went in search of Phil and Tony. After some time they located them in the forecastle head locker, where they were keeping out of the way of Kirton and anyone else who may be looking for them. They sat and smoked as Tony brought them up to date on what had been going on. Kirton had been on their backs all the time that Paul and Mike had been gone.

He had arrived on the scene shortly after Paul and Mike had left for home, and was very annoyed that they had gone as arranged with his predecessor. Obviously he had wanted them to remain on board. This was going to cause problems when Kirton realised they were back.

In the last five days, the apprentices had little or no spare time. It was as if Kirton was carrying out some dreadful personal vendetta against them. Paul and Mike slumped onto a coil of rope as the news slowly sank in, and they began to wish again that they had not bothered to come back.

If this was to be the bad news, then it was difficult to know what to make of the news of the initial ports for the next voyage. It was not to be, as they had hoped, another voyage to New Orleans, Galveston and back to Liverpool. This time they were really going globetrotting. The first two ports were in Cuba where she would load sugar for Japan.

On any other day, Mike would have been ecstatic at the thought of travelling through the Panama Canal and crossing the Pacific Ocean to Japan. Here he was, only eight weeks into his apprenticeship, about to have one of his wildest dreams come true. But then his thoughts returned to Kirton, and the fact that this voyage was going to be a lot longer than seven weeks.

Although they knew that they would be discharging in Osaka and Tokyo, nobody knew what was to happen after that. The possibilities were endless, and would lead to constant speculation until the truth was revealed. At this point, the favourites were a grain cargo from either Australia or Canada, back to Japan. Then the same voyage would be repeated until a homeward bound cargo was found. This could take anything up to the two years of their contract.

The rope locker was silent as the four of them considered the news. They were still in Liverpool, so one possibility was to pack their bags and head home. There would be very little likelihood of another company taking them on if they walked off a ship.

Tony, who had previously endured similar conditions on *M/V La Estancia* and was near to the end of his indentures, considered that he had no alternative but to stay. Paul was almost in the same situation, as he was well into his second year and shared a belief with Tony that all things pass, even the forthcoming voyage with Kirton as their tormentor.

There was a possibility for Phil and Mike that they could write off the last two months as a terrible mistake, and find other employment. Mike had only ever considered being a Deck Officer Apprentice in the Merchant Navy. He was not interested in anything else. He had faced this situation previously when he had reported for the eye and lantern test in Hull.

He had known that he would not be allowed to train as a Deck Officer Apprentice if he failed the sight, colour blindness or lantern test. The sight test of reading the letters on a wall chart, and the colour blindness test posed no problems. He had done them before at school and he was fairly certain that he had no problems.

The lantern test was unnerving. He was left in a completely blacked out room for his eyes to become accustomed to the dark. After what seemed like a very long time the examiner, an extremely gruff Scotsman who was the Chief Examiner for Masters and Mates, joined him. The two would meet again four years later, but fortunately did not know that at the time. Mike was told to look into a large mirror at the end of the room where he would see different lights appearing and tell the examiner what the colours of the lights were.

They started simply with single lights, green, red or white. Then they progressed to two colours alongside each other. By the time they reached the slides with three lights, Mike's eyes appeared to be swimming as he strained in the darkness to see the different colours and name them correctly. The earlier confidence he had felt with the single and double lights had gone completely. The realisation that if he did not answer correctly his career would be finished before it started did not help.

The tiny pinpricks of different colours seemed to be in rings of white as he continued to strain his eyes. "Red, red, white," "White, white, green," "Green, green, red" he shouted out as the slides came up one after the other. After what seemed like an eternity, the room light came on and Captain McQuaid told him that he had passed the test. He gave a huge sigh of relief, collected his certificate, and headed for the train back to Bridlington. This was the first time he had ever had to consider the possibility of not embarking on a career in the Merchant Navy. The process had left him stunned, and he pushed the thoughts of what else he could do to the back of his mind.

Now the thoughts of an alternative career had returned, and still he wanted to put them to the back of his mind. He would have problems if he left the ship, and he did not want to be a disappointment to his family. He would have to face the teachers, who thought he was a waste of space, and his friends. All these things went through his head before he agreed with the others that they would have to make the best of it. Reluctantly they headed for their cabins, and whatever the new voyage would bring.

By the following day the holds were virtually empty. The bulk grain had been discharged whilst Mike and Paul were on leave, and now just a few bales of cotton remained. The crew had signed on, and with just a few exceptions they were virtually all new. The officers with the exception of the Captain and Chief Officer were the same as the previous voyage. The new crewmembers were all Scousers with the traditional Scouse sense of humour, knowledge of Union rules, and reluctance to overwork themselves.

Preparations for going to sea began with the empty holds. Their beams were replaced, together with the hatch boards and covers. The bars and wedges were knocked in next prior to the crew lowering the derricks and making fast the guys. As the stevedores finished discharging the residual cotton bales from each of the remaining holds, the crew and apprentices battened them down in the same way.

By mid afternoon, the ship was ready for sea and they awaited the arrival of the Pilot and the tugs. In due course, they arrived. The accommodation ladder was hauled up and stowed away, the crew departed to their stations for leaving port and the ropes were singled to a headline, stern line and a spring fore and aft. Within a few minutes, the engine room telegraph rang. There was a massive hiss of compressed air as the five cylinder Doxford burst into life for the first time in eleven days. The stern tug swung the ship out into the dock, and she began the slow passage through the dock system. She made her way into the lock before passing through the lock gates and out into the Mersey.

As soon as she had cleared the lock and come onto course

for her journey towards the open sea, the tugs were let go. The forecastle and decks were cleared of ropes, which were stored in the lockers fore and aft. The apprentices prepared the pilot ladder for when they reached the end of the pilotage, and the crew headed to their quarters for dinner. Only Kirton and the carpenter remained on the deck, as they would continue to do until they were clear of the river. They remained huddled in the cold wind for safety purposes, should they need to anchor in an emergency following an engine failure or collision.

Paul and Mike stood in the very cold February evening by the rail, watching as the lights of Liverpool faded on the horizon. The pilot cutter was on its way to collect the Pilot and very shortly their last contact with home would be gone into the approaching night. The thought depressed them, but they had made their decisions and it was too late to go back now. Paul had the four to eight watch with Kirton for the first part of the voyage, and Mike had drawn the eight to twelve with the Third Mate. So as soon as the Pilot had departed, Paul headed for his bunk, and Mike went to the bridge for four hours freezing in the increasing westerly wind.

Directly ahead of them were the lights of local fishermen, ferries from Ireland and the odd cargo ship heading for Liverpool. Beyond that, the Irish Sea and the Atlantic, and a very unpredictable voyage to the other side of the world.

CHAPTER 11

The next morning, they were given a taste of things to come. By 0705 hrs they were in the hold ready to start the clean-up operation. Some of the holds that had held the bales of Cotton were still strewn with dunnage to be stacked, and the hold needing sweeping. Then the process of laying the dunnage could begin again ready for receiving sacks of sugar. This was a filthy job, and because of the damage that the dunnage could do to the hands, one that the apprentices were glad that they were not doing.

For a few moments Tony, Phil and Mike congratulated themselves on not being given this job. Then the Bosun gave them their own job. On the face of it, theirs was a fairly obvious job, to clean the holds that had held the grain cargo. After they had taken off a few hatch boards to give some natural light, they lowered brooms and buckets made of old five-gallon paint drums into the hold.

A short time into the job, they realised that it was not going to be that easy to sweep the hold. The loose grain swept up easily enough, and between them they heaved up dozens of buckets full and threw it over the side. This was tiring work as they only had a single block and pulley system to lift the buckets, and the rope bit into the hands of each of them in turn.

Still they were pleased that they were not working with the dunnage, until the penny dropped as the ship rolled slightly more than normal. Water seeped from under the bilge boards onto the hold floor. Why should there be any water in the bilges? Then the extent of Kirton's sadistic streak slowly became apparent.

Prior to loading the grain in Galveston, they had covered the bilge boards with heavy brown paper, which was held down by thin wooden battens nailed to the boards. In a few places, the paper had torn and exposed the cracks between the bilge boards. The thousands of tons of cargo on top of the boards had forced grain into the bilges. This in turn had mixed with the condensation running into the bilges from the hold bulkhead and formed a vile smelling sludge, which had blocked the extracting nozzle for the bilge pump. In places, the water stood three feet deep, with six inches of grain at the bottom. This then was to be their job for the next few days.

On the freezing February morning, they had to lie on the wet hold floor with half their bodies hanging into the bilges, with their upper arms in freezing cold water and putrefying grain. This initially was the only way they could scoop out the wet grain. Eventually they had a brain wave, and found empty paint and cocoa tins. They pierced their bases to dredge out more grain. Still they could only work for a few minutes at a time, as they could no longer feel their fingers and arms with the cold and had to get up to allow the circulation to return.

The apprentices took turns working in the bays where there was more grain than water, but even scooping out the slimy, foul smelling, wet grain was almost as bad. By the time they had removed the bulk of the grain in these bays, dredging with the small tins was all that was possible.

When 1700 hrs arrived, they ran to their cabins and fought to be first into the hot shower. Dinner passed all too quickly and Mike settled down to try to warm up before going onto the bridge at 2000 hrs. He was only just recovering from the numbness caused by the icy water, so he crammed on several layers of clothing under his oilskin coat before heading to the after mast house to make the tea.

By now, they were in the Atlantic and the long well spaced waves on the starboard bow were causing her to roll with a corkscrewing motion. Periodically small amounts of spray would fly across the deck, but as she was sitting so high in the water, this was not a problem. Mike had taken his place on the port bridge wing so that he would be sheltered slightly by the wheelhouse. The wind was coming from a southwesterly direction, which should be considerably warmer than the wind that was blowing on him. He doubted he was ever going to feel warm again as he pulled up his collar to reduce the skin area exposed.

They were one day into the new voyage, and already the situation was becoming unbearable. There would be at least one or two more days' work in the hold in which they had been working, as the other side appeared to be in a similar state. When they finished the first hold there would be another. The one cheering thought was that they were heading for the Gulf Stream and the Caribbean, which should mean a substantial increase in temperature. It was some consolation as he stood there counting down the hours until midnight.

Only three days ago he had sat in front of a large fire in the living room at home in the company of his Mother, two younger brothers and sister. The food and relaxation he enjoyed after the previous voyage lingered in his memory, as did the evening he took Julia to see *The Pyjama Game* at the Regal cinema.

Although they had been friends since they had broken up two years before, they had never spent an evening solely in each other's company since then. In the glow from the screen Mike looked at her and realised why she had been his first, and one of the only, serious girlfriend to date. He still thought she was one of the most beautiful girls he had ever seen. The two preceding years had only helped to confirm it. Her naturally blonde hair was cut in a fashionable bob and framed her face in a very attractive way. Her figure had developed from that of an early teenager into that of a young woman. She caught him looking at her and smiled, squeezing his hand before looking away in embarrassment.

They had walked hand in hand from the cinema to the coffee bar opposite, and talked and talked until they were politely shown the door by the owner closing for the night. Still hand in hand and unwilling to let the evening end, he had walked her home. Her mother, with whom he had always enjoyed a good relationship, invited him in for supper. Together with her father, they talked until late. Eventually they stood on the doorstep, where they had stood so many times before. This time he was not so nervous, and took her face in his hands before planting the first of many kisses on her lips. They had both learnt a bit about kissing since their previous relationship, and neither of them wanted to stop and say goodnight.

Eventually they had to stop, if only to discuss where they were going from here. Julia knew Mike's commitment to his career in the Merchant Navy from many conversations in the past. She also was well aware that she would not change this commitment, nor would she try. There was only one sensible solution to the dilemma which they faced and at this moment. They did not really want to face it.

Julia was not about to sit at home for anything up to a year waiting for Mike to come home. In return, Mike would not even consider suggesting that she did and so they agreed on a solution that would appear unusual to some. When Mike was home, and on the assumption that neither Julia nor Mike acquired another partner, they would be a couple, enjoying each other's company and everything that went with a normal boy and girl relationship during the period of his leave. They would revert to single status upon his return to sea. It seemed eminently sensible on that cold February night and lasted for several years to come.

After setting things right they kissed and cuddled on the doorstep until the time came to say goodnight and goodbye for some considerable time. He turned and looked as he headed down the path to the road and saw the light reflected in her eyes, which had suddenly become very wet. He waved, blew her a kiss and set off to walk home for his last night in his own bed before leaving in the morning.

Now as he stood on the bridge wing clutching a mug of cocoa, he pondered on whether he had made the right decision or not. Whether he should have stayed at home and built a career for himself so that he could be with the lovely Julia. As things appeared at that time he had probably made the wrong decision, but that was not unusual.

The next day was very much like the previous one, thrusting their arms into the icy water as they continued to dredge the grain from the bilges. By early afternoon, they had almost finished the port side. They took the non-return valve apart and cleaned out the grain that had lodged in it. Re-building and returning it to the end of the pipe, they left nothing but the water in the port bilge. It could be pumped out once the starboard side was finished.

When the paper and battens were off the starboard bilge, Kirton came down to tell them to get a move on. He ranted at them as they struggled to lift the bilge boards, and grabbing one of the heavy boards he threw it across the hold. After he had done the same to three or four other boards, the four apprentices started bailing the grain out of the bilge in the hopes that he would go and annoy someone else. But he continued to pace like a huge gorilla, hurling insults at them and telling Mike that he desperately needed to build up his upper body strength, and to put some effort into it.

They were miserable enough in the icy water, with most of their clothing soaking wet without Kirton's continuous carping and criticising. Kirton eventually gave up and stormed off to harangue the Bosun over the time that the crew was taking to sweep and lay dunnage in the other holds.

For the whole of the next day, they continued with the starboard side of the same hold, the misery only relieved slightly by the increase in temperature as they sailed south. By 1700 hrs they had cleared the non-return valve and were able to ask the engine room to pump out the bilges. There was a huge sigh of relief as they watched the water level drop until the pump was sucking on air and they were able to report that the hold was ready for the next phase of preparation for cargo.

The following day was Sunday and they spent the day in the warmth of their cabins, cleaning in readiness for the Captain's inspection. By comparison with what they had been doing during the week, the cleaning of the brass work and the polishing of the bathroom seemed pleasant. In addition, there was Sunday lunch to anticipate and the new round of soups.

Promptly at 1100 hrs, Captain Eyre-Walker began his weekly inspection, first in the forward accommodation where he collected Kirton and the Chief Steward, then to the midships accommodation and the home of the apprentices. He still walked around looking as if he had an unpleasant smell under his nose, but now after seeing *La Pradera* Mike understood why. He ran his finger tips along the edges of the wardrobes and the back of the settee in Phil and Mike's cabin in the hopes of finding long-term dust, but there was no way that they were going to be caught like that. He nodded his satisfaction with his inspection, probably to the disgust of Kirton who stood behind him with an unpleasant sneer on his face.

The inspection was over, and they were able to get on with washing and mending clothes and possibly the worst job of all, writing home. Whilst they could not wait to receive mail in port, none of them actually enjoyed writing back and it was always the last job, unless a post deadline was facing them.

By the following morning, all thoughts of relaxation and enjoyable meals had been erased from the memory as they headed down into the second hold that had carried grain on the last voyage. The port side was not as bad as the first hold, but the starboard side had several bays completely filled with grain.

Whether it was the rest the day before, or the rise in temperature, the job did not seem anywhere near as bad as it had. They pressed on with it, stopping periodically for a smoke and a coffee at 1000 hrs. The revolting smell had not changed, and they attempted to heave all the wet grain out of the hold as fast as possible so that they could throw it over the side.

The work became more difficult as the ship developed a steady roll of around twenty degrees as the wind started to increase. A gale forecast in their area for the next day was likely to make things worse due to the way the ship was sitting high in the water. Even with the water ballast tanks filled, she sat like a cork bobbing on a bowl of water. After they swung the five-gallon drum out of the hold and onto the deck, they timed the run to the ship's side so that they got downhill to the rail as she started to lift again. In between rolls, they lifted the drum onto the rail and then emptied on the next roll.

Lifting out the grain was becoming difficult, and it was making the dredging of the grain in the bilge water steadily more unpleasant. The more grain they dredged out, the easier the remaining filthy water flowed. At the time when they reached the furthest point of the roll, their heads were going under the water. The secret was to take a very deep breath and hope that you avoided a mouthful of filth.

They had finished the port side by the end of the day, leaving the bigger problems of the starboard side until the next day and the worsening weather. They battened down the hold, and headed for the accommodation and their evening meal before either bed or watch keeping.

Five days out of Liverpool, and they were back to the glorious sunsets. Despite the increasing winds, it was warm. In four days' time, they would be in Cuba and tropical heat.

On the next day, Mike celebrated his seventeenth birthday, although it could hardly be called celebrating. They headed back down the hold, clinging onto the ladder while they descended, while the ship rolled even more in the strengthening wind. This was the first birthday he had spent away from home, and he intended to keep it quiet so that nobody would be tempted to bump him, or worse. He had certainly spent better birthdays than the one facing him.

They spent the day scooping the grain out of the bilge bays without encountering any problem with the water that lay in the bottom. The work was preferable to dredging the water for grain, but arduous. They regularly lost balance when they moved in the bays, and were thrown against the ship's side or the bilge boards. By the end of the day, they were bruised all over, but had taken all the loose grain out and disposed of it over the side. This left the wet grain and the water to tackle on the next day. They hoped that the rolling would lessen as they headed out of the path of the gale.

Mike dragged his body to the bridge at 2000 hrs, hanging onto the silver teapot as he climbed the ladders to the bridge. Each time the ship rolled, he hit the rail and winced. There was hardly any part of his body that had not collided with the metalwork in the hold. He felt every step of the ladders. He poured the tea for the Third Mate and himself, and headed out onto the port side bridge wing. Even though the gale was still blowing, it was noticeably warmer and not unpleasant. He stood in his own little world with just his thoughts to keep him company for four hours.

He thought about his birthday, and how life was changing in his late teens. He was drawing away from his friends. Not only was he absent at sea, but he was the only one of the group to leave school. Whilst he had enjoyed his evening with Julia, the evening he had spent with his best friend Jono was a bit of a disappointment. They had regularly gone for a pint at a pub in Bridlington where their age was unknown, but this time Jono seemed to be intent on drinking the pub dry. Mike enjoyed the odd pint, but had not developed a taste for more than one or two.

In addition to the drinking, Jono's relationship with Alison had become far more intense and all consuming. Mike believed that they had probably reached the stage where they were sleeping together and, although he envied Jono, he had far too much to do in life before he wanted to find himself in a similar restrictive situation. Mike thought of the mad things they had done together, and regretted the changes in their relationship.

Mike's thoughts automatically moved on from Jono and Alison to Julia. Would their relationship ever develop? He doubted that he would be able to develop it as long as he stayed at sea. She was certainly not the type of girl who would happily sit at home for months on end whilst her boyfriend/fiancé/husband travelled around the world, uncertain of when he would return. Still, there was always the hope that their newfound romance could blossom substantially without unrealistic commitment. Mike hoped so, and he thought in detail of the possibility, promising himself that she would not be able to complain of him being slow. Then he was rudely pulled back into the real world by the Third Mate telling him to call Phil.

By morning, the gale had eased considerably. Despite all their aches and pains from the battering their bodies had taken on the previous day, they climbed down into the hold to finish off the last section. They started at the forward bay, and one by one dredged all the grain out of the water, until all that remained was the bay in which the pump suction head lay. In due course, they emptied this, stripped the non-return valve out, cleaned it and replaced it ready for the pumping out of the bilges. Paul headed for the engine room and within a few minutes, the water level dropped appreciably on both sides of the hold, concluding with the slurping noise as the pump started to suck air into the system.

By lunch time they had heaved all the wet grain out of the hold, disposed of it over the side, cleared away all the gear they had been using, and were ready to start the next stage in preparation for cargo, laying dunnage.

The dunnage in that hold had been stored in the tween deck whilst they were in Liverpool. Now it was dropped into the lower hold for spreading out to receive the sacks of sugar. They dropped half the stack into the hold, and set about laying it athwartships. They had almost finished the first layer when a voice from the darkened tween deck shouted at them to straighten the lines and lay the planks tidily. Kirton had decided that they were not working hard enough and required more supervision.

For the next hour, he continued to annoy them. He sat in the tween deck and barked out instructions to them. He wanted most of the first layer be re-laid. The second layer was treated in the same way as the first, and even when they finished the job at 1700 hrs, he was still dissatisfied.

During the final day of the passage to their first port of call they saw land in the distance on the starboard side. This proved to be the Turks and Caicos Islands, but thought little of it. By the time Mike went up to the bridge for his watch they were very near to Guantanamo Bay. The heat, even at this time of night, was probably as great as anything he had experienced before in England. He was sweating after climbing the ladders to the bridge. But above everything else, he noticed the smell, the sweet, all pervading smell of sugar.

After the Captain had stopped the engines and allowed the way to be taken off the ship, he shouted "Let go," and the carpenter let go the anchor. Mike and Paul hoisted the anchor lights and "Finished with engines" was rung on the telegraph. They had arrived in Cuba.

CHAPTER 12

They were called to go out on deck at 0500 hrs. The Pilot had been booked for daybreak, and as it was only a short pilotage to the wharf where they would be loading, the Captain wanted everybody at their station. Tony headed for the bridge to take the wheel, Phil headed for the forecastle, and Paul and Mike prepared the ladder for the Pilot prior to joining the Second Mate on the afterdeck.

In the distance as the sky lightened, they could make out the shape of a small boat heading their way. Within a few minutes the Pilot was alongside, and beginning the long climb up the ladder of the empty ship. Not an easy job at the best of times, but one to be avoided like the plague when the ship was rolling. He greeted them in Spanish and guessing that he wanted to know the way to the bridge, Mike escorted him there. This was the first time Mike had needed foreign language skills, apart from a short visit to France with the school, so Mike spoke very slowly and precisely to the Pilot on the way to the bridge. When he arrived in the wheelhouse, the Pilot introduced himself to the Captain in fluent English with a very heavy American accent.

The sun was beginning its rapid ascent as the telegraph rang and they began their passage into Guantanamo. It was already too hot for working and they had dressed in t-shirt, shorts and sandals. As they neared the land, sugar was all that they could really smell. As the sun rose, so the smell increased with the higher temperature.

The pilotage was indeed short, and soon a wharf with lots of ramshackle sheds on it appeared on their starboard side. The heaving lines were made ready and secured to the spring and stern lines ready for throwing to a bored looking man on the wharf. The first throw did not reach him. The line fell in the water only just short. Mike coiled in the wet line as the man made some comment in Spanish, which probably cast aspersions on Mike and the English in general. The second throw was on target, and the monkey's fist in which a heavy steel nut had been secreted hit the man squarely in the chest. This provoked another round of comment from the man as he pulled the heavy manila stern line in towards the quay and secured it on a bollard.

The spring was sent out next and secured on a bollard amidships, followed by another stern line and a combination wire rope. The ropes were wrapped round the winch, and slowly the ship was pulled in towards the quay until she sat alongside. The telegraph rang "Finished with engines." They were in their first real foreign port.

They next lowered the accommodation ladder onto the quay to enable the most important man in Cuba to come aboard, the ship's agent with the mail. The usual procession of immigration and health officials, together with police, headed for the Captain's cabin where they would study the ship's documents and be suitably placated with bottles of whisky and cartons of cigarettes. Then they would give the all clear for work to start on the loading of cargo. It was unbelievable how many officials were needed to study the documents. Mike realised he was receiving his first lesson in the Hispanic custom of oiling the wheels. He watched them all leave the ship, clutching more than a full case of whisky and the best part of 3,000 cigarettes.

By the time they had eaten breakfast, the Chief Steward was distributing the mail. Mike received a large number of birthday cards, which totally gave away the secret he had kept from his colleagues. Within minutes, they were making plans for a party as soon as they went ashore that evening. For a short time peace reigned in the accommodation as the mail was read and the news from home assimilated, but it could not last.

They had wondered what work Kirton would find for them to do whilst they were in port. Would they be painting the ship's side? Or would he find something really unpleasant for them to work on in the heat? They did not have long to wait before they knew their fate. Kirton duly arrived and told them that for the duration of their time in Guantanamo Bay they would be tallying the cargo as it was loaded. Once again, on the face of it the job seemed reasonable enough. Find a comfortable seat out of the sun and count in the sacks of sugar. A pleasant change from the awful work they had been involved in during the voyage.

By the time they went out onto the deck, the hatch covers and boards had been stripped off, the steel beams taken out, and the derricks swung out over the quay ready to start lifting the slings of filled sacks. The stevedores were the most motley crew that Mike had ever seen, and resembled pictures of beachcombers he had seen both in magazines and in the cinema. They were dressed in colourful shirts, vests and t-shirts, and a mixture of faded denim jeans and shorts. Almost to a man, they wore very worn, sweat stained straw hats that they used to keep the sun from their eyes. They were useful to place over their faces whilst they grabbed a siesta in the hold when the foreman was not watching.

Phil had been designated as night watchman during their stay in Guantanamo, and so he had returned to his bed before starting work at 1900 hrs when the other three boys would be able to go ashore. Mike headed for his position alongside the hold armed with a clipboard and pen, ready to check every sling. A long procession of the oldest and most rickety lorries he had seen were queuing on the quay. Each one was grossly overloaded with bags of sugar, which were over-hanging the side and tail, waiting to be placed in slings and winched aboard the ship. Mike thought this would be fun and sat on a box waiting for the first sling. A tallyman from the sugar producers sat alongside him and smiled in introduction.

The first sling that was swung aboard contained ten sacks of sugar. It was lowered into the hold and the stevedores there carried the sacks to the extremities of the hold. Mike and the tallyman agreed there were ten sacks in the sling. This was a good start, but was destined not to last. After a large number of slings had been winched into the hold, Mike noticed that the next sling appeared to contain only nine sacks. The sacks had been arranged in a different way so that it was not obvious that a sack was missing. Mike queried the figure with the tallyman, who assured him that there were ten sacks in the sling. He immediately stopped the sling from being lowered, and raced down the ladder into the hold to count the number of sacks. There were only nine sacks.

War had been declared. Possibly nobody had queried the tallyman's mathematics before, but Mike had the choice between keeping the tallyman happy, or keeping Kirton happy. He had no doubt which he preferred. He checked carefully every sling as it was lowered into the hold and suspected that there was a conspiracy going on to cheat the company. Every twenty or thirty slings they would send at least one sack short. Periodically they would put in an extra sack just to confuse Mike. He had told Kirton when he came on deck what was going on, and for the first time ever he grunted a type of thank you. This had quite shaken Mike and he watched, probably with his mouth open, as

Kirton shot off to the foredeck to check if the others had noticed the deception.

The Third Mate relieved him for lunch and managed to cause more trouble with the tallyman. He queried every sling that came aboard. By the time Mike returned, he doubted the wisdom of going ashore that evening. He would probably end up with a knife between his shoulder blades. He was very slow in accepting that this was yet another Hispanic custom, and he was supposed to turn a blind eye. The mood amongst the stevedores in the hold was becoming ugly as they realised that they were not going to make much extra from this ship.

On average, the stevedores were loading around 350 sacks of sugar an hour, so by the time they finished for the night there were just under 3,000 sacks in the hold, covering the deck totally with one layer, with a second layer over large areas of the hold. Mike's tally was nearly thirty sacks lower than the tallyman's and so he refused to sign his sheet at the end of the day. This produced a further stream of invective that fortunately he did not understand.

After dinner, they set off to paint the town red on the few pounds they had been able to draw from the Chief Steward. It was clear that there would only be one opportunity for a sub whilst they were in Cuba, so the £5 Mike had drawn would have to last throughout their time in their second Cuban port, Manzanilla, as well. What he did not know then was that on that particular evening he would not need to spend any money. The other apprentices and the engineers had laid plans to ensure that his seventeenth birthday would be memorable.

They walked for some time up the track, which purported to be the main road, until they reached a dilapidated large wooden building. The advertising signs on its weather beaten walls suggested that it was a bar. There was no sign of any other shops or buildings, so this would be as far as they travelled. The beers were ordered and they settled down at a large table. Mike would have been quite happy with a Coke, but as the beers had been ordered it seemed churlish to refuse.

Shortly afterwards a second round of beers were ordered, followed soon by a third and fourth round. By this time, four local girls who seemed very keen to join the party had joined them. Mike thought how beautiful one of the girls was. Her skin was a light coffee colour and her long hair jet black. She appeared to be around Mike's age, but was dressed in an older but quite provocative fashion. Lois was, without a doubt, the loveliest sight Mike had seen since leaving home.

As soon as Mike had finished his beers, he was introduced to a cubalibra, a mixture of the local rum Bacardi and Coca-Cola. This was more to Mike's taste than the beer he had been drinking. Anyway, he was feeling rather befuddled and could not be bothered to argue. The drink had been invented to celebrate the guerrilla struggle that was going on in Cuba. President Batista was almost universally disliked, and a guerrilla force led by a charismatic leader named Fidel Castro was up in the mountains, fighting to take over the country and oust Batista.

All the locals were far more enthusiastic about the possibility of Castro winning the struggle, as Batista had ruined the country and probably bled it dry whilst in power. They did not have the nerve to say too much about it for fear of the secret police. If you listened to the stories, the police were on every street corner waiting for someone to shout abuse at the Batista government.

Mike was far more interested in the lovely Lois than guerrilla warfare, and tried to engage her in conversation. With her smattering of English and his patience, they were making themselves understood. He wondered what she was doing in a place like this. The cubalibras were coming thick and fast and Mike was starting to lose his power of straight thinking. One of the last things he remembered before his head hit the table was a remark he had heard on the voyage to Cuba, "Watch out for the bars. Every bar is a brothel and every brothel a bar".

When he started to come to, he could not work out where he was. He lay on a bed, still fully clothed, but with the gorgeous Lois sitting on the edge of the bed, clad only in white bra and panties, which set off her colouring vividly. At first, he was convinced that he was dreaming, but his headache and inability to focus his eyes properly told him that it was not as simple as that. He closed his eyes again and tried desperately to remember what had happened during his last moments of consciousness. Where was he? What was he doing there? Where were his friends? What was this beautiful apparition at the end of the bed? How was he going to get out of the situation?

Lois spoke to him, dragging him out of his befuddlement, and although he had not really understood a word of what she said, he briefly answered her. At least she would know he was alive. She leant over him, and gave him a gentle peck on his forehead. He squeezed her hand as he made the effort to lift his head and at least part of his body off the bed. Eventually he managed to sit up and Lois administered first aid in the form of a glass of iced water. Mike could never remember water tasting that good before and he started immediately to feel better. If someone would only stop the pneumatic drill working inside his head, he would be fine.

He gave Lois a sheepish grin and immediately apologised for whatever he may, or may not have done. At that moment, he was not sure which was applicable. She moved closer until she was sitting alongside him, still clad only in her underwear. Mike realised that this is what he would have given anything for earlier, but somehow the enthusiasm had gone now. Slowly she started to tell him in a mixture of English, Spanish and sign language what had happened. Mike's thoughts went back to the last thing he could remember before the drink took over. Every bar is a brothel and every brothel is a bar.

It did not take Mike long to realise he was in a brothel, but nothing could make him believe that Lois was a lady of the night, a working girl, a woman of ill repute, a whore. No one as lovely as Lois could be involved in anything like that. No matter how many times he realised that it was a fact, he would not accept it. She told him how all his friends had told her that he was a virgin and had clubbed together to pay her to, as she put it, break him in.

Even in the state that Mike was in, he realised that there was no way that she had been successful. Even now, he found it hard enough to raise a smile never mind any interest in things sexual. He apologised to Lois again for being a nuisance, and she gave him an affectionate kiss and quick cuddle before jumping off the bed and slipping into a dress. Mike slowly stood up, and after the initial dizziness stopped, waved goodbye to Lois, headed for the door and the dirt track road leading back to *La Cordillera*.

As he wandered along the road to the ship, he tried to work out what would be waiting for him when he arrived. Almost certainly, he would be the butt of bad jokes for some time to come, but if the word got around what would the Captain say? What would Kirton have to say about it? He had promised in the indentures that apprentices had to sign that he would keep out of houses of ill repute. What would they have to say about it? Would it get back to his parents? All these things rotated in his mind during the seemingly interminable walk.

Mike considered for some time what he would tell the others. They had set him up. Should he tell them the truth, or should he elaborate a bit so that he could have the pleasure of watching their faces? He had been taught at school that revenge is a dish best served cold. He therefore resolved to make them suffer when he revealed what had happened to him that evening, and how Lois had begged him to stay with her, rather than go back to the ship.

Phil greeted him at the gangway by telling him what he had already heard from the returning apprentices and engineers. It was as Mike had feared. He would be the butt of their jokes for the rest of the voyage. Phil commiserated with him. He was well aware that if it had not been Mike, it would have been him, as the other new boy. Phil was already the subject of many jokes, as he would not use any swear words, either when working or conversing. This made him stand out significantly. Mike was impressed with the way he would not change, despite all the ribbing.

Mike went to his cabin and bunk, but not before taking a couple of painkillers in the hopes that his head would feel better after a few hours' sleep. His last waking thoughts were of the story he would tell when he had to face the other two apprentices. When he had finished they would have to accept his word, as they would be unable to disprove it.

After a very short night, it was back to the counting of the bags of sugar. Mike felt awful, and had a problem with staying awake in the hot sun. The slings of sacks passing before his eyes had a soporific effect, causing him to experience intense pain from his already aching head banging against the accommodation bulkhead. This reoccurred on several occasions during the course of the day. The tallyman seemed much happier with him, so it was reasonable to assume that they had loaded substantially fewer sacks than they should have done.

The lunch break was shortened to thirty minutes. The stevedore gangs did not break for lunch and the Third Mate had relieved Mike prior to having lunch himself. As a result, he spent very little time with the others. Despite their remarks, he hinted at the wonderful night he had spent with Lois. It was worth the lying and the headache just to see their faces. They were an absolute picture.

He returned to the cargo tallying feeling better than he had in the last fourteen hours and vowed to continue the storytelling later in the day. In the meantime he would try and restore the cargo figures by disputing every sling, hoping that by the time they stopped for the day he would be somewhere near to the correct figure. It would take a Herculean effort to stay awake, but now it was starting to seem worthwhile.

After dinner, as predicted, the engineers, the Electrician, Paul and Tony came round to the cabin he shared with Phil. Their sole intention was to extract the Michael from Mike, and try to humiliate him. Mike greeted them by thanking them for the greatest night of his life. For a minute, the cabin was quiet and so Mike gave them a blow-by-blow account of what had happened once he had made it to Lois's room. By the time he had graphically described the striptease she had performed for him you could have heard a pin drop. This was followed by a hint of what had happened next and how Lois had continued to ravish his body through the night.

They wanted to disbelieve totally every word Mike uttered, but they could not be sure, so they pressed him on some of the details. Mike explained that a gentleman did not go into such details, and so they left him and went ashore to the bar for another evening's entertainment. Mike breathed a sigh of relief and headed for his bunk in the hopes of catching up on his sleep.

They completed loading the scheduled quantity of cargo from Guantanamo Bay the following day and prepared for sailing to Manzanillo. By sunset the hatches were battened down, the Pilot was aboard and they were underway for the overnight journey around the coast. Mike stood and watched as the port slowly slipped astern of them, and reflected on the experience gained from his very first really foreign port.

By sunrise, they were awaiting the arrival of the Manzanillo Pilot, and within a short time were heading into the port itself. They completed the berthing and started again readying the ship for the loading of cargo. This time Mike was blessed with a seemingly honest tallyman. The whole day passed without a single dispute on sling content. He had invested in a large straw Stetson, and sat on his chair overlooking the hold with the intention of enjoying the time in port. He would probably have continued to enjoy the respite from the normal routine, if Kirton had not come along during the afternoon and told him to climb into his bunk. He was night watchman with effect from 1900 hours.

The time between 1900 hrs and 0200 hrs passed reasonably quickly, as most of the ship's company had gone ashore and were returning at different times and in different states. Several crewmembers were literally dragged back aboard the ship by their mates as the night wore on. Mike helped them aboard, and continued to check the ropes fore and aft on a regular basis. By two o'clock, he was starting to flag. The Cook had left bacon, eggs and sausages out for him to cook for his meal, so he passed the time by lighting the galley range and cooking himself a fry up.

After finishing his meal and making a mug of tea, it was still only three o'clock. He still had four hours left to kill before he would be relieved. Despite the time, he was still dressed in shirt and shorts due to the heat and humidity. The mosquitoes had noted this and were taking every opportunity to bite him. He had covered himself with mosquito repellent earlier in the evening, but this appeared to be wearing off so he covered himself again with the awful smelling liquid.

He walked to the forecastle to check the forward ropes and then down to the stern to check the after moorings. Someone had left a chair near the No 5 hold, so Mike sat down to pass some time as the clock moved pathetically slowly towards 0700 hrs. He must have dropped off to sleep almost immediately, and was wakened by something moving on his foot. What he saw ensured that he stayed awake for the rest of the watch, and every other night on night watch thereafter. Two large rats had just walked over his feet, which were shod only in sandals.

He was awakened by the noise of the cargo loading just after lunch time. He had been so tired by the time he collapsed into his bunk that even the horror of the rats walking over him had not caused him a problem. Almost certainly it would in the future, but not today. He dressed, determined to enjoy the one perk of night watch, going ashore in the daytime and seeing the port when the shops rather than the bars were open.

The port of Manzanillo was a typically Cuban town. The buildings were old and for the most part weathered by the hot sun. The paint on them was peeling and bleached, but the welcome from the inhabitants was genuine. Mike was impressed with the lack of urgency and the laid-back attitude to everything. He enjoyed his time, shopping until most of his currency was gone. He kept enough to buy himself some Coca-Cola that he could enjoy during the night's work.

Two days after this pleasant shore leave, they were battening down the hatches that were virtually full of sugar, lowering the derricks and making ready for sea. This would be their last port of note until they arrived in Osaka. The thought of the journey ahead excited Mike, and particularly the destination. But before Japan, they would have to pass through the Panama Canal, one of the world's greatest engineering achievements.

CHAPTER 13

Apart from a brief glimpse of the coast of Jamaica on the next day and the ever-increasing heat, they had little to talk about during the passage to Panama. They had spent the working hours chipping paint as usual. As a result, in the absence of sun tan oil, they were all badly burnt. The straw hat had been a great help keeping the sun off Mike's head, but his arms, legs and back were painful and starting to peel. The one cheering thought was that if he could keep the tan that he would eventually acquire, it would be a great talking point back in Bridlington.

They had expected that they would be chipping paint and painting for the majority of the voyage to Japan, but Kirton told them in an extremely unnerving and conspiratorial way that he had a special job for them once they cleared Panama. He had said there would be money in it for them, but gave no further details. Whilst Mike risked being called cynical and pessimistic, he did not believe that Kirton would be involved in anything that would benefit the apprentices. They spent all the time available for talking thinking of any possible work that they could do that would bring in money. They could not between them come up with any job that would be legal. They had to assume that it was illegal.

Almost exactly two and a half days after leaving Manzanillo the clang of the engine room telegraph was heard whilst they were having their breakfast. They dashed out onto the deck to see ahead of them a large number of ships at anchor, awaiting their turn to transit the canal. Although they would be requiring a Pilot for the canal, initially they would have to anchor and wait their turn in the queue. They organised a very much shorter ladder for when the Pilot arrived. The ship was sitting so low in the water that ten or twelve rungs were quite sufficient, whereas they had needed the whole ladder plus an extension when they arrived at Guantanamo.

Mike had been asked many times since leaving Liverpool whether he was saving carrots up for the mules in Panama. On the first occasion, he had fallen for it, not realising that they were talking about the mules that would assist them in their passage through the three series of locks that made up the Panama Canal. The mules were like small locomotives with a cab at each end. Between the two cabs, a large winch like drum carried a heavy steel cable. Four mules, two on each side, would pass their cables to the ship to ensure that the ship could be moved through the locks without scraping the huge stone walls, and to hold her steady whilst the water was allowed to fill up the lock.

The ship would be lifted over eighty feet up to the level of the Gatun Lake before beginning the journey towards the Pacific Ocean. To achieve this incredible feat, fifty two million gallons of freshwater would be drawn off the lake. With the type of rainfall experienced here, it was not a tremendous sacrifice through most of the year. The incredible sacrifice that had built this eighth wonder of the world was the number of people who had died from Yellow Fever during its construction. For every foot of the narrowest part, the Caillard Cut, a man had died. A sobering thought when considering the wonderful achievement.

The first attempt at crossing the isthmus was still visible to the side of the canal, Ferdinand de Lesseps the successful builder of the Suez Canal had started construction of a canal back in 1881, but the conditions and disease forced its abandonment a few years later. The need for such a canal was never more obvious than at the time of the Cuban American war when it took sixty-seven days for the American battleship *Oregon* to sail from San Francisco, around Cape Horn to Cuba. The building of the canal reduced the journey by eight thousand miles, and ensured American interest in its construction.

Mike had read much about the Canal and had seen pictures of it in Geography classes at school. In fact, his Father had set the start of the book he was trying to write on board a ship making the journey through it. He was therefore more excited than most to be actually making the crossing from the Caribbean to the Pacific. The day seemed to pass slowly as they waited their turn, and they started to contemplate the thought that they may have to wait until the next day. The priority for those ships passing from the Atlantic side towards the Pacific expired in the late afternoon, when priority would switch to the ships making the opposite crossing from the Pacific. They were now in the afternoon.

Presently a high-powered American military launch came alongside and the Canal Pilot came aboard. Their time had come, and they were to be the next ship into the locks. Stand by fore and aft was called and the crew went to their stations. According to the older hands, they were likely to be there for some time, as a fast passage through the canal would be at least ten hours. But with the amount of ships they had seen ahead of them, it was more probably going to be more like fifteen to twenty hours. A large proportion of this time would have to be spent at their stations whilst they moved through the three sets of locks. For those not on watch, there would be some sleeping time as they travelled from Gatun Lake to the Pedro Miguel locks, but it was almost certainly going to be a very disturbed night.

The next launch to arrive carried the customs, immigration and health officials, but far more importantly the ship's agent with the mail. Immediately everyone's thoughts turned from the canal to what mail they would be receiving shortly. Would there be a letter from Julia for Mike, and if so what would she have to tell him? As it had only been six days since they had mail in Manzanillo, he could not imagine that there would be anything for him at all, but he never the less hoped that there would be. They did not have long to wait until the Chief Steward came to their stations and distributed the letters, Mike and Paul had letters from their Mothers and some of the crew had letters, but in general, as expected there was not much mail, which upset most of the crew.

By the time they had finished reading their letters they were approaching the first of the Gatun locks. Ahead of them, they were confronted with the incredible sight of the ship that had preceded them into the locks, towering eighty-five feet above them. If Mike had been impressed before, the reality of what the Canal actually did was brought home to him in dramatic style. On each side of them the mules were getting nearer as they made their way down the track towards the lock gate. Within a few minutes the crew had thrown heaving lines to the waiting handlers on the lock wall and dragged the wire ropes attached to the forward mules winch drum over to the ship, where they were made fast.

The ship moved forward slowly into the lock, the mules took the strain and within a few minutes, the ship was positioned exactly in the middle of the lock. The after mules were made fast and the huge gates closed. Mike had expected the movement of the ship in the lock to be imperceptible. Within seconds, the surface of the lock turned into a maelstrom as the one hundred gravity fed inlet valves started to fill the lock with water from the second lock and the ship was lifted steadily up to the first level. As soon as the level was reached, the gates ahead of them opened, the mules began their forty-five degree climb on their funicular rail line, and the ship moved through into the second lock. The process was repeated for a second and then a third time, to lift the ship eighty-five feet up to the level of the Gatun Lake.

The gates of the third lock opened, they let go the mules and once again they were on their own as they started to move across the lake. Mike was struck by the intense green of the tropical vegetation surrounding them and he could well believe that this was one of the wettest places on the American continent. Today the humid heat was oppressive and he could only imagine what it must be like when it rained to give the amount of water needed to keep operating the locks. Astern of them and receding into the background was the Caribbean, their last look at this part of the world for some time as they headed towards the immense Pacific Ocean.

Once they had cleared Gatun, they were allowed to stand down and they headed for the cabins and the saloon. Mike noticed that in the alleyway where their cabins were, a small queue of sheepish looking engineers, stewards and seamen had formed outside the Chief Steward's Office/First Aid room. He mentioned this to Tony and Paul who laughed and explained that they were waiting for their jabs. Mike continued to pursue his line of questioning.

Eventually Paul explained that the crewmembers were in fact waiting for penicillin injections to counter the gonorrhoea infection they had contacted in Cuba. This was a sight that he was to get used to as the voyage unfolded, and more and more members found themselves unable to resist the charms of the natives.

There were always the stories from some of those involved that they had not been to brothels. There must be some mistake as the girl they had slept with was a nice family girl, and not a lady of easy virtue. Paul recounted an experience on his previous ship where they had been in a bar in Recife.

The owner of the bar was attempting to persuade Paul that the gorgeous young girl behind the bar whom Paul had been watching for the past two nights was a virgin waiting to start her profession working with the other girls in the bar. Although tempted, Paul steadfastly refused to weaken and go upstairs with the girl. The Third Engineer, who was not going to wait for Paul to make up his mind, brought the matter to a head. He greedily paid his money and took the girl to a room upstairs. The whole incident would have been forgotten were it not for the Third Engineer appearing outside the Chief Steward's Office four days out of Recife, celebrating the enlightenment of his virgin.

They had made good progress by the time Mike began his watch. They were about to enter the Gaillard or Culebra

Cut, the narrowest part of the canal. It was just three hundred feet wide here for eight miles. Although work had already started to widen the Cut to five hundred feet, it was not expected to be finished until the seventies. The Cut had been re-named Gaillard in honour of the engineer in charge of its construction. Without any doubt, it had been the most difficult part of the canal to construct. There was huge loss of life and devastating landslides, but it represented a substantial reason for the canal to be considered the eighth wonder of the world.

At the end of the Gaillard Cut were the Pedro Miguel locks that would start the lowering process. Everyone returned to their stations fore and aft. The whole of the lock area was brilliantly floodlit, to the extent that you had to look into the distance to realise it was night. They went through the same process of securing the mules and began the transit into the lock. The gates astern of them closed and the lowering process began. Thirty-two feet later the gates ahead of them opened, the mules guided them to the end of the lock and were let go. The darkness rapidly enveloped them and they were on their way to Miraflores and the Pacific that lay on the far side of its locks.

After the feverish activity of the lock transit, the bridge was comparatively calm. Mike made his way to the wing where he had a wonderful view of the action. The night was the type that would live in memory for many years. It was hot and steamy, and above the thump of the engine could be heard the noise of crickets and other inhabitants of the jungle on either side of them. The stars above were bright, but there was no moon, the only light visible being the navigation lights on either side. The Pilot was in conversation with the Captain, and the Third Mate hung onto the engine room telegraph as if someone was about to take it away from him. Periodically the Pilot would call out a course change that would be repeated by the seaman on the wheel, but at this stage there was very little to do until they had to go to their stations. It was the kind of night that made Mike realise why he had wanted to be here.

By the time Mike had adjusted to the peace and quiet it was over. Ahead of them were the brilliant lights of the Miraflores locks and it was time to stand by fore and aft again. The same procedure was gone through again with the mules, only this time they would pass through two locks as they made their final descent through fifty-three feet to the level of the Pacific. Within the hour, they had let go the mules, said goodbye to the Pilot, and rung "Full ahead" as they entered the Pacific Ocean and began to look forward to reaching Japan.

CHAPTER 14

By the time Mike went out on deck the next morning the frenetic activity of the previous day had vanished. In the distance on the starboard side, there was a vague suggestion of land as they headed south out of the Gulf of Panama. The canal lay some sixty to seventy miles astern of them and the ship was racing through the clear, flat calm waters at a good speed of around twelve to thirteen knots. This to Mike was what it was all about. A heavily laden ship steaming at full speed across a wonderfully blue sea, not a cloud in the sky, not a ripple on the surface of the water.

The oppressive humid heat of the canal zone had been replaced by a very hot day tempered by a warm breeze caused by the speed of the ship. In the accommodation, it was swelteringly hot. They had tried to fix cardboard scoops onto the portholes in the hopes of forcing cooler air into the cabins, to little avail. Unfortunately, the first person to walk down the starboard alleyway in the dark didn't have much sense of humour as his face collided with the scoop. Nevertheless, plan B was on the drawing board for action later.

Ahead of them on the starboard bow lay Punta Mala on the Peninsula De Azuero. This stretch of coastline, terminating at Punta Mariato, would be the last land they would see before they adopted a westerly course that would bring them to the approaches to Japan, some eight thousand miles and around twenty-nine days away. This would be the longest time at sea to date, and Mike wondered what work would be found for them to occupy them for that continuous length of time.

The immediate prospects were not bad. Tomorrow would be Saturday when they would work together to clean and scrub out the wheelhouse. This would probably be a job and finish where they would work like Trojans to complete the work during the morning so that they could have an afternoon free. On Sunday, they would be cleaning the accommodation in readiness for the Captain's inspection. Once again, they would finish by 1100 hrs with the added bonus of Sunday lunch. All in all life was looking rosier. But could it last?

By Monday, everyone had settled once again into the sea-going routine. The sea state had altered, causing a slight roll and a temperature drop of a few degrees to a more manageable level. This was just as well, as Kirton had told them of his money making plan. The apprentices had been right in assuming it was probably illegal, it most definitely was! He had persuaded the stevedoring company in Cuba to supply several bundles of spare sacks in case any of the sugar sacks had been damaged in loading.

His scheme was based on the assumption that the number of sacks loaded in Cuba would tally accurately with the number unloaded in Osaka and Tokyo. If he was able to produce far more sacks than originally loaded he would be able to negotiate a selling price with the agent in Tokyo, he would then split the money with the officers and apprentices. On the promise of twenty pounds each to spend in Japan, which was the equivalent to Mike of two months wages, they would create more sacks of sugar.

Armed with knives, shovels, scoops and bagging needles they climbed down into the No 1 hold and rigged a series of lighting clusters. They turned the hold ventilators around as much as possible to force some air into the holds, but most of them were rusted and immovable. As a result, the temperature in the working area on top of the cargo was similar to a sauna, with the added cloying smell of sweating sugar. They had already stripped to a pair of shorts and a mutton cloth bandanna around their foreheads but the sweat was running down their faces and bodies.

They unpicked the stitching on the top of a sugar sack, scooped some out into an empty sack, then sewed the top up again using some thread pulled out of a piece of old sacking. The original sack did not look suspicious. This was repeated eight or ten times until the empty sack was filled. It was then sewn up and stacked separately so that a close watch could be kept on the numbers created.

Gradually they formed a production line, one of them unpicked the stitches on the existing bags, two of them scooped and shovelled the sugar, and the fourth one sewed up the bags. They changed jobs at a regular interval to relieve the boredom. In the first hour with Kirton supervising, they created one new sack of sugar. Realising that at that rate they were only going to produce eight sacks per day, he started to use his over developed strength to drag two sacks at a time to the point where the apprentices were working. This had the effect of producing one extra sack in the second hour and again in the third. After lunch, they were just able to maintain three new sacks per hour. Despite Kirton's efforts to make them work faster, they did not increase on that hourly figure.

By day two Kirton had decided to reduce the number of sacks to be opened to six or seven, taking more sugar out of each one. This reduced the amount of sewing and unpicking. Immediately the number of new sacks increased to four per hour and then five in the next hours. At the same time, it was more apparent that the donor sacks had been tampered with. Kirton stated that he wanted fifty new sacks per day, but even with him working all day, they did not increase on the figure. Assuming they worked every working day until they arrived in Osaka, they would have produced over six hundred sacks.

Day three found the apprentices on their own. Kirton had started to tire of the idea of working in a sauna after losing weight at an alarming rate and causing him to worry about his muscle-bound figure. He had, as expected, issued instructions to the apprentices to work harder to make up for his absence. The good news was that, apart from a regular visit to check the number of new sacks, they saw very little of him during the next two weeks. They were also losing weight rapidly, and were making up for it by eating colossal amounts of food.

Breakfast out on the No 3 hatch top consisted of cereals, a large curry or kedgeree, bacon, eggs, and a pile of flapjacks, followed by toast. If they ate outside on the hatch top at lunch time, their plates were piled high. They had three courses, and sometimes three helpings of pudding. As they had to appear in the saloon at dinner time they only had normal helpings then, but they went right through the menu. Vast quantities of liquid accompanied every break, mostly tea and coffee. Occasionally they had water that had passed through the main refrigerator, the tap to which was padlocked to stop the ship's complement using it all the time. The copious amounts of fluids helped to stop them de-hydrating at a worse level than they had been.

The crew were allowed to buy three cans of beer per day from the Captains bond, but the apprentices were only allowed cordial to mix with the tepid water. After a day in the hold, even this proved extremely inviting.

On day four, they moved to the next hold. They had

hidden the new sacks under untouched cargo, so that what had happened would not be apparent. But one hundred and twenty new sacks, plus the six or seven hundred that had provided their content took some hiding. In hold No 2, they started all over again dragging the sacks from one end of the hold, to creating a large pit where the underweight sacks could be hidden.

All four of them were feeling totally drained by the oppressive heat. Despite regular water breaks and smokos up on deck, there was no way the number of new sacks per day were going to increase. The thought of the money in either Osaka or Tokyo drove them on. A quality 35mm camera or cine camera for ten pounds was the spur that Mike needed to push himself to the limit.

Mike's abiding passion had always been photography, as it had been his Father's before him. He had his first Box Brownie at the age of eight and had never looked back. Two years later, it was a Kodak Duoflex, which he carried everywhere possible, and which subsequently accompanied him on the *Rossallian* to Russia. Next came a series of Zeiss Ikons and Kodak folding bellows type cameras, which inspired him to join the Bridlington School Photographic Society. Home processing followed shortly after with the gift of a contact printer for his birthday and the basic chemicals to go with it. This was followed quickly by access to the school darkroom out of school hours.

The society had a top of the range enlarger that had a glass negative carrier capable of handling most sizes of negatives, and chemical dishes that would accept prints up to twenty inches by sixteen inches. Two of the masters were avid photographers and were only too pleased to pass on their skills to Mike, probably because they knew of no other way of gaining his interest. He spent hours dodging with pieces of card and metal under the light from the enlarger's lens in the hope that he could alter areas of light and shade on the negative and ensure the perfect print. Over a period of time, he produced prints that other people thought were very good, but found little that he was satisfied with.

By the age of twelve, he had his first job delivering evening papers to the north-eastern corner of Bridlington. Two years later, he added delivering Sunday newspapers for another newsagent at a remarkable wage of half a crown. Together with five shillings for a week's work from the evening round, he had enough money for the specialist photographic papers he needed to indulge his passion. First, he tried Kodak's Bromesko range for its black and white accentuation, but quickly settled on Agfa's Brovira and Portiga papers that gave superb blacks, whites, and texture to the prints.

The fact that he was now producing acceptable quality prints led to more expense. He was persuaded to enter prints in the school society's exhibition. To do this he had to purchase exhibition mounting card and mounting tissue.

As a result of this, the number of prints being consigned to the rubbish bin grew. This led to a further job, this time for Saturdays during the summer months. He joined the huge ranks of seasonal workers in Bridlington who relied on the thousands of visitors who made the annual pilgrimage from Leeds, Sheffield, and the industrialised areas of Yorkshire.

Along with several other boys, he had identified a need for transporting suitcases from the railway station to the bed and breakfast establishments around the town. At the height of summer, the trains arrived almost every minute, disgorging many hundreds of people. The railway station stood at least half a mile from the nearest guest houses, and in some cases over two miles away. Most of these people were on a very limited budget and were not inclined to take taxis. Mike and the other boys queued at the station gates with a wonderful selection of old prams, or pram wheels that were capable of carrying a family's suitcases.

Dependent on the distance to the guesthouse they received anything from one shilling to half a crown for each journey. They were able to complete between four to six journeys per day. On a good day, he made twelve to fifteen shillings for the Saturday to share with his younger brother. It all helped him to keep buying film and papers.

By the time he was ready to go to sea he had graduated to an Ilford Sportsman 35mm camera, which had been handed down from his father. The controls on it were limited, but he had been reasonably happy with the results he had produced using Ilford Pan F and FP2 black and white film. He had his own enlarger and dishes and was able to take a job in photography shortly after his sixteenth birthday.

A close neighbour had a large photographic processing business on the Promenade in Bridlington. His main business was collecting exposed films from shops and caravan sites in the area, developing and printing them during the next day, and returning the prints for collection within twenty-four hours. At the height of the season, they would process in excess of five hundred films per day. At Easter and in September they rarely dropped much below two hundred films per day.

To Mike, it seemed that all his Christmases had come at once. He was going to be paid to spend all his holidays processing films. If pushed, he would probably have done it for nothing. But what he did not know was that the job would introduce him to his other all-time abiding passion: motor cycles.

His new employer intended to teach Mike to ride a motorcycle, a BSA Bantam, so he could cover the film collection round each day. The round covered some twenty miles around Bridlington itself, out to Sewerby, Flamborough and North Landing. On the first day, he was given one lesson in the controls and theory of gear changing and was left to practise on waste ground and around the town before starting his first run.

His Mother insisted that he wore a crash helmet when riding the Bantam. Rather than risk losing the opportunity, Mike reluctantly agreed. Even though the spring had not really arrived, he did not notice the cold. The adrenaline was sufficient to insulate him against bad weather. He made his first calls in the week before Easter on the south side of Bridlington and slowly made his way to the north of the town. From there it was out into the country and a chance to wind the throttle open on the way to Sewerby and Flamborough. The last calls were at North Landing, and then the wonderful run through the countryside back to the shop. Could life really be this good?

Mike could hardly wait for the summer to arrive when he could work full-time in the processing laboratory, and collect and deliver the films in the evening. In the meantime, he was happy to rush home from school, jump on the Bantam and complete his round. His only problem in life during spring was that he had to attend school in between one collection and another.

Mike even thought of taking the Bantam to school, but resisted until the lunch time when he found he had a puncture in his bike's rear tyre. Thinking it would be a good excuse to ride the Bantam to school and be the envy of his peers, he set off to school. Afterwards he realised that it would have been sensible to enter the school premises by the main road, but he elected to ride up the long drive, where the Gym Master saw him. Mike was not one of the Gym Master's favourite pupils due to his lack of effort in all things connected with PT.

Problems followed far faster than expected, as the first period of the afternoon's timetable was PT. Within ten minutes of the start of the lesson, he found himself outside the Headmaster's office. On at least two occasions, this had ended painfully for Mike, and he was anxious to ensure that this visit did not end in the same way.

His brain went into overtime concocting a story to explain him arriving at school on a motorcycle. In the end, the truth was sufficient. The Headmaster discussed motorcycles and cars with him for five minutes, and sent him on his way with a warning not to bring the Bantam to school again without permission.

Five weeks after the dream began, it ended very abruptly. Kevin, his neighbour and employer, was heading home from the shop on a rainy day and was involved in an accident with a car on the Promenade. The Bantam was badly damaged and the insurance company spent the whole summer deciding whether to repair it or write it off. Mike was destined not to ride a motorcycle again until 1962. The film run became a car journey with Mike as a passenger. The magic had disappeared forever.

Now Mike had the chance of earning sufficient money to purchase a camera of his choice in Japan. It would have interchangeable lenses, but would he be able to afford one of the new single lens reflexes? Tony, Paul and Phil had similar ambitions. This was Thursday and they would hopefully have two days out of the holds at the weekend to act as an extra spur, but it was getting more difficult by the day to keep going. Their hands were calloused and sore from sewing sacks and dragging of them across the hold. The constant sweating and the roughness of the sacking was also making their arms, legs and chests equally sore.

They managed to drag themselves through Thursday and Friday somehow, and almost welcomed the cleaning of the wheelhouse and accommodation on Saturday as a means of getting out of the holds. Mike had never been so keen to polish the brass engine room telegraph on the bridge wing. It ensured that he stayed in the sun and fresh air for at least an hour. The smell of the sugar no longer filled his nostrils. It was only just perceptible when the air from the hold ventilators was blown towards the bridge.

On watch that evening, he had time to be able to reflect on the Pacific Ocean. They had been in the Pacific for just a week and had a further two weeks to go before they would see land. They had taken a course that would keep them away from land until they reached Japan. Already the majority of the ship's company were bored with no change in the pattern of work and eight hour watches. In contrast, the apprentices would have enjoyed the opportunity to taste boredom, unless there was a change of heart they faced ten hours in the holds working on Kirton's scam plus four hours on watch in the evening.

The ocean was exactly as its name suggested. For the majority of the past week it had been flat calm with hardly a trace of a ripple. The ship seemed to speed through the water without leaving an impression other than its wake at the stern. The sunsets of purple, gold, green, turquoise and blue were even more incredible than those enjoyed in the Caribbean. The bow wave, wake and ripples turned into an incredible spectacle. Phosphorescence in the water caused them to light up in a display of turquoise luminosity of unbelievable depths and staggering brightness.

Mike ran to the bow to make the most of the phenomenon and looked at the water below him. Every little drop of spray flashed with iridescent colour. Even the odd fish surfacing looked like a sign from Blackpool's illuminations. The wake astern of them boiled in a fluorescent turquoise maelstrom. On either side, quick flashes of light could be seen as spray droplets shot through the air. He thought to himself that it was probably worth a week's work in the hold for the chance of visions such as this.

They spent the next week in the No 2 and 3 holds,

doctoring the sacks of sugar. By the end of the second week, they calculated they had created well over four hundred extra sacks. Early in week three, they hit five hundred while working in the No 4 hold. Although told by Kirton to keep going, mysteriously they were withdrawn suddenly from the hold and spent the remaining days at sea working on chipping and painting in readiness for their arrival in Japan. Whether the Captain had suddenly realised where they were, or whether he was worried about what might be said about their uniforms hanging off them, they did not know. Either way, the scam was at an end and they just had to wait for their money.

The temperature dropped markedly as they approached Japan. They changed back into their battle-dress uniforms, putting their whites away until such time as they travelled south again. The sea state had also gradually changed, starting with a gradual roll of five to ten degrees in a very long swell to something a bit more obvious. The ship was rolling steadily around fifteen to twenty degrees. Things slowly began to slide off desks and shelves if they were not secured.

They continued on relatively light duties, chipping, scraping and painting around the amidships accommodation. No mention had been made about the sugar scam, and they assumed that they would have to wait until they completed the discharge of the cargo in Tokyo before being paid their share of the money. They had all mentally spent the money and it would only be a matter of travelling to the Ginza in Tokyo to collect their dream purchases.

As they approached the Kii Suido, the sea leading to the port of Osaka, they turned into the swell causing the ship to start a pitching motion. At the same time, the water depth was reducing from around 2,700 fathoms to 1,100 fathoms, causing the sea swell to alter dramatically. The apprentices had been given the job of preparing the ship for entering port and they were hauling out the mooring ropes from the after rope locker when Mike suddenly noticed that the ship was pitching far more heavily than beforehand. He looked up and froze in horror at the scene before him.

From their position on the afterdeck, the ship appeared to be diving straight into a massive wave, the crest of which was above the top of the foremast. He shouted to his colleagues. This was probably going to be the end, and he was unable to disguise the terror he felt. But just as it looked as if the mountainous wave was going to crash into them, the bow lifted. For a moment, they sat on top of the wave before beginning an even more frightening sleigh ride down the other side of it.

For what seemed like an eternity, but in reality was about an hour they fought their way through the fearsome sea. Eventually the waves reduced in size, as they saw on the horizon their first sight of land for three weeks. The relief soaked through Mike. His mind went back to the storm he endured on the *Rossallian* and the calm that followed. Perhaps prayer worked after all!

They busied themselves preparing for the Pilot, and put more effort than normal into all their preparations to wipe the last hour from their memories. The Pilot boarded shortly afterwards and they headed for their stations fore and aft. Around them lay a land unlike anything Mike had seen before, the excitement began to mount as their recent experience was forgotten and they arrived in Japan.

CHAPTER 15

On the next morning, they were out on deck by 0700 hrs to witness a sight unlike anything they had seen before. From a long distance, the ship looked as if it was being attacked by ants. Hundreds of stevedores had come aboard, stripped the hatches of all their covers, boards and beams, and were already positioning the derricks for the first slings of sacks to be deposited on the quay. Whilst they were arranging the derricks, their colleagues had already made up several slings of sacks ready for the hook to lift them.

The contrast between what they were witnessing and the manana attitude of the Cubans who loaded the sugar was breathtaking. The Japanese appeared to be enjoying the work. They wanted to complete it as quickly as possible, whereas the Cubans' sole intention seemed to be to make the job last as long as possible. By 0715 hrs, the first slings were heading shoreward. The pace was maintained for the whole day with a short break around lunch time.

Occasionally the stevedores would take a drink of water from the wooden bucket they had brought with them, using the carved wooden ladle on a stick. Although simply made, it struck Mike as a thing of beauty. When he eventually drank from it, there was a whole new dimension to the taste of the water. The wood had an unusual fragrance and was probably from the pine family. He decided there and then that he must have one of these before leaving. Two days later when he surreptitiously removed one from the hold to his cabin he found that he was not the only one with the idea.

By the end of the first day's work, it became very apparent that they would not be staying more than three days in Osaka. Roughly half the cargo was to be discharged in Osaka prior to their voyage around the coast to Tokyo. At least double the amount loaded in a day in Cuba had been discharged, including all the extra sacks they had produced during the voyage and they waited excitedly for the pay out they would receive in Tokyo.

After spending three weeks at sea, their priority that evening was to go ashore. Mike had been able to draw the sum of £10 as a sub on his wages. This was a fortune in a country that was still suffering economically twelve and a half years after the end of the war. Already many traders had been aboard the ship with a huge range of products, some incredibly beautiful, some very tatty copies of American products such as Zippo lighters.

Mike had been struck by the eggshell china tea services, which were extremely popular amongst the whole crew. He selected a wonderfully gaudy one incorporating dragons in red, gold and green. The spout on the teapot and milk jug were in the form of a dragon's head. The tail was raised a half inch off the surface of the china, winding over the lid towards the handle, which was also part of the tail, in gold with individual white scales. The cups matched the dragon theme and seemed almost too delicate to pick up without crushing. The cup handles also had the raised scales and formed the tail of the dragon. Traditionally when raised to the light a delightful picture of a Geisha was visible.

Mike paid a total of £3 10s 0d for the tea service with teapot, milk jug, sugar bowl and six cup and saucers. He was a slightly nervous about parting with his money, as the tea service would not be delivered until just before they sailed from Osaka, but those that had been to Japan before said that it would turn up on time. He was also advised that the tea service would arrive in a wooden crate. Under no circumstances should he open it, as this would be considered to be very bad manners, implying lack of trust. In addition, it would be impossible to re-pack in the way that the potter had packed it.

After what seemed an age, they finished work, showered and dressed ready for going ashore. The whole ship's company had been warned as to their behaviour in the city. The Americans were not popular in this area of Japan, and the British were not too far removed from the Americans. There were apparently many brothel/bars on the way to the city, and the apprentices were specifically told to stay out of them. After Guantanamo, Mike had no interest at all in entering another for the foreseeable future.

The stories of what awaited the sailor who frequented the Japanese brothels ensured that the majority of the ship's company got no further than the road to Osaka itself. Lured by the tales of bathing ceremonies, erotic massages and Japanese troilism, their interest did not extend to shopping and sightseeing, nor to the study of life in this teeming city.

The apprentices put themselves above all this and started the walk to the city. On the way, they passed several groups from the ship's company, standing outside bars, discussing the qualities of the girls on view inside. They were not swayed. The sight unfolding before them amazed them. The area on the outskirts of the city was virtually unlit with the exception of the light coming through the walls of the houses on either side of them. Although they were looking at poverty on a large scale, they were struck by the cleanliness of the area. Many of the workers in this area were in the textile industry, and evidence of this was on most corners with material for kimonos stacked in huge piles.

Eventually they reached the city, which was exactly the opposite of the area they had walked through. Every type of light you could imagine, raw, naked electric light bulbs, oily black smoking torches, delicate paper lanterns, made a blaze of colour that seared the eyes. There were banners and signs in brightly coloured script the meaning of which they could only guess. There were unbelievable smells, some appetising, some decidedly not, and despite the time everywhere there were crowds of people hurrying between the shops and restaurants.

Having missed their evening meal and done a hard day's work, Paul, Phil and Mike were feeling very hungry, but were reluctant to enter one of the tiny restaurants that abounded. Eventually the pangs overtook them and they entered a small but clean looking establishment just off the main street. The owner bowed low before them and they self-consciously did the same in return. They were shown to their table and a menu placed before them. As soon as they looked at the menu, they realised that they were in trouble. The only recognisable symbol on the paper was the yen sign. If they wanted to work to a budget, this would be useful, but there was no indication whatsoever of the food on offer.

One by one, they tried using hand signals and animal impersonations to communicate the type of food they would like. Eventually the whole of the small restaurant came to a standstill as the strange foreigners communicated with the owner. They settled for some sort of pork stew, or so they thought.

With an intense feeling of trepidation they settled on their seats and looked first at the tea they had been served. No milk and no sugar. How were they going to drink it? In due course, the fact that they had not had a drink since the afternoon tea break prompted them to try the tea. To someone brought up on milk and two sugars, it came as something of a shock, but was not unpleasant. In the absence of anything else, they started to drink.

Presently their meal arrived, together with the chopsticks with which they were supposed to eat it. Phil and Mike had never even seen chopsticks before, and relied on instruction from Paul who had used them on one previous occasion. By this time, they had the feeling that all eyes in the restaurant were upon them. In fact the other customers were probably far too good mannered to look at them. The dish presented to them was a cross between a thick soup and a stew, the ingredients of which would forever remain a mystery.

Bravely and hungrily, they set about their meal. Shortly, they were chasing lumps of something around the table top, as they tried in desperation to use the chopsticks. In deference to their inexperience and fruitless chasing of the best part of the meal around the table, the waitress had produced very ornamental spoons. The boys gratefully used them to eat the meal before it became cold. Despite the look of it, with shredded cabbage and other vegetables, in reality it was a very tasty meal, or was that the hunger talking?

They left the small restaurant, and thanked the owner, who bowed profusely. After this, they thought themselves very worldly-wise and would not worry about strange food again. They returned to the brightly lit street and the main job of the evening, spending the small amount of money they had in a country where their money appeared to be worth ten times its value in England.

Despite the small number of western visitors to Osaka, many of the shops were selling souvenirs aimed at the western market. Miniature, and not so miniature, samurai swords were in abundance, copies of Zippo and other lighters, some marked "Made in USA", a small area of Japan. Some small dolls particularly took Mike's attention, around six inches high and clothed exquisitely in the ceremonial kimonos of the traditional geisha. He purchased one for his sister and one for Julia. Then as an investment for his future in attracting girlfriends, he purchased a further two. The total bill came to just two pounds.

As they were so confident that Kirton would make the promised pay out in Tokyo, they were happy to spend most of their money on their one night in Osaka. Eventually, tired and loaded with presents, they headed back to the ship. The walk to the city centre had been dark and winding. Now with virtually all lights extinguished, the walk back to the ship was going to be very long, and fraught with problems should they not be able to recall the route. In many places, they had only the light of the moon to guide them and regularly tripped over objects and holes in the road, until in the distance they saw the neon lights of the brothels where they had last seen the majority of the crew. The relief they gave was of an altogether different type to that advertised.

On the next day, they lost the first crewmember of the voyage. One of the junior engineers had enjoyed the affections of a young Cuban girl in the brothel in Guantanamo Bay, and subsequently had not responded to the ministrations of the Chief Steward and his doses of penicillin. It was therefore decided to send him to hospital in an attempt to clear up the problem. No decision would be made about his future and how he was to get back to the UK until it was known where *La Cordillera* would be when he was suitably recovered. This once again had become a source of great speculation, with Vancouver the favourite for a grain cargo for the UK or Japan. Australia was second favourite for a cargo of coal or grain for Japan. The speculation would have to end shortly, as they would be in Tokyo.

During the course of the fourth day in Osaka, the stevedores started to leave the ship as each of the holds reached the required level. In the same way that they came aboard and stripped each of the hatches, so they replaced the beams, hatch boards, cover, bars and wedges, quickly and efficiently. Leaving only the derricks for the, somewhat speechless, crew to lower and secure, they left to go to the next ship along the quayside. Within minutes it was difficult to realise they had ever been there.

The younger members of the crew who had ordered tea services and other presents when they arrived in Osaka were becoming increasingly nervous as the ship made ready for sea. The older hands assured them that they had no need to worry. They would arrive. Just one hour before they were due to leave, the presents arrived. The tea services were packed in solid wooden cases and Mike itched to open his to ensure that he had received the correct one. He was advised again to leave it alone and stow it away until they reached home. This was a real leap of faith for someone who had just spent over a third of a month's wages on something he could not see. Still he left it alone, and many months later was not disappointed.

They left Osaka sorry that they were leaving a beautiful part of the world. Despite the problems of only a few years before, they had been treated with friendship and courtesy. They were excited that on the next day they would be in the nation's capital, Tokyo, and would be very much richer than they had been in their lives before.

His evening watch passed quickly as they sailed along the coast. Hundreds and hundreds of small fishing boats, each with one lantern burning brightly dotted the sea and horizon. Coupled with the lighthouses on the shore, they gave a magical quality to the scene. So fascinated was he that when he was relieved at midnight he had completely lost touch with the time.

Mike awoke the following morning ready to start work on deck at 0700 hrs. The sun was rising slowly on the starboard side and going through the cycle of glorious colours of a clear sunrise as he walked out onto the deck. The sight that greeted him on the port side would live with him forever. In the distance was the unmistakable shape of Mount Fujiyama, as shown on all photographs, its upper slopes covered in snow. As a result of the sunrise, the slopes were painted a beautiful deep pink. He longed to have a camera with colour film to record this breathtaking sight, but this would have to wait for a few more days.

Later that morning they sailed into Tokyo. They were met by the same sort of hustle and bustle that they encountered in Osaka. Here there appeared to be a different form of intensity, and not quite the same friendliness. The holds were stripped, and very quickly again the cargo was on its way ashore.

The crew were working themselves up into a frenzy recounting stories from previous voyages of what delights were waiting for the seamen ashore. Bathing sessions with semi-naked girls administering to their every need came near to the top of the bill, but at the very top were the stories of the Queen Bee, a hostess bar in the centre of the city. Here, if the crew were to be believed, were 1,000 hostesses waiting for the first seaman to arrive and select his companion for the evening. They were therefore to get ashore quickly to ensure they had the best choice of girl. Clearly, the Chief Steward was going to be busy after they left Tokyo.

Eventually Tony, Phil and Mike were able to go ashore leaving Paul on night watch. The road from the dock area was very similar to that in Osaka. A shanty town almost, with just lanterns to light the way. But when they arrived in the city, there was little or no similarity to Osaka. Tokyo had already been westernised and their eyes were assailed by thousands of garish neon signs.

Dozens of shops with cameras, radios and other similar products of the new Japanese technology were everywhere. Prices were totally unbelievable, around a quarter or less of the similar product in the UK. Mentally they spent their bonus that would be with them any day. Mike wondered what the school photographic society would have to say when he returned with his top of the range 35 mm camera with a complete set of interchangeable lenses. They spent what money they had left on presents and returned to the ship to await their big payday.

Three days later the majority of the cargo had been unloaded and the excitement grew by the second amongst the apprentices. Their biggest worry was whether they would receive their money in time to spend it in Tokyo, or whether in fact they would have to wait until the very last sacks were unloaded and the tally sheets checked. This would almost certainly mean that they would sail before they had a chance to go ashore. Although this would be an enormous disappointment, they would have money to spend in their next port, wherever that may be.

On the fourth day total catastrophe struck. They had argued for the past two days as to who should approach Kirton about their money. As the senior apprentice, Tony was the natural choice, but understandably he did not want the job. Time was now running out, and reluctantly he headed for the amidships accommodation and Kirton's cabin. When he returned he was white with anger. Kirton had just shrugged the matter off and told him that despite all the new sacks they had created, the tally only showed the correct number of sacks of sugar discharged and therefore there would be no money. Not a word was said, but the looks on each of their faces spoke volumes.

They had spent two weeks in intolerable conditions, had shed so much weight that they all looked emaciated, had pinned all their dreams and hopes on the money they would be receiving, and worse still had trusted Kirton. Now everything lay in tatters. All that could keep them going would be the knowledge that possibly they may be heading home shortly, a pathological hatred of Kirton, and the need to get their own back, no matter what.

The first of their crutches looked for a short time to be a distinct possibility. They were told two hours later that their next destination would be Portland, Oregon to load a grain cargo. The ship's movements from there were unknown, but there was a strong chance that they would head for a port in England to discharge and the freedom they desired. In the three weeks that it would take to reach Portland, they would once again have to clean the holds and rig the shifting boards, but the thought that they could be homeward bound would sustain them and lift them from their present mood of deep despair.

Somehow, they lifted themselves and went back on deck to carry out their day's work, but they could not fail to notice Kirton go ashore in the afternoon and return laden with many presents and every conceivable sample of Japanese technology. He must have spent hundreds of pounds, which even on a Chief Officer's salary needed some explaining, but not to the apprentices.

They left Tokyo on the evening tide. Everything they had enjoyed about Japan had been pushed into the background by Kirton's treachery. Now they turned all their thoughts to the United States and the hope of a homeward bound cargo.

CHAPTER 16

The voyage did not get off to a good start. In addition to the feeling of total depression, they had to contend with bad weather. Despite all the ballast tanks being filled, they were riding very high in the water. They were, cork like, totally at the mercy of the big waves. Adding to this, the propeller was spending an inordinate amount of time out of the water and causing the engine to race. This in turn was making it difficult to sleep in their cabins as the engine racing caused a thundering vibration throughout the accommodation.

They started the hold cleaning at 0700 hrs on the next morning. The dunnage, which had been so unpleasant to lay, was still as difficult to handle as they piled it up ready to lift it into the tween deck for storage. The splinters were still piercing their gloves and causing painful cuts that would be extremely sore later.

Where sugar had spilt from the sacks after the splinters stabbed holes in them, it had mixed with the sweat running around the deck forming an awful sticky mixture that clung to everything, particularly their clothing. Fortunately, it was Friday and they had the weekend to look forward to, but all too soon it would be Monday.

The unpleasant working conditions were made worse by

the rolling and pitching of the ship. No sooner had they stacked the dunnage in a pile, than it slid all over the hold again. As they chased the dunnage, the ship's motion propelled them towards the bilge boards and the steel bulkhead beyond. Sometimes it threw them into their colleagues, who were trying to maintain their balance as well. Very predictable language resulted.

Despite the hellish conditions as they cleaned the holds, it was infinitely preferable to what they knew was coming next. The thought of rigging the shifting boards in the current weather was almost too horrible to contemplate. They hoped that the storm they were in would move away over the weekend. They fully believed that the storm would be a typhoon by the time they got back into the holds on Monday.

Mike was even more depressed as they settled into the long Pacific crossing. They had rotated the watches and he was now on the graveyard watch, the 12-4. On the positive side, he did not have to start work at 0700 hrs with the rest of the crew. He could lie in until 0730 hrs and get up for breakfast at 0800 hrs. On the down side, he had to go to bed around 2000 hrs, and get up again at 2330 hrs, moving from a warm bunk to a freezing bridge wing. The two sessions of three hours in his bunk left him tired and less resistant to the conditions than normal.

On the basis that the shortest route between two points on

the earth's surface is a curve, they were taking the northern great circle route to the USA. This took them from Tokyo well up towards the Aleutians, before turning towards Portland. This meant that the weather would get progressively colder as they headed almost towards the edge of the Arctic. Already this was becoming noticeable as the ever-present icy spray soaked them whenever they went out on deck.

Possibly one of the few good things to remember about Japan, along with the scenery and the people, was the fact that he had received plenty of mail. There had been several letters from his Mother as usual, a letter from Jono, and most welcome of all one from Julia. He was not often homesick, despite the problems they had endured on the voyage, and he tried hard to wrap himself in the excitement of what he was doing and seeing. However, when he sat and re-read the mail, his mind was taken back to Bridlington.

The town was starting to wake up from its winter hibernation, as people started to paint the entire visitor attractions and amusements. The caravan camps opened and the greatest harbinger of all, the *Yorkshireman* arrived from Hull. The *Yorkshireman* was a large sea-going tug belonging to the United Towing Company, which spent its summers as a pleasure boat operating out of Bridlington and its winters working in the Humber on general towing duties. Together with the *Thornwick, Yorkshire Belle, Boy's*

Own, Bridlington Queen and *Britannia,* it carried thousands of tourists across Bridlington Bay towards Flamborough Head and beyond.

Each year, from the time he had been old enough, Mike would travel on the train to Hull just before Easter and travel back to Bridlington by sea on the *Yorkshireman.* Most of the people travelling would head to the bar as soon as she left Corporation Pier and not be seen until they arrived in Bridlington, apart from coming up on deck to be sick as they turned out of the Humber into the North Sea. It would be a jolly affair, as the accordion player played current and old popular tunes and the progressively inebriated passengers sang along to them.

As the years went by, Mike was joined by his two brothers. Whilst not totally sharing Mike's enthusiasm for the sea, they still enjoyed the bracing voyage around the coast. Because their father knew the Skipper and Mate, they were able to spend a large proportion of each summer travelling on the *Yorkshireman* on its shorter trips to Flamborough Head and Selwicks Bay, and the longer ones to Scarborough and Whitby, at no cost to themselves. To Mike it was the most wonderful way of spending the summer holidays, if he was not working.

One of the more memorable occasions in his life had started with the 1953 pilgrimage from Hull at Easter. They had arrived home after a day at sea to discover a shiny X television aerial on the roof, the only X television aerial in the road of H aerials. Life would never be the same again. Up until then only one of the local children had television and they would ensure that they played as a gang with him on the nights when *Kit Carson* was on, in the hopes that his mother would invite them in to watch the tiny screen. Now they could watch every minute of television on their own set. They became the area's most popular children, when good programmes were on.

The television played a large part in shaping his views on what he wanted to see and do in the world. The cinema, his geography lessons, and school visits to various places of work such as the Hull docks, Cook Welton and Gemmell's shipyard, Premier Oil and Cake Mills, and the Yorkshire Main colliery confirmed his ideas. Television was to a certain extent responsible for him being where he was.

The letter from Jono showed he was even more heavily involved with Alison than Mike had feared when he last saw them. Mike in his best globetrotting, man of the world, view believed that Jono would benefit from spending time at sea, and realising that there was more to life than a steady girlfriend and beer at the age of sixteen. He was unlikely to convince Jono, and in reality if Mike had been Alison's boyfriend, he would probably have found it harder to come back to sea after the first voyage. When he last saw her, her short dark hair in an elfin cut framed her face beautifully. She wore a gypsy blouse that exposed her shoulders, and gave a wonderful hint of what lay beneath it. With this picture in his mind, he was not sure that he could give any sensible advice to Jono.

He saved the letter from Julia to last. He had wanted to receive this letter so much, but having read it so many times, did not know what to think about its contents. When they had parted on his last night at home they had made the pact that whilst he was away, she would be like any other normal teenager of her age, enjoying her freedom to date anyone that she liked. Now she had built a relationship with one of Mike's good friends, Derek.

What had seemed so sensible and adult just three months ago now emerged as sheer stupidity. Whilst criticising Jono for his involvement with Alison, he realised how much the thought of one of his close friends dating Julia hurt. Names like Cassius and Judas sprang to mind. The apparently treacherous Derek would not even have approached Julia if Mike were home.

He hoped that the friendship would die before he arrived home, that they would resume their relationship, and he would enjoy the same feelings again. He knew that even if this relationship did not last there would be many others, unless he gave up the sea. He was left with the other part of the pact to hope for. If they were both free, they would enjoy each other's company.

An unbelievable amalgamation of Julia and Kirton had

started to make Mike wish for a speedy conclusion to the voyage. Despite the conditions, he was not worried about descending once more into the holds. If it would bring his return that much nearer, he would work hard to make the time pass. If as popularly forecast they were heading to the UK from Portland, he could be home again in around seven weeks' time, which would be more than worth the hard work ahead.

The new-found commitment lasted until Monday afternoon. They had cleared out two of the holds of their dunnage and sugar mixture. They were dirty, sticky, bruised from being thrown around the hold, and bleeding from several cuts to their hands and arms caused by the dunnage. The time had come to break out the steelwork for the shifting boards. They had known it would have to come, but had hoped that common sense would prevail and that they could have waited for more clement weather.

Initially, and very worryingly, they had to raise a single derrick so that they could lift the steel centrepiece into position. Lifting one of the heavy derricks whilst the ship was rolling was considered to be verging on suicidal. It would have to be undertaken with extreme care if an accident, or worse, was to be avoided. They detached the guys and shackled them to the deck, one either side of the hold, making the ends fast to a cleat so that they could fully control the movement of the derrick once it left its clamp.

Eventually the derrick was at a height where its wire hung vertically over the centre of the hold, ready for lifting. Next, all the covers had to come off the hold so that a couple of hatch boards in the centre could be removed, and the wire passed down to the tween deck. The steel central upright was shackled on and dragged from the furthest point of the tween deck, until they could rest it on the edge of the hatchway. A rope was made fast to the lower end of the upright, with a view to limiting the amount of swing once they started to lower it into the hold.

As soon as it was lifted high enough, the steel upright shot across the hold as the ship rolled heavily. The rope raced through two pairs of already bleeding hands, burning them painfully. The upright crashed into one side of the hold before heading back towards them as the ship rolled the opposite way. They managed to control it this time, but the problem started again as the rope had to be dropped into the lower part of the hold. The upright flew from side to side, smashing into everything in its way. Eventually three of them controlled it and held it in place until a bolt could secure it to the deck in the lower hold. Immediately they also bolted the top of the upright to the beam in the tween deck. For a few brief moments, the excitement was over. The hold was covered up and battened down again, and the derrick very gently lowered into its clamp.

With great difficulty, the support cables and bottle screws were made fast to the bulkheads. Paul and Mike clung onto the ladders as they attempted to tighten the bottle screws on either side. All the time the ship continued to roll violently from side to side. They dropped the spikes that they were using to turn the screw, as they clung frantically to the cables to stop themselves falling to the deck.

The fitting of the shifting boards was very difficult during the first voyage towards New Orleans, but that had been a Sunday afternoon stroll. The boards were too heavy to follow the rule of one hand for the company, one hand for themselves. Their length meant that the person holding the end in the tween deck had to lean over the edge of the hold as the board was slotted into the upright channels. They had no way of saving themselves as the ship rolled, other than to drop the heavy board into the hold below. This would risk the possibility of dragging their colleague from the beam in the centre of the hold.

It was no use telling Kirton that the job was too dangerous. He was not interested, and on previous occasions had ordered them to get on with it. Fortunately, the Bosun believed that it was too dangerous to work in the holds during the bad weather. For once Kirton listened to the Bosun and the crew was found something less dangerous to do. The apprentices were sent to start chipping on the upper decks of the amidships accommodation. It was certainly safer, but in the cold weather and icy spray, it was marginally more unpleasant. Unbelievably, they found themselves wishing for better weather so that they could return to the holds and the shifting board rigging.

For two more days, they worked chipping and scraping as the ship bobbed around like a cork on the top of the huge waves. They were cold and miserable, and wetter by the minute as the waves broke over the bow, to be followed seconds later by the spray showering them with its freezing droplets. It seemed to the four of them that this had to be one of the most stupid ways of passing time going. They were breaking up the rust and paint on the deck, reducing the surface to bare metal, only to have the polished surface soaked in salt water. When they coated it with boiled oil, the salt and damp was trapped in.

Overnight the wind dropped and the sea flattened dramatically, but this brought more problems. They were approaching the northernmost point of their voyage, and now they had the weather seafarers most feared and hated: fog. When Mike left the bridge at 0400 hrs the air was cold and clear, but he was woken at 0600 hrs by the ship's whistle as the sound vibrated through the ship every two minutes. By the time he was called for breakfast at 0730 hrs, it was difficult to see the forward accommodation from amidships.

Although they could now resume work on the rigging of the shifting boards, they were down to just three of them. The fog meant that a proper lookout had to be kept at all times. Each of the apprentices had to stand their daytime watch on the bridge.

This was another terrible job, as they strained their eyes looking towards the horizon, which in reality was no further away than the forecastle head. At the same time as straining to see around them, they had the responsibility of timing the interval between the whistle blasts. It was impossible to take their eyes off the view ahead to look at a watch face, so the seconds had to be counted down each time. Meanwhile the Officer of the Watch spent his time equally between the radar screen and the horizon.

At the end of the four-hour watch, Mike's head was aching from the strain on his eyes as he peered into the fog. The sun shining brightly made it very difficult to look into the fog, and the constant noise from the whistle behind him on the funnel ensured a blinding headache. Half way through each count, he became confused as to whether he was in the first or second minute of the count. Had he sounded the whistle at the end of the last count, or not?

The slotting of the shifting boards into the upright channels had become considerably easier. They no longer had the constant rolling of the ship as they tried to maintain their balance on the edge of the hold, and the boards were going into place in rapid succession. By the time they finished for the evening, all the boards were in place. They could concentrate on building the feeder in the tween deck during the following day.

The fog had lifted by the time Mike arrived on the bridge at midnight, but it had been a noisy night up until then. The continual blasts on the whistle kept him awake for some time. As he stood on the starboard bridge wing in the cold, clear air, he clutched tightly his pint mug of cocoa and sipped it whilst it was still very hot. The sweet, thick mixture made with condensed milk burnt his throat as he swallowed, but he could feel the warmth down in his chest as it travelled down into his stomach.

For a moment, he turned his thoughts to Portland. He had enjoyed the United States so much on the previous voyage. The other crewmembers said that the west coast was infinitely preferable to the east and south coasts. The people allegedly were more friendly and the scenery stunning.

All this, plus the hopes that they would be heading for home after leaving Portland, made him feel happier than he had been for some time. Even allowing for the bad weather they had just experienced, the crossing should only take about twenty-two days. They should be in Portland before the end of May. After leaving Portland, they should be home by the end of June, which would be a great time to be in Bridlington. The weather would be good, and there would not be too many tourists. These thoughts sustained him through the rest of the watch and he returned to the work in the holds next morning with a spring in his step.

They completed the first of their holds on that day. The heavy feeder boards were rigged vertically around the tween deck. The huge tie bars held it all together right across the hold and through the horizontal bars on the other side. A locknut was tightened, for insurance, before their team headed for hold No 3, to start all over again.

When they started on hold No 3 on the next day, there were few surprises. They collected and stacked dunnage, cleared out the bilges and swept the hold. With the change in the sea-state there was nothing like the stress. Talk was on the subject of going home. Kirton visited them during the day and promised cash if they completed the rigging of the shifting boards before reaching Portland. Although the boys did not believe a word of it, there was no harm in thinking about the possibilities when they went ashore in the port.

A day before they arrived off Astoria at the head of the Columbia River, all five holds were completed. The ship was ready to load her grain cargo as soon as she docked and the whole ship's company could hardly contain their pleasure at the thought that they would soon be heading home. Anything that could be done to hasten this was to be welcomed.

It was still daylight when they took the Pilot aboard and headed for the river mouth. They were quite stunned by the scenery and the proliferation of pine trees. After the dirty, ramshackle ports they had visited, this was a beautifully rural way of approaching a port. Unfortunately as night was approaching they would miss most of the scenery, but by the time morning arrived, they would be in Portland.

The majority of the ship's company had turned out to see the Pilot come aboard. Mike should have been heading for his bunk, but he was too excited to sleep. They watched as they passed the lights of Longview and saw the locals heading home in their pleasure boats. At times like this, it was worth all the problems of the past three weeks to enjoy the tranquillity of this scene.

Later in the evening, before going on watch, Mike had occasion to visit the engine room. Because they were on pilotage, the engine room was a hive of activity as the telegraph rang its various speed changes. Normally the whole area smelt of hot oil and diesel, but suddenly and dramatically there was an incredible smell of wonderfully fresh pine. Mike realised that he was standing under one of the huge cowl ventilators. Air was being forced down into the engine room by the speed of the ship.

It was a memorable night that would live with Mike and he dashed back onto the deck to get the full effect of the pine forest stretching on either side of the river. Later he was fortunate enough to be on watch as they continued to pass through this stunning scenery. Despite only climbing into his bunk twenty minutes after coming off watch at 0400 hrs, he was up again at 0700 hrs to witness their arrival in Portland's harbour.

In the distance were snow-capped mountains, on their left Mount St Helen's and Mount Adams, and on their right Mount Hood. Further back into Washington was the even bigger Mount Rainier. The pine forests were still around them. Without doubt, this was the most beautiful place he had ever seen. He knew little about this part of the world except that according to Lonnie Donegan, ahead of them lay the Grand Coulee Dam. This knowledge was unlikely to prove very useful.

CHAPTER 17

As soon as they were alongside, the usual procession formed on the quayside, awaiting the lowering of the accommodation ladder. There were the immigration people, customs, and health authorities. Following them was the most popular of all, the ship's agent, bearing mail. After them came the stevedore's agents and the surveyors to inspect the shifting boards before cargo could be loaded. Because of the disasters that could ensue as a result of grain movement, their word was law. If they were not happy with the way the boards were rigged and the feeders constructed, the whole lot would have to come down and be re-built.

The Captain gave the personal mail to the Chief Steward, who treated its distribution as the highlight of his existence, being the only time when he could achieve any semblance of popularity amongst the assembled crew. He therefore took his time, milking the situation as much as possible and creating drama where he could. The apprentices gathered their mail together and headed for the cabins to enjoy a part of their life that they felt almost completely cut off from, but would soon be able to resume. By their calculations, there would be one last mail opportunity, going through the Panama Canal, before arriving in the UK.

Mike had several letters from his Mother together with a letter from Jono. He opened his Mother's letters in the order they had been written and posted, and read them avidly. His Mother had always been great at recording things that she knew he would be interested in. Reading the letters was like reading a potted history of what had happened in Bridlington in the past weeks. There was news about his friends at school, news about the goings on at the youth club and news about Julia and her friends.

He saved Jono's letter for later as they were summoned back on deck to uncover the hatches for the surveyors to carry out their inspection. They took very little time in declaring themselves totally satisfied with the standard of work and the stevedores were given permission to start loading. In no time at all, they had stripped the hatches and the giant elevator pipes were spewing wheat into two of the holds.

Assuming they would not work over the weekend there would be about five or six days' work before they would be heading for home. However, in view of the beauty of the port, it was not going to be any great hardship to remain patient and stay here for a few more days.

In the evening, they were allowed to draw their subs, but in view of the amount they had drawn in Japan, the maximum Mike could draw was $10. Somehow, he felt it would not take him very far, but at least he would enjoy a few milk shakes and strawberry shortcakes.

To their enormous surprise when they went to the saloon to collect their money, they were given a further $6 each as a reward for the work they had done on the shifting boards. Apparently, the ship had been saved many thousands of dollars by the crew completing the rigging, depriving the local carpenters of a chance to do the job. What Kirton had taken as his share, no one knew, but they were grateful to have something after the disappointment in Japan. Suddenly life was looking good. They had money in their pockets and were about to head for home.

They headed for the shore as soon as they received their money and after finding the bus route, went for downtown Portland. Their first stop was a diner where they gorged themselves on milk shakes, ice cream and apple pie, together with the obligatory strawberry shortcake that Paul had introduced them to back in New Orleans. Shopping came next. Presents for those members of the family not catered for in Japan and souvenirs for themselves.

It was the first occasion for some considerable time that the three younger apprentices had been able to relax and enjoy their leisure time together. They made plans for what they would do on Saturday and Sunday, once they had completed the usual cleaning duties.

Just sitting in the diner, listening to the latest in pop music and absorbing the movement of life in Portland was brilliantly relaxing. The Everly Brothers had made it to the top of the local charts and *Till I kissed you* was blaring out from the jukebox and the radios. Across the road, the west coast premiere of *South Pacific* was advertised, and queues were forming for tickets. They knew nothing about the film at the time, otherwise they may have made an effort to see it, to be one up on their friends back home.

They started painting the ship's side on Friday morning using rollers on six-foot canes to reach a greater area. Kirton had given them a job and finish, with the intention of keeping them busy for Friday and Saturday. He obviously had still not realised what the apprentices were capable of, because after a Herculean effort they finished by mid-morning on Saturday.

Once the ship was loaded, it would look very smart, but as she was being loaded the area they were painting was slowly going below the water surface. They were experiencing major problems as the rollers went into the water. What it would look like once she was unloaded they could only imagine. While they were painting from the quayside, the crew were painting the other side from a punt made up of old paint containers, dunnage and stages lowered from the deck. They were not moving as fast as the apprentices were, so their side would have large gaps where the men on the stages and the punt were unable to cover the area before it submerged.

The rush to finish the job meant that large amounts of black paint were floating on the water, on the quayside, in fact on virtually everything including the apprentices. This would be the next job to tackle. A wash down with paraffin and paraffin soaked rags followed by a shower before the skin started to really burn. Then a quick lunch and the trip ashore.

Again, on Sunday they were able to get ashore after they had completed their usual cleaning regime. For a change, they decided to explore the area and headed up a road leading up the hill to the east of Portland. They walked and walked, as the road first became a lane and then a track. There in front of them was an incredible sight. They had climbed to the highest point around Portland. From the area alongside them were able to look down on the harbour and see *La Cordillera* in the distance. Around the harbour were the pine forests and behind them the mountains.

The breath taking scenery left them speechless. Then they realised that they had a grandstand view of a powerboat race. They settled down making the most of the view and were eventually disturbed by the owners of the garden they were unknowingly sitting in, coming over to talk to them.

On arrival back at the ship, they were met by a local couple. They had come down to visit the ship and enquire whether anyone would like to go to church. Having been in the church choir from the age of seven and a sidesman from the time he left the choir, Mike had missed going to church over the past five months. Phil had accepted the offer, and so Mike agreed to go with him.

They drove through Portland until they reached a building the size of a concert hall in a wonderful woodland setting. The Church was unlike anything they had ever seen before, huge, modern and airy with lots of beautifully polished wood. The choir were arranged in many tiers and filled the whole of one end of the church. The congregation filled virtually every remaining space.

Although one or two of the hymns were unfamiliar to them, Mike and Phil did their best to join in with the service. They were struck by the enthusiasm of the congregation and the willingness with which they took part. Neither had experienced the American gospel style where members of the congregation testified to the way that they had been helped in their lives by their faith. Mike was struck by the obvious sincerity of the people that went forward and by their complete lack of nerves.

The boys had been made to feel welcome, not only by the couple that had collected them from the ship, but also all the members of the congregation. When it became general knowledge that Phil and Mike were from England, they became the focus of lots of attention from all areas, particularly young ladies. This was due largely to the proximity of Oregon to British Columbia where there was a lot of interest in England and everything English.

When the time eventually came to return to the ship, they were sorry to have to leave. This was possibly one of the most enjoyable evenings since leaving home and the new friends they were making, especially amongst the girls, made them wish the evening would last. It was certainly the first time Mike could remember being happy to stay in a foreign port for longer than necessary. However, they were buoyed up by the thought that they would be home in a few weeks' time.

Loading commenced again on Monday morning and the apprentices were back to reality. They had painted as much as possible of the ship's side before the weekend and now started on the accommodation exterior. No Captain or Chief Officer would take a ship home with paintwork dirty or showing rust, if they wanted to retain their job. The likelihood now was that painting and chipping would be the priority until the end of the voyage.

Along with the rest of the crew, the apprentices did not really care what work they had to carry out. They were going home and anything that helped to pass the time was welcomed. Each day the position of the ship in comparison to the quay was noticeably lower as one by one the holds were filled to capacity and the trimmers were employed to shoot the grain into the corners, prior to filling the feeders.

The greatest source of conversation amongst the whole ship's company was the destination port for the cargo. Would it be a return to Liverpool, favoured by the crew, as most of them were from that area? Would it be Avonmouth, a big grain port, Newcastle, Southampton or, Mike's favourite, Hull? The thought of his family and friends being able to see *La Cordillera* appealed to him enormously. But really, it was not important, as they would sign off and go on leave regardless.

The odd Jonah amongst the ship's company threw up a few what if scenarios based on the ship being diverted to Antwerp, Rotterdam or Hamburg. But nobody would take them seriously, and pretty soon they joined the pack in speculating which English port it would be. With only one day to go before they were due to sail, speculation had become rife. Everyone was betting on one port or another.

Although it was unusual not to be officially notified roughly where they were bound, it was not unique. Many of the older officers and crew had experience of similar situations. There again, even after being told the destination it was not unusual to have the cargo bought and sold several times before arriving off Land's End and being notified of their destination.

Later that day came the news of their destination. News that caused them unbelievable depression and heartache. News they would have given anything not to receive.

News that would take days to sink in. Their destination was not Liverpool, Avonmouth or Hull. Nor even Antwerp, Rotterdam or Hamburg. Their destination was to be Calcutta.

CHAPTER 18

At the time, the news of their new destination was considered the worst possible news. Within days, the rumourmongers had worked on it and turned it into something far worse. What was known definitely was that they would leave Portland and proceed to Yokohama where they would take on bunkers and stores, thence to Borneo where they would once again bunker. From Borneo, they would be going via the Straits of Malacca to Vishakhapatnam on the east coast of India to discharge part of their cargo, as they would not be able to navigate the Hooghly River to Calcutta fully loaded.

Once they arrived in Calcutta, they would discharge the grain prior to loading gunny bales for Cuba. Gunnysacks were the rough hessian type sacks into which sugar was bagged, their original cargo to Japan. The total expected turnaround time in Calcutta would be six weeks. This was official and was in writing. What had not been seen in writing was the next part, which had been given credence by those in the know.

From Calcutta, they would go to Cuba and discharge the cargo, then load sugar for Japan, and then they would travel to the United States or Canada for a grain cargo for India. This could be repeated ad infinitum for the full two years allowed before a change of crew would be forced on the owners.

On the strength of this news, they lost the next member of the ship's company. An Able Seaman, who had been particularly unhappy, had disappeared when the time came to check that everyone was aboard before sailing. He had apparently jumped ship. He had made friends with somebody he could stay with in the short term. In the longer term when the authorities caught him, he would be repatriated to the UK on the first available vessel.

A number of the crew spent time on reflecting on the plusses and minuses of this. Effectively you would be unable to resume a career at sea, but you would not have a problem ashore. The chances also were that he would be back in England long before the remainder of the crew.

Eventually one by one the holds were filled to capacity, the hatch boards and covers were put on, bars and wedges were in, the derricks lowered and they were ready for sea. By comparison with the crew that had entered Portland, the one leaving was dramatically subdued. They lined the rails as the slow journey down the Columbia River began, it was every bit as beautiful as it had been a week ago, but now no one seemed to notice. In their minds, they had been about three weeks from home. Now they were at least six months away, maybe much longer.

At a time when they would have benefited from having

plenty of work to do, the apprentices were on stand-by. Each one of them took their turn on the wheel during their own watches, working two hours on and two hours off with the crew. This, for Mike, was the only enjoyable part of the day, having a grandstand view of the river as they made their progress down it to the sea. The ship was very low in the water, so was answering to the wheel in a much more positive manner than normal, making the river passage a pleasure for the man at the wheel.

When they were not on the bridge, they watched, mostly in silence, as the magnificent pine forests swept by. Occasionally they were broken up by small areas with fishing and hunting lodges, with their boats bobbing around when hit by the wake of the ship. The wake formed small waves that washed along the shoreline through the trees. Anything not tied down was lifted by the water, and transported a hundred yards down the riverbank.

Presently darkness fell as they reached the mouth of the river. They said goodbye to the Pilot and watched as the lights of Astoria disappeared slowly into the distance. Apart from being the place where the bad news was imparted, Portland had proved to be a wonderfully welcoming port, and one which Mike sincerely hoped he would have the chance to visit again. They would need to remember their last trip ashore, because although they would be calling at two ports before they arrived in India, they would not have the opportunity to go ashore until then. The bunkers would be taken aboard either from a barge or an offshore buoy, not tied up alongside a quay.

That night on the bridge there was still the occasional light to keep an eye on and a few fishing boats to stay clear of, but on the whole both the Second Mate and Mike wanted to be alone with their thoughts. Mike moved out to the extremity of the bridge wing, nursing his pint mug of cocoa and the Second Mate retired to the chartroom to catch up on his Notice to Mariners corrections to the charts.

He had hoped that he would not have to make any corrections other than those to the Atlantic charts, Panama and the English ports. Now he would have to correct the vast majority of all the charts on board. It was a huge time consuming job, that would entail reading through dozens of copies of the Notice to Mariners, noting changes to lights or any other navigational aids, wrecks, new quays or jetties and marking changes to every chart. This was unlikely to make him a great conversationalist on the bridge at night and Mike would be left to keep his own company.

On the whole, Mike was probably happier being left alone on the bridge wing. Like his colleagues, he had pinned all his hopes on going home. Not that he was unhappy travelling to Cuba, Japan and America and seeing the incredible sights that his friends back in Bridlington would give anything for the chance to see. Rather it all centred on the one person, Kirton. Without him, the ship would be a much happier place. The thoughts that someday soon, somebody may drop a hatch board or a steel block on him from a great height and so remove him from the ship appealed to Mike.

The voyage started pretty much as they expected. Out came the chipping machines and the chipping hammers, and as soon as they had finished breakfast work started on removing years of rust from the deck. With only pauses for coffee breaks, lunch, darkness and the weekend the cacophony continued day in and day out. With no masks or ear defenders available, they wrapped sweat rags around their noses and mouths and persuaded the Chief Steward to give them cotton wool for their ears.

The makeshift protection had little effect and they were caked in thick black and red dust that permeated everywhere. When they showered in the evening, the water ran black for some time as they initially washed their hair and bodies, but much later, if they sneezed or coughed they produced large amounts of thick black mucous. Worse than this was the continual vibration in their hands.

Although they were travelling in very northerly latitudes as they followed the same route as they had travelled from Japan, the weather was considerably warmer. They spent most of the day in shorts and t-shirts. This left them even more exposed to the flying rust chippings from the chipping machine, giving them cuts and bruises. This went on day after day, broken only by the weekend, until their bodies were covered in cuts and red blotches.

When Mike had first decided that he wished to pursue a career at sea, he had known that it would be hard work and that the apprenticeship would probably seem long. What he had not bargained for was the consistent sixteen-hour days of hard labour. He had listened to his Father's stories of the hardships when he was an apprentice, but had thought that times would have changed nearly thirty years on.

On the bridge that night, he thought of the story that both his Father and Grandmother had recounted of his Father's time as an apprentice. His Grandmother was a wonderful, if somewhat imperious, lady. Mike always thought that she reminded him of Queen Mary. In all probability, she had never wanted his Father to go to sea. Grandfather was the Managing Director of a company manufacturing bitumastic products, and had supplied those used for the construction of the Mersey Tunnel. The photographs of the opening of the tunnel by Queen Mary were imprinted in Mike's brain, so many times had he been shown them.

Grandmother had decided to visit his Father's ship when he had returned after a voyage and did not expect to have time to come home. She did not think to tell him of her decision, but just to arrive at the dockside as a surprise. In the late 1920s, ships were coal-fired and the bunkering of the ship took a considerable time. There was also an enormous amount that had to be moved by hand, using the apprentices as cheap labour. It was a filthy job with large amounts of coal dust clinging to their sweating bodies. The boys appeared to be natives of somewhere far warmer than England.

In the absence of any officers, Grandmother reluctantly approached one of these filthy urchins and enquired whether he could direct her to the part of the ship where she could find her boy Jim. The boy looked up at her and said, "Mum." The shock endured for some considerable time after the encounter and never again did she visit the ships unannounced.

For the first ten days of their voyage to Yokohama, the weather was very pleasant with hardly a ripple on the sea surface. Only a very slight rolling motion gave them a clue that they were travelling in the world's largest ocean. In view of the way the ship lay in the water, it was just as well. However if the first ten days had been pleasant, the next few were far from it. The wind had started to increase in intensity and had whipped up the sea until she began rolling heavily. Then, as the wind veered around to the west, she began pitching into the waves.

Breaking heavily over the forecastle, the water raced down both working alleyways. The spray covered the bridge, making the job of lookout very wet, unpleasant and frightening. One second you were looking up at the stars, the next you were taking cover under the bridge dodger as the water came crashing down on the bridge and shooting down the ladders onto the next deck. It was scary during the day, but at night was far more sinister as you could not see what was coming next.

The only positive side of the weather was that the chipping of the decks had to be abandoned temporarily. Instead, they found themselves painting in the accommodation. This in turn had its own dangers. All the necessary paraphernalia required for painting, the paint, brushes and rollers were all stored in the forecastle head. This was spending a large amount of time under water. The secret of gaining access to the forecastle was to wait for the bow to come up. Then, very quickly, let the water race past you and run up the thirty or forty degree slope of the wet deck, grab the door of the forecastle head, open it, get inside and close it before the bow plunged into the next wave.

If gaining access to the forecastle was difficult, then returning was far more dangerous. With hands full of painting equipment, they had to open the door when the water cleared, get out onto the deck, close the dogs on the door and run down the wet sloping deck to the safety of the accommodation, gain access to the accommodation and close the door before the next torrent of water shot down the alleyway.

On the first day, three of the apprentices, Paul, Phil and Mike made it to the forecastle head. They collected everything they needed and then considered returning to the accommodation. At the same time, they had to attempt to keep their balance as the bow plunged into the wave and the ship shuddered. This was followed by the feeling of weightlessness as the bow came up, and hovered for a second before plunging again.

Phil went first and made it past the first hold before his feet went from under him and he hit the bulkhead at speed. He recovered just in time to make it before the water rushed past the place where he had fallen. He had held onto the paint but lost everything else. Mike went next, filling his pockets with brushes and rags and making it to the accommodation before his feet went. He saved his can of turpentine substitute and made it to his feet, opening the door just as the water struck. This proved very popular with the inhabitant of the first cabin.

Paul, who had watched both of them from the forecastle, collected several paint kettles which he tied onto himself, together with paint and more brushes and bided his time before achieving a perfect run down the deck. He entered the accommodation where the others lay nursing their bruises after their collisions with the steel bulkheads. This was supposed to be easier work than chipping.

Once the gauntlet between accommodation and forecastle

had been run, the theory was that the work would be easier. In reality, as normal, there were problems. Attempting to retain their balance whilst cutting-in a straight line between bulkhead and deck head or deck was virtually impossible. Wavy lines were testament to this.

The weather did not change substantially during the next seven days. The ship continued to be battered by the storm, but by then they were within two days of reaching Japan and the lea created by the land. They awoke on the second day to the same wonderful sight that had greeted them upon their last visit to this area of Japan. The snow covered slopes of Mount Fujiyama in the early morning sun. It was on mornings like this that everything they had gone through suddenly seemed worthwhile.

CHAPTER 19

Yokohama came and went all too quickly. They connected up to a bunkering barge. The Agent came aboard together with the usual officials. The stores arrived alongside and were taken aboard. All this, together with the mail distribution, was achieved by lunch time.

They were surprised during the morning when a boat came alongside with the Junior Engineer who had left them originally in Osaka. It had taken all this time for the Doctors to cure his problem, which according to the more lurid stories had resulted in his testicles swelling to the size of footballs. He had hoped to be flown home to the UK, but the agents realising that the ship was coming into Yokohama to bunker had decided, much to his disgust, to re-unite him with his colleagues.

As soon as he was aboard, the telegraph rang and they were heading southwest towards their next destination, Miri, on the border between Sarawak and Brunei. In this major oil producing area the fuel would be cheap, so they had taken a small amount aboard in Yokohama.

They anticipated a voyage time of seven days to Miri, but if the weather were anything like the past seven days, it would be considerably longer. They had averaged just over nine knots from Portland to Yokohama, which was two to three knots below normal. As soon as they cleared Tokyo Bay, it was apparent that the weather was considerably better than before. There was a gentle swell and brilliant sunshine as the double ring "Full ahead" was sounded on the telegraph.

The voyage would take them well into the tropics and by the time they altered course to go north around Singapore, they would pass within one degree of the equator. There had been lots of talk about what would happen to members of the crew crossing the line for the first time. Mike was happy to put off the moment for as long as possible. They would have to cross eventually on their voyage around the Cape of Good Hope, but that was a long time away.

On the next day normality returned. Out came the electric chipping machines together with the chipping hammers. They once again began the monotonous job of taking the paint and rust off the afterdeck. To add to the normal unpleasant nature of the job, the sun was now becoming a major problem. They were already sun burnt, and each day spent chipping was agony. As well as enduring the burning, the chippings hit the burnt areas of their bodies. Later on in the shower, washing the gritty particles off hurt.

If the days were painful, then the nights were relatively pleasant. They were able to sleep with the portholes open. Even on the bridge at midnight, Mike could wear shorts and t-shirt. The sunsets were becoming more spectacular and the huge amount of phosphorescence in the water made the nights magical.

On the fifth night out, they had an electrical storm, which was the most magnificent of all. As Mike stood on the bridge, the forks of lightning danced one at a time all around the horizon, lighting up the whole sky and sea. At times it slowed down, then moved faster and faster until it seemed as if hundreds of bolts were in action at the same time. The most awe inspiring of all was a bright blue flame dancing on the cross-trees of the foremast. The finale of this show would live long in memory.

There was no thunder or rain to follow and life returned to normal as if it had never happened. The Second Mate returned to his chartroom and Mike to the remaining two hours on lookout. He wished Julia could have been there to witness what he had just enjoyed. However if the letter he had received in Yokohama was anything to go by, he would not be seeing much of her upon his return. She was continuing to see his ex-friend and there was no sign that she would be available when Mike returned. If he were to listen to the rumourmongers on board the ship, she could be married and have children by the time Mike returned to Bridlington.

If Julia remained unavailable, he wondered idly whether Marcia would have him back. Marcia had been the one love interest in his life after breaking up with Jane and before taking up with Julia again. They had sung together in the choir, and were members of the youth group. During the months leading up to Mike's departure they had been inseparable, and Mike still could not really explain why they had broken up. Marcia was a beautiful girl, one year Mike's junior, with medium length auburn hair and a stunning figure. She was now about to go to college and dressed in a much more grown-up style that Mike found very exciting.

Although, technically, they had been going out together for some time, in reality they had spent very little time on their own. They always seemed to be in the company of others or in large public places. Each night he had walked her to her home near his old school. Occasionally he was seen by some of the boarding pupils from the school, and had to put up with their ribald comments the following day. If he was invited into the house, there was always her Father, Mother and brother sitting there with him, if they went to his home, his Mother, brothers, and sister would be there as well. Privacy was in very short supply. They managed the odd goodnight kiss or two, but that was as far as it went. He was happy in her company and she appeared to be the same in his.

Presumably, life would have gone on in the same way if it had not been for Jessica's Christmas party. Jessica was Marcia's best friend and was currently going out with Paul, the son of the Harbour Master. Her parents had, somewhat surprisingly, given her permission to hold a party whilst they were away for the weekend. Jessica wasn't one to pass on an opportunity like that, especially if she could be with Paul.

The guest list consisted entirely of Marcia and Mike's friends. The underage partygoers drank some alcohol, but it was nothing stronger than Black Velvet made the poor man's way, with cider and Guinness. Most of Mike's friends were in the same situation as he was. They were never able to spend any time alone with their girlfriends. Like Mike, the majority were at the grammar school, and had no contact whatsoever with members of the opposite sex, other than at weekends or at social events during the week.

As a result of this deprivation they were only interested in playing games such as Sardines or Murder, where the lights had to go out for some time. In fact the lights were out for nearly an hour at a time, or until someone decided to come up for air. Mike and Marcia took up residence in one of the main bedrooms, where they lay together under the bed, just in case someone started to play the games in the way they were meant to be played, and forgot the real reason for playing.

Mike cuddled Marcia close to him and watched as the moonlight streaming through the window lit up her hair. Together with the beautiful silvery dress she had bought especially for that evening, it was a sight so magical that it was truly memorable. She sighed and moved her body closer to him. Slowly she began to tell him what Jessica and Paul had been up to during her parent's absence. Jessica had told her that they had been sleeping together, after extracting the usual promises that Marcia would tell no one.

Mike wondered why she was telling him this intimate piece of news. While it made him feel quite envious, it was beyond where Mike wanted, or felt able, to go at this time in his life. He started to think back to Jane and the way she had goaded him into going further than he really wanted to. He had the promise of the career that he had always wanted. He did not want to ruin or miss out on it now.

He asked her if the reason she had told him was that she wanted to be like her friend. As he expected, she denied that she wished to emulate Jessica. However, he knew that things would probably change now and that simply kissing her goodnight was not going to be sufficient anymore.

Mike did not have long to wait until their next meeting, and to discover what she had planned. They met up, as was normal when they were going out anywhere other than the town centre, equidistant between their homes. It was a glorious sunny winter's day and Marcia fancied the idea of a cycle ride to Danes Dyke, three to four miles east of Bridlington along the coast. Danes Dyke was known as a place where boys took girlfriends in the absence of privacy elsewhere. Lots of grassland, bushes, trees, and cliffs that put off casual walkers, and more to the point, peace and quiet where you were unlikely to be disturbed.

They were both dressed in thick jackets to ward off the cold, but by the time they had cycled to the Dyke, it was unlikely that they would be needed. Red in the face with the cold and the exertion of the ride, they parked their bikes. They made their way hand in hand through the woods on the eastern side of the great chasm until they were nearly on the cliff-top itself. The view was spectacular. The whole of the distant town and the bay were bathed in the wintry sunshine and small white flecks sat atop the waves coming into the bay from the North Sea. Mike stood with his arm around Marcia thinking, for the first time, what it was going to be like to leave her for his forthcoming career.

Hours later, they made their way back to Bridlington after a memorable afternoon. They had not been in each other's company since that wonderful afternoon, and Mike had come to the conclusion that he would never understand women. Right now, he would give a lot to be in her company again.

He gazed out over the horizon thinking about where Marcia would be at this time, probably at college whilst he stood out on the bridge wing in the vast darkness of the ocean. At least, it had been darkness, but his eyes were suddenly drawn to something on the port bow. He thought at first that he was seeing things but sure enough, there was the occasional lume of a flashing light. After several days without seeing any land, he had spotted the north west coast of the Philippines. He rushed into the chartroom to tell the Second Mate, his mind firmly back in the present.

Apart from being their first contact with the land, the north west coast of the Philippines marked something far more sinister. They had entered the South China Sea. From now on, during the hours of darkness, they would not only be looking out for land and ships. They would be keeping a special lookout for pirates.

If Mike had been reading some boy's adventure book, he could have understood it. But now in the late nineteen fifties? The stories of pirates in this area were quite horrific. Instead of large sailing ships, they now had very fast motorboats. During the hours of darkness and particularly the early hours of the morning, they would approach and board a large cargo ship. They would slaughter the people on watch and anybody who got in their way, quickly making away with money and any valuables they could find, together with small bits of valuable cargo.

Other than possibly a pistol in the Captain's safe and the emergency Verey pistol, the ship did not carry any weapons, and certainly nothing to compare with the automatic weapons the pirates were known to favour. In reality, the only weapons at their disposal were fire hoses. Admittedly, they were powerful, but against automatic rifles? Their main hope was to maintain a keen lookout during darkness to ensure no other vessel was able to get near to them. For the next few days, they would be vulnerable until they had passed through the Singapore Straits and back into the open sea. One thing was certain. There would be no daydreaming during the night watches.

On the next day, they arrived off Miri. Off being the operative word. In the distance on the shore, amongst the jungle, there was probably a settlement or a town, but from all they could see they might just as well be at sea. They dropped the anchor, and within a short time a motor launch left the shore and headed for the ship. On board were the officials from the bunkering company, the port officials and everybody's friend, the ship's agent.

They could do little whilst preparation was being made to take on the bunkers. For a change, the engineers and donkey men were running around the deck as the fuel lines were hoisted aboard and coupled up to the respective pipes. The decision was taken to go and pester the Chief Steward in the hopes that he would collect the mail, that had been brought aboard by the Agent, from the Captain's cabin. The ploy worked to some extent as the Chief Steward set off towards the Captain's cabin, but he was then invited to have a drink with the officials, which left them all waiting again for the mail.

Mike had noticed as they waited that the sky had darkened perceptibly and that the land was no longer visible. This probably meant a shower was on its way and for a few minutes a coolish breeze could be felt as a change to the oppressive heat. Then with almost no warning other than the breeze, the heavens opened. Rain unlike anything he had experienced before soaked him to the skin in seconds. The drops were massive and descended like the proverbial stair-rods. Within seconds, water was streaming along the deck, the metalwork steaming from the cool rain hitting it. The shower ended as it began, suddenly, his first experience of tropical rainstorms was over, but certainly not forgotten.

The rain coming as it did, after the fuel lines had been connected, did not affect the bunkering process. Within a short time, sufficient fuel had been taken aboard to last until well after they left India. The officials departed, somewhat unsteadily, armed with the usual packs of cigarettes and bottles of spirits, the anchor was weighed and they were heading for India at full speed. Mike mentally noted that at no time did he want to be involved with tankers, if this was all they saw of a port.

The temperature continued to rise steadily as they headed southwesterly towards the Straits of Singapore. Work on deck during the day was becoming almost unbearable, but still Kirton had them out in the blazing sun chipping the decks. By the time they had eaten breakfast the decks were so hot that the skin needed protection of some sort, to avoid contact. They tried sitting or kneeling on coir mat fenders to keep off the deck, but now and then the bare skin would touch the metal, provoking a stream of obscenities aimed at Kirton, providing he was not in earshot, the ship, the company, or just life in general.

On the bright side, the red raw burning on their skin had painfully peeled and they were now quite brown from the constant exposure to the sun. All four of them would easily pass for natives of any warm country. Daily they continued to burn, the only respite being the hours of darkness when they were on the bridge. The cabins were oppressive despite the portholes being wide open. The heating system was blowing even warmer air, so the bridge afforded a draught of slighter cooler air. Even then, they did not have a lot of time to enjoy as they made their way through the small chains of islands, any of which could be home to the pirates.

By the third day, they began the turn through the Straits of Singapore and the Straits of Malacca. They passed Singapore at night and saw nothing more than the lights, but this was spectacular. In the morning, they could still see Malaya on the starboard side and Sumatra on the port. But they were left with only the thoughts of what it would have been like to go ashore as they headed for the Andaman Sea.

One week after leaving Miri, they entered the Bay of Bengal. The sun continued to blaze down on them, but at least they were clear of the area in which the pirates operated. They were grateful for the fact that it was Sunday. Apart from the time spent cleaning, they could find somewhere out of the sun to sit and attempt to find some cool air. In two days' time, they would be in India and would lose even the cool air from the ship's slow passage.

Mike was unsure of his feelings towards their destination. On one hand, people still referred to India as the Jewel in the Crown of the Empire. On the other, there were those whose comments were somewhat pithier as they had served there, and were only too pleased to get out of the country. Unknown to him, the next few weeks would make an impression on Mike that would not be removed.

CHAPTER 20

As they made their approach to Vishakhapatnam, the scene could have been taken from any Indian travel advertisement. There was not one cloud in the sky. The scorching sun was creating a heat haze on the glass-like blue ocean, and in the haze fishermen stood in their small canoe-like boats, eking out a most precarious living. Nothing that they could see gave any real clue to the dirt, misery and poverty that was waiting for them a few miles ahead.

A clue to the kind of things they were going to witness came when the pilot boat approached. The Pilot stood, god-like, in full naval uniform, waiting for his crew to hold the ladder steady for him. When everything was positioned perfectly he finally made an effort to come aboard. This contrasted dramatically with all other pilots they had seen, who jumped for the ladder and scrambled up after the boat had made one quick run alongside the ship.

Having ascended the ladder, he stood on the deck and did not acknowledge the "Good morning," from Tony and Phil, but waited for the Third Mate to arrive and escort him to the bridge. This duly done he spoke briefly to the Captain and then issued the first of his commands to Tony, who by now had taken the wheel.

Slowly the ship approached the quay, which consisted of a corrugated iron roofed warehouse and a few huts. The quay was lined with officials and their helpers They all wanted to come aboard and be bribed with cigarettes and spirits to complete their paperwork rapidly. In the background, dozens of workers surrounded a man who appeared to be deciding how many of them would work on the ship.

Within a very short time the ship was alongside, the moorings secured and "Finished with engines" rung. Prior to them arriving alongside the apprentices and crew had raised all the derricks to ensure that work could commence immediately. They expected to open the holds, but the huge gangs of workers descended on the ship like a plague of ants and very quickly stripped the hatches of tarpaulins, bars and wedges. Following this, they took off the hatch boards and removed the supporting beams.

Only after this amazing show of efficiency did it become apparent that when it came to discharging cargoes, they were really in the Stone Age. There were no grain elevators to suck out the grain. Every bit had to be removed manually. The men worked in teams of five, two men held open a gunny sack, two filled it using metal scoops and the fifth sewed the top of the sack closed when it was full, using a large bag needle and hessian string.

Because of the size of the feeders, initially only two teams could start in each hold, but by the time they had cleared the feeders and the tween deck up to ten teams were in each hold. Over two hundred men were working in the holds, plus winch operators and deck workers. It was a truly incredible sight, but one that made Mike think how this could be reconciled with the number of people who desperately needed the grain to ward off starvation. Surely, it would be better to invest in the technology to discharge a ship within hours so that the cargo could get where it was urgently needed. The argument against this was that over two hundred people were employed discharging the ship, and therefore earning a wage.

If that was the first lesson Mike was to learn about India, then the second was very quick in coming. Mike noticed a young girl with a small child, obviously begging for food on the quay, which was level with the ship's rail. Some grain had dropped from the sacks as they were being swung ashore, and she was trying to sweep it up from the floor. Mike scooped up a few handfuls of the grain from the deck, and put in on the quayside so she could pick it up.

Further up the quay stood a large cow that had decided that it would have the grain and made a move towards it. Mike jumped onto the quayside and attempted to drive the cow away, but was grabbed by two of the crewmembers. They thought they had better stop him from provoking an international incident. In his rush to help the girl, Mike had forgotten that here the cow was sacred and that whatever it wanted to do, it could do without let or hindrance.

He watched in disgust as the cow ate the grain he had put down and decided on another tack. Finding a piece of rag, he filled it with grain from the deck, knotted it and threw it to the girl, who caught it successfully and gave him a smile of gratitude. His action provoked a rush of beggars from further along the quayside.

Mike and his colleagues found the extreme poverty upsetting, but the older more experienced hands said that if they could not stand poverty, then it was no use coming to India. They could expect far worse in Calcutta. There they would see the most abject poverty imaginable side by side with enormous wealth, which was probably more objectionable than the situation in Vishakhapatnam.

Their thoughts on the problems of India were interrupted by Kirton, who came to inform them that he would require two apprentices on night watch instead of the usual one, due to the expected pilfering of cargo and stores. Paul and Mike would work nights and Tony and Phil days.

They did not have long to wait for their first intruder. Mike and Paul had taken the opportunity of sleeping in the afternoon, prior to starting their watch at 1900 hrs. They had gone into the saloon for dinner with the others and the four of them were sitting out on the deck prior to the changeover. The hatches had been covered for the night, as the crowd of stevedores left. Mike saw a figure entering the door to the No 2 hold, and they realised they were dealing with a trespasser.

How they were going to handle the problem provoked much discussion. None of them wanted to go into a dark hold on their own, not knowing who was down there. So first they fetched a couple of lighting clusters from the forecastle. While they were there collecting these, they noticed a bundle of axe and sledgehammer handles lying on shelf and armed themselves with one each. Tony recalled that one of the engineers had a Webley air pistol, so this was quickly procured, as well.

They plugged in the clusters and one by one descended the ladder into the tween deck. There was no sign of anyone in the tween deck of either the No 1 or No 2 holds. For a minute or two, they tried to talk each other out of the idea that they had seen someone.

The next alternative was to descend into the main hold and search amongst the grain. They tried this with no success in No 1 hold and dropped down the short distance into No 2. They shone the cluster around until they were convinced that the hold was empty. Only then did Paul notice that one of the holes in the boxed area where the tween deck bulkhead joined the hold deck head was obscured by something. All the other holes right around the edge of the hold were clear, with this one exception. All four of them moved quickly, with the cluster, to this one area. There, cowering in the box beam was a man. He made no attempt to run, but jumped down into the grain begging them not to shoot or hit him.

None of the apprentices would either shoot or hit this terrified creature. They all felt pity that someone should be reduced to stealing grain. After a long discussion, they locked him in a locker in the forecastle until a decision was made. They half hoped that they could let him go, and that his arrest would be a lesson to him, but they realised that the decision would be taken out of their hands.

No sooner had they locked him in the forecastle, than the Police, who had been called by the Second Mate, arrived. Three turbaned officers armed with large rattan canes came aboard and asked for the prisoner to be produced. They dragged him down the accommodation ladder. As soon as he was ashore, they began systematically beating him with their canes until he lay cowering on the quayside. Only then was he dragged off for justice to be administered.

The four sat in the cabin after the Police had gone. They were disgusted with what they had witnessed, and their part in it. There and then, they made the decision that, within reason, no matter what happened during their time in this country, they would not involve the Police again. They would sort out their own problems.

The week passed terribly slowly. Due to the rate at which the cargo was being discharged, they did not appear to be any nearer to the point at which they would be able to navigate the River Hooghly. Eventually some of the sacks that were being filled with grain were laid in rows across the hold as a precaution against the cargo shifting during transit. The shifting boards had been removed and stored in the tween decks, ready for the next grain cargo. Although the forecast was good for their short coastal voyage, they were taking no chances of any cargo movement that could prove disastrous.

Paul and Mike were feeling the strain in particular. They were finishing the night watch at 0700 hrs and attempting to sleep after breakfast. It was impossible to open the portholes due to pilferage problems and the general hubbub of people walking on the working alleyway. The external daytime temperatures were in the nineties, making life in the cabins intolerable. They had little sleep by the time they started night watch again.

In addition to the sleep problems, dysentery was starting to sweep through the ship. Paul had succumbed to the disease, but never the less was struggling to keep going. Those that were not already suffering were resigned to the fact that they too would be.

Exactly one week after arriving, they left Vishakhapatnam for Calcutta. Nobody was sorry to be leaving; yet neither were they looking forward to Calcutta. Mike attempted to be philosophical and positive about visiting a city of that size and reputation. It would be one step nearer home, whenever that was going to be. Illness however was causing most of the officers and crew to look upon death as a better alternative.

If Mike was trying hard to be upbeat about the situation, then this came to a sudden halt just after leaving port. As was customary after a longish voyage they were changing watches. Paul moved to 12-4, Phil to the 8-12, and Mike as he had dreaded, the 4-8 with Kirton. He had known that it would eventually happen, but he had put it to the back of his mind, ostrich like.

By the time they cleared the port they were into the Third Mate's watch, so his first watch started as soon as he finished his dinner. It passed fairly quickly with little or no contact with Kirton. The dining saloon had been almost empty, as nearly half the officers were ill. Paul and Tony were suffering badly and not eating. Tony had always looked thin and drawn. Now he looked skeletal and haggard. Paul had lost a lot of weight due to the illness, dehydration and the lack of sleep in port, and was probably nearing collapse.

Mike relieved Paul at 0400 hrs, and listened to the stories about how he and the Second Mate had spent most of the watch running to the lavatory. As one arrived back on the bridge, so the other left. Both of them were trying hard to hang on in the hope of some treatment when they arrived in Calcutta. They expected to arrive in port during the late afternoon, so Mike would not have to stand a watch again until they left Calcutta. That was possibly the most positive thought he had that day, as he started to feel a bit queasy later on.

The Pilot came aboard in the late afternoon with a similar amount of ceremony as his counterpart in Vishakhapatnam, again immaculate in full naval uniform. This time though, he was lifted, seated in a throne like chair onto the ship's deck. Within a short time they had crossed the sand bar that had necessitated them discharging part of the cargo elsewhere and continued to make steady progress up the Hooghly. On each side of them, the poverty was obvious. Large birds, which later he was to discover were vultures, wheeled overhead and periodically swooped on an animal corpse in the river or on the bank. Young and emaciated children stood on the banks and waved.

Gradually the riverbank became more urbanized, until it built into a huge sprawl of extremely basic housing and factories teeming with people. In the distance were large houses, well away from the dock area and the slums. Presently they could see the dock area, identifiable by rows of cranes and ship funnels and ahead of them the dock gate. They had arrived in Calcutta!

CHAPTER 21

Aided by two tugs they made their way down the dock to a space on their port side, which had obviously been reserved for them. It was the only space in a long dock that had ships in every berth. Some were moored side by side. Each one was teeming with hundreds of workers. Many of the ships were owned by an Indian company, The Scindia Steam Shipping Co. To Mike's astonishment they had large swastikas on their black and yellow funnels. The Second Mate noticing his expression pointed out that the swastika was a very lucky omen in India.

Once again, the obligatory line of officials stood on the quayside waiting the lowering of the accommodation ladder and the rush to the Captain's cabin. Various crewmembers approached the ship's agent to ask if a doctor's visit had been arranged for their colleagues. They received only a shrug of the shoulders, suggesting that nothing much was going to happen. Each day saw a few more people suffering, with over half the ship's company now taking to their beds at every opportunity.

Within minutes of coming alongside the hatch covers and boards were off. The same sized multitude descended on the cargo, slowly filling the sacks, stitching them closed and placing into a sling ready to be swung ashore. In a place like Vishakhapatnam, it had seemed an anachronism. Here it was just ludicrous that nothing better and more efficient had been discovered.

Mike discovered subsequently that further down the river there was a modern grain elevator and silo, which lay rusting from lack of use. This had been a gift to the country to attempt to address some of the famine problems. A ship the size of *La Cordillera* could be discharged in around fourteen hours, as opposed to the three to four weeks it would take in total on this occasion. Once again, the problem was the number of people it would employ, in the region of six or seven instead of the two hundred currently in the holds.

Shortly after the crowd of officials left the ship clutching their cigarettes and spirits, it was announced that a doctor would be coming aboard to administer cholera inoculations. Whilst this was preferable to the disease, according to the old hands, it would be a close run thing. Apparently, if you took to your bed or rested after the inoculation, it would take the best part of a week of pain before you were able to fully use your arm. If you continued to work, you would only be in pain for two days.

The apprentices got used to the idea of being in pain for two days and were not disappointed. The morning after the injection, Mike could not lift his left arm. His three colleagues were the same. Despite this, they were sent into the holds to stow away the shifting boards and lash them to the bulkheads.

With great difficulty and a lot of bad language, they descended into the tween deck and worked throughout the day, doing as much as possible. Paul and Tony were still suffering badly from dysentery and were finding the added pain of the cholera inoculations even more difficult. When it came to climbing the ladders to take them back on deck, which normally they would have scurried up at great speed, they found every rung difficult and had to cling on, exhausted. Eventually they made it to the main deck, and sat on the deck in an attempt to recover.

Phil and Mike, who were still, mercifully, free of dysentery decided to go ashore on the Saturday. As promised, the pain from the cholera injection had disappeared. Many of the stewards and crew who had taken to their beds were still suffering and unable to move their arms.

They seriously believed that things would be much better when they were able to get away from the filthy, run-down dock area. Quickly this notion dispelled as beggars accosted them continually all the way to the city centre. Here it was much worse. They faced for the first time beggars, many of them children. Some, as children, had been deliberately deformed by breaking their limbs and allowing them to set at unnatural angles.

They made the grave mistake of giving some of the

children a few coins, and were then besieged by the others. Eventually, they had to seek sanctuary in a modern looking cinema, where they could have tea and coffee and wait until it was safe to go out again. For the first time, they experienced the wonder of air conditioning, and sat taking their time over the drinks to enjoy the fabulous coolness. Never having experienced it before, they were not ready for the down side of air conditioning. The heat and humidity hit them like a huge hammer when they walked out onto the streets.

Within a day both Mike and Phil were in the first throes of dysentery, joining the rest of the crew, most of whom were now sufferers. Like the others, they wanted to curl up in their cabins and die. As long as Kirton, who by now was also a sufferer, could make it out onto the deck, they had to work.

The Captain, who claimed continually to be suffering from constipation when all around him were dropping like flies, had finally sent for a doctor. Medicine was dispensed to everyone, but keeping it down was a major problem that faced all of them. Within a week, a study of the condition of the ship's company would almost be reminiscent of the pictures taken at the opening of a prisoner of war camp, such was the loss of weight and condition.

The four apprentices found their uniforms hanging off them when it came around to Captain's inspection. The loss of weight through illness, lack of food and heat was enormous. Tony and Paul were just skin and bone, with Phil and Mike not much better. They found they had to use belts on their tropical uniform shorts just to keep them up, where previously they had been a tight fit. By any standards, they were all seriously ill, and not showing many signs of improvement.

By the end of the second week all four of them were eating again, but were still very weak. They showed a complete lack of interest in anything other than their immediate survival. Although Kirton, due largely to his own illness, had not bothered them much in the past week, it soon became apparent that he was involved in very questionable practices.

As they had been moving up river to Calcutta, he had ordered them to stack all the bags of grain that had been used to stop the cargo shifting in a corner of each of the holds. Now he wanted the holds uncovering after the workers had gone so that these bags could be discharged separately. There was no doubt in the minds of the apprentices that this grain was being sold by Kirton and the proceeds possibly split with other officers. He had made a casual comment about seeing them right, but they would not be holding their breath after the sugar fiasco in Japan.

The slings of sacks quickly disappeared over the side straight onto a small lorry, which took them away and returned quickly for the load from the next hold. One by one the holds were uncovered, the sacks discharged and all evidence of the operation removed. Within two hours, only those who knew the sacks had been stored in the recesses of the holds would have known that anything had occurred.

After they had finished work, the four of them sat in the cabin and discussed how they too could earn similar money. It had been the apprentices, and they alone, who had done all the hard work on the sugar dodge and now the sacks of grain. They knew it would be easy enough to obtain a large supply of sacks, but filling them and selling the grain was a different matter. They resolved to find a buyer and then come up with a plan.

The selling proved to be no problem at all. By the next day, they had a slightly crooked stevedore who was only too willing to buy any amount of grain they could produce. The problem was a logistical one of where could they store it so Kirton would not see it. Days of thinking did not achieve much, until one day when they were sitting on the hatch boards of the No 4 hold. Suddenly it dawned on them that there was an empty space where no one usually entered: the ship's hospital bay. As she had been built to carry some passengers, a special room had been created which opened straight onto the deck, and was fitted out with a hospital type bed.

Although the apprentices had seen the inside of the hospital, to their knowledge no one ever went into it. It was kept locked, with the keys hanging on a hook in the Chief Steward's cabin. It was the perfect place to hide something. The decision was the easy part. How were they to obtain the keys, and how would they physically carry the grain sacks in their weakened state?

The key acquisition fell into place just one day later. Mike needed a plaster for a cut he obtained whilst moving the shifting boards. As he was almost certain he would, the Chief Steward told him to take the first aid room key and help himself. He returned the keys to their hook in his office, and temporarily borrowed the hospital key.

They inspected the hospital bay that night. They calculated that they would be able to load thirty or forty sacks, or maybe more, into it. They just needed to fill them and get them out of the hold. If they could store a further twenty to thirty sacks in the hold they would be able to earn around sixty pounds. When split equally, this would equate to several weeks' pay.

The thought of the money helped them to galvanise their much weakened bodies into action. Each night they took it in turn to fill some sacks in the No 4 hold and store them in the tween deck where they could not easily be seen.

Eventually they had filled sixty sacks. They were ready to try to move them to the hospital, but, as was becoming customary, things immediately began to go wrong. They were notified the following morning that the berth in the main dock area was urgently required for another ship. They would have to move *La Cordillera* down river to Rajabagan, a village on the outskirts of Calcutta, to moor in the river and remain until the cargo was fully discharged and the new cargo loaded.

Where previously they could sell the grain to someone with a lorry, they now needed someone with a barge or boat. It would now take time to sell the sacks again. More time for them to be discovered in their hiding places.

They began to move the ship after lunch. The remains of the crew who were still standing went to their stand by positions and slowly she was manoeuvred into the river. On the face of it, they would tie up to buoys fore and aft and continue discharging the cargo. The whole movement should be finished very shortly. However, as usual, there was to be far more to it than they had so far been told.

None of them had heard of the Hooghly bore before, but very shortly they were to become experts on the subject. The bore, as with the Severn bore in England, was caused by particularly high tides being constricted by a narrow estuary, forcing the water in the form of a tidal wave up the river. The Hooghly bore was due in three days' time, and that was the reason they had been forced to move out of the docks. They were light in the water by comparison with the ship that had taken their place in the dock, and would stand a better chance of not parting their moorings when the bore arrived.

The boys had visions of a twenty-foot tidal wave racing up the river and sweeping all before it. The reality was somewhat different as the bore was unlikely to be more than two or three feet high, but never the less lethal in the force it could exert.

The preparations they were making suggested an enormous force. They were moored facing up river towards Calcutta, and they ran out four headlines to the buoys on either side of the bows. At the stern, they had already run out four lines using the huge manila ropes and combination ropes. In addition, the wire springs were doubled back and made fast, giving eight lines in total.

The work involved in putting out all the lines had left everyone totally exhausted, but much worse was to come. They were planning to use anchor cable both fore and aft as insurance. The huge anchors had to be separated from the enormous chain and swung off. It was unlikely that the anchors had ever been separated from the chain in the life of the ship. Eleven years of paint and rust seized them solid.

Fortunately, a specially trained local Indian crew came aboard to do this work, or the bore would have arrived long before the work was completed. The anchors were swung off, and half the anchor chain on each side run out until they located a joining shackle. The chain was then split, and half the chain was taken to the stern to be shackled first to the buoy and then to the ship. For this purpose, huge bow shackles had been purchased, with four-inch diameter steel pins securing them at each end. This was repeated on both sides, and the remaining chain was run out and secured to the forward buoys. Looking at the finished work, it seemed like total overkill. They were convinced that even a ship permanently moored as a visitor attraction would not have been secured like this.

Work returned to normal, and the discharging of the cargo resumed. The apprentices were very conscious that their sacks were still laid in the hold. They would have to be moved soon if they were to avoid detection. Their health was improving very slowly, and so they decided that they must make a move that evening otherwise they would probably be discovered.

By 2300 hrs, the decks were deserted with the exception of Mike and Phil who were the official night watchmen. Tony and Paul had been excused, because of their poor health. They had to take a boat to go ashore because of their position in the river, so the crew had decided not to bother. There were no apparent lights in the cabins, so Tony and Paul were summoned and the hiding of the sacks began.

To make the work as surreptitious as possible, just two

hatch boards were lifted from the forward end of No 4 hold, right outside the hospital bay. A rope was lowered into the tween deck, and one by one the sacks were pulled up onto the edge of the hold before being carried into the hospital. In total forty-five sacks were hidden, under the bed, on top of the bed, in the bathroom and on the deck. The curtains were drawn, the door locked, and the key hidden so that if the worst happened the sacks would not be traced.

The remaining fifteen sacks were hidden under an old tarpaulin in the tween deck and the hatch covered. Then they could allow themselves to collapse on the cabin settee, and Phil and Mike resume their night's work.

During the following day, Tony and Paul were able to discuss the disposal of the grain with the original contact. He agreed to have a boat alongside that night at midnight. They all had their worries about what they were planning. Mike considered that theirs could be short but eventful careers. Phil and Paul agreed, but as Tony had less than a year left, he had seen many other similar situations, so he was not overly concerned. When they really came to analyse the situation, they were probably the only members of the ship's company who had not indulged in a bit of trading. Kirton and one or two others had sold sugar and grain. It was also fairly obvious that some of the ship's deck stores had gone from the forecastle, and boxes of provisions from the galley or storeroom had magically disappeared. In all cases, wild parties in the after accommodation normally followed this.

The more they talked about it, the more they convinced themselves that what they were doing was right, or at least, not really criminal. When midnight arrived, they headed for the No 4 hold. Tony and Paul took a lighting cluster down into the tween deck and Mike and Phil fractionally opened a space between the hatch boards so that they could pass the hook from the derrick down to the two below.

The first problem they encountered was that the power to the winches had been cut off when work on deck ceased. This immediately involved them in something they had not considered. One of them would have to go down into the engine room without being seen and put in the correct power breaker. Mike, who had always shown an interest in things mechanical, was nominated. He set off on a very lonely journey into the engine room. Just being there would almost certainly mean the end of his career, never mind actually touching anything, he told himself as he descended the metal ladders. If there was anyone awake and moving around on the port side of the accommodation, they could not fail to see him. He was also convinced that although he was moving slowly to avoid noise, they would be able to hear him all over the ship.

Did they have any alarms set on the electrical control

panel? Would he pick the correct breaker at the first attempt? All these things rushed through his mind as he approached the area where the whole of the ship's electrical system lay. He looked at the line of breaker switches and selected the one marked afterdeck, grabbing the large handle and pushing it in towards the main panel. Nothing happened as far as he could tell, no bells, sirens or any other noise, so he headed back up the engine room ladders as fast as he could move and arrived exhausted on the afterdeck.

He climbed up onto the deckhouse and tried the port winch. The winch hummed into life, much more noisily than he would have liked, and he lowered the hook down into the hold, coming back on the starboard winch at the same time, which doubled the noise. Meanwhile Paul and Tony had put all the sacks into a rope sling and waited for the hook to connect it to the sling. As soon as the hook was in place, Phil signalled Mike to start lifting on the port winch, to drag the sling out of the tween deck and over the main hold.

As soon as the wire was hanging vertically, he began to lift the sling towards the underside of the hatch boards. The plan was to stop as soon as the sling touched the boards. Then Paul and Tony could come up from the hold, and together they would quietly take off enough hatch boards to allow the load through. Very gently and slowly, the wire ran back onto the winch drum until there was the slightest movement on the board nearest the wire. Mike immediately stopped and descended onto the deck.

As he turned at the foot of the ladder, he froze. Another nightmare was about to start! Standing at the end of the alleyway leading to the afterdeck was Kirton.

For what seemed like ages, but in reality were milliseconds, his brain raced. How much had he seen? Could they talk their way out of it? Would he notice the cluster lead and realise that something was happening in the hold? Could Paul and Tony be stopped from coming up on deck? Had Phil seen Kirton, and would he be able to think on his feet? All these questions would be answered, but the last one was answered first, Phil stood transfixed and like Mike tried to get his mouth into gear.

Kirton spoke first, which gave them a few more seconds to think. "What the hell are you doing and why?"

The seconds had proved invaluable. "We noticed some hatch boards were not properly positioned and were trying to close up the hold" was Phil's first offering.

Mike joined in, "We've just been down into No 4 to see if they had been deliberately left open and if there was anyone down there". He said this near the door leading to the hold in the hopes that Paul or Tony would hear, and not shout out. At the same time, he took out the plug for the lighting cluster, plunging them into total darkness.

The removal of the cluster plug would do one of two things, it would either back up his remarks to Kirton, or it would have Paul and Tony shouting obscenities at them. He naturally prayed for the former, and his prayer was answered. There was not a sound from the hold. Kirton muttered to himself, and then told them to ensure they kept a good lookout and not go to sleep. With that, he was gone just as quickly as he had arrived.

With a huge sigh both Phil and Mike slid to the deck, both of them visibly shaking. Not a word was spoken, until they suddenly realised that Paul and Tony were still in total darkness, with the huge drop into the hold in front of them. Mike pushed the cluster plug back into its socket, and slowly Paul and Tony made their way out of the hold. They were both intelligent enough to realise that something was wrong. They too slid to the deck when the story was recounted.

In the middle of the panic, they had completely forgotten the contact who was buying the grain and who was standing in his boat along the starboard side of the hold. Fortunately, he had not called out a few minutes ago, otherwise the game would have been up.

Pulling themselves together, they stripped off sufficient hatch boards for the sling of sacks to be lifted out of the hold and swung over the side into the boat. Next, they checked the forward accommodation to ensure that there was no sign of any lights before going back to the hospital and wearily dragging out the sacks. These went into two slings and were lowered into the boat, which disappeared rapidly down river after its occupant had given Tony 900 Rupees.

For one moment, they were wealthy. But what were they to do with their 225 Rupees? None of them really wanted to go ashore again, and they would not be able to spend it aboard the ship. If they tried to return it via the Chief Steward to the ship, it would be obvious that something was wrong. None of them had taken more than 80 Rupees out as a sub.

Their choices were to go ashore and blow it all on presents, save it until they arrived home and pay it into a bank or attempt to buy dollars around the ship in case anyone had them leftover from Portland. The latter option would be the best, as they would be able to spend dollars in Cuba or anywhere else they may go, but equally the sight of impoverished apprentices changing money would cause raised eyebrows. In the end, it had to be a mixture of all three.

CHAPTER 22

The night finished quietly. Phil and Mike cooked their nightly meal, settling back into their normal routine. Tony and Paul headed for bed. Regardless of all the excitement during the past evening, the next day was expected to be special. Around 1500 hrs the Hooghly bore would hit them. Mike and Phil left instructions to be called after lunch so that they could witness this at first hand. They would probably be called anyway due to the number of sick crew. Regardless of whether they were fit or not they would have to be on deck.

By 1500 hrs all the members of the crew, sick or not, with the exception of the Captain, Third Mate and Tony who were on the bridge and the engineers and donkey men in the engine room, were lining the rails of the afterdeck. There were seamen and stewards who had been ill for days putting in a special appearance. The workforce had gone ashore as they appeared to be very frightened of what might happen. They told stories of ships being swept away by the awesome power of the bore.

The three apprentices, together with the Second Mate and three crewmembers, were on the poop deck with a grandstand view of the river and everything that would happen as the bore approached. The Second Mate's view of the situation was that they would all get out of the way at the sign of any rope parting and worry about it after the danger had passed. There were to be no heroes. The bore was due to reach them at 1520 hrs. Almost to the minute, they could see a disturbance down river, as small boats were carried up onto the bank and the water rushed along the fields at the top of the banks on each side of the river. Rapidly it approached them, but as a tidal wave it was a great disappointment, being only two or three feet high at the most. In terms of force, it was awesome. The ship was carried forward. One by one, the huge ropes parted, followed by the anchor cable.

For a few seconds panic reigned as they struggled to heave the parted ropes aboard, so that if they used the engine they would not foul the propeller. The Third Mate kept sounding intermittent blasts on the ship's whistle, as if it could have had any effect on any other ship in a similar predicament. But almost as quickly as it had all happened, it was over. Five lines of all types had parted, and it was necessary to pass the other ends out to the boat that had originally helped them moor to the buoys, so that they could be made fast again.

The Bosun cursed as the parted lines were dragged aboard. He, together with one or two of the able seamen or apprentices would be given the job of re-splicing the ropes and springs. This was a difficult job at any time, but particularly so with the large number of damaged springs and combinations. When normality had returned they heaved in the damaged anchor cable to discover that the huge bow shackle had spread apart and the giant pin dragged out and lost, an incredible demonstration of the force of nature.

The arrival of the bore had enlivened the ship. People who had not been seen for many days due to the illness had mysteriously reappeared. Many of them were still suffering quite badly but, unlike the apprentices, they were able to take to their beds to recover. In all cases, the sight of the majority of the ship's company was quite frightening, all of the officers and crew had dramatically lost weight through their illness, but some were so emaciated that one could almost doubt their chances of a full recovery.

A large number of the crew were back working on deck and had started the job of painting the ship's sides. This was being done in two ways, the first by using wooden stages on ropes made fast to the main deck and lowered by the people working on them. The second using a painting punt, which was little more than a large metal box that floated, with two people and a large quantity of paint in it.

Because people were working over the side, all crewmembers were asked to check before using lavatories that discharged on the side being painted. All crewmembers were suffering with dysentery, that is with the exception of the Captain. He was still boring all the officers with tales of his own constipation. Work progressed throughout the day. Suddenly, just after lunch, an enormous scream followed by a string of obscenities stopped everyone in their tracks and had them racing to the ship's side. An Able Seaman climbed up the ladder from the painting stage, a living testament to the end of the Captain's constipation.

By the middle of the third week, the discharge of the grain was finally completed. They could turn their thoughts to loading the new cargo and the departure from this nightmare port. With virtually no break between the last of the grain and the start of the loading of the gunny bales, the apprentices were limited on the amount of preparation work they would have to do. For this they were incredibly grateful, as the temperature in the holds was frightening and sweat ran off them simply by standing there.

They had hoped to escape almost entirely, but as usual quantities of grain had leaked into the bilges and had to be removed. Once again, the heavy boards had to be taken up and the grain scooped out so that water from the sweating of the bales could run freely in the bilges and be pumped out. This had not been an easy job last time, but in their continuing weakened state, it was totally exhausting. The addition of many rats running through the bilges did not encourage them.

Phil and Mike started on the work as they were on day

work for a short time prior to starting again on nights. Fortunately, they did not have to lay the dunnage for the new cargo as the native crews were completing it. For once, they looked forward to returning to the night watch. The cooler air on deck was a pleasure when compared with the hold.

The hardest part of the night's work was between 0100 hrs and 0630 hrs when the ship was totally quiet. Sleep beckoned should you make the mistake of sitting down somewhere comfortable.

They had experienced some attempts at thieving whilst they had been moored in the river. The anchor cables and the big ropes were a source of temptation for people in canoes on the lookout for anything not locked up. Now and then, the temptation would prove too strong and they would climb up, making their way around the rat guards that were secured to each rope or cable.

For that purpose only, Phil and Mike armed themselves with axe handles, the Webley air pistol being thought to be too extreme, and regularly checked around the stern and bow lines. That night was more productive than most. Several canoes were spotted on the river. On one occasion, they spotted a man standing on one of the after mooring buoys ready to begin his ascent. Upon seeing the two boys, he disappeared rapidly and was last seen paddling furiously down river.

Later when checking the bow lines, Mike spotted a canoe tied to one of the buoys and realised that its owner was halfway up one of the anchor cables. He signalled to Phil, who quietly moved to the hawse pipe to await his arrival. Presently a head appeared at the top of the hawse pipe and Phil struck with his axe handle. There was a slithering, follow by a loud yell, and a splash as the intruder slid back down the cable. Later he was seen paddling slowly away from the buoy reflecting on his misfortune. Whether the incident had, or had not, scared the would-be thief, it had most certainly opened Mike's eyes. Phil had always been the quiet, gentle, non-swearing member of the four. The idea of him being some type of vigilante was a complete shock.

By the third week in August, the holds were over half-full of cargo and work was progressing steadily, but somewhat slowly. They had all been ashore for one last time to buy presents with their ill-gotten gains. Mike had bought some delicate filigree jewellery for his Mother and sister. Between them, they had spent what money they had set aside for presents. They were pursued all the way to the city and back by beggars, making the trip an experience they did not wish to repeat. This would definitely be the last visit, no matter how long they were moored in the river.

Over the final week, the river was to reveal one further horror that would make them even more resistant to any return. Shortly after the bore had passed higher up the river, a ferry carrying several hundred passengers had overturned, drowning most of its passengers. Now slowly day-by-day bloated bodies were drifting down river. On the bank alongside them, vultures were tearing at human carcasses. This last nightmare vision was one that would stay in Mike's mind and colour his views on India for the rest of his life.

They prepared for sea on Thursday the 28th August, having been either in Calcutta or moored on the river for six weeks. Soon they could head for Durban, for which they were duly grateful. The holds were battened down and the derricks lowered after some stores had been taken on board. Normally the stores were loaded without comment, but on this occasion whilst loading meat an observant steward noticed that instead of wool on a lamb carcass, there was fur. From that point on any dish purporting to contain lamb was avoided like the plague.

Late that afternoon the Pilot came aboard and they made their slow progress down river to the open sea beyond. As the pilot boat disappeared into the distance, Mike sincerely hoped that he would never have to return.

CHAPTER 23

Even the thought of being on watch with Kirton did not initially detract in Mike's mind from the fact that they were back at sea. They had missed the air being pushed into the cabins as the portholes had been closed for the past six weeks. For the first time for nearly seven weeks, they were able to sleep properly. Although they were heading for the equator, meaning even warmer weather, the slight breeze caused by their movement was a huge improvement.

Kirton had been at his most unpleasant on the first day out of Calcutta. He had noticed that one of the enormous bow shackles was missing in addition to the one wrecked by the bore. All four of the apprentices searched the ship from stem to stern in an attempt to find it.

On being told yet again that it could not be found, he lambasted all four of them and told them to look again. Eventually they spent the whole day looking for it with no success. They did not expect to be successful as Paul and Tony had used the pin for a weight when fishing in the river. It had proved too heavy for the line, causing it to part, leaving the pin at the bottom of the Hooghly. Realising the problems it would cause, they had put the remainder of the shackle over the side under cover of darkness. They decided a day spent searching was infinitely preferable to the alternative.

The thought of the impending crossing of the equator filled Mike with dread. They would be at the crossing point in about five days' time and the Captain had spent most mealtimes discussing how they would celebrate the crossing of the line. He was already preparing his costume for his part as King Neptune, and urging all others to consider their parts in the ceremony. The electrician, heeding the Captain's bidding, started to prepare an electric chair to plug into a deck lighting socket. The voltage could be cranked up as required.

No matter how much they tried to concentrate on other things, the crewmembers who had not crossed before could not avoid the subject. A large structure, formed from a hatch tarpaulin, was taking shape on the top of the No 3 hold. Initially they were not told what it was to be, but eventually after it was filled with water, they realised that this was where they would be thrown after all kinds of unspeakable things had been done to them.

The older hands gloated each time they saw Mike, Phil, the Fourth Engineer, the junior engineers, several crewmembers and stewards, giving them various ideas on what was to happen to them. The condemned men assembled in a cabin later to discuss what could be done, but realised that no matter where they hid, they would be found and dealt with. Most agreed that they would not give up easily, but possibly that was what was wanted by the perpetrators of the misery.

Wednesday the 3rd of September dawned hotter than ever. Whilst Kirton had been taking his morning star sight, Mike stood by the chronometer in the chartroom ready to note the time on Kirton's mark. He looked at the chart in front of him and at the estimated position. By his reckoning, they would cross the equator at around 1500 hrs that day. In the hopes of catching them by surprise, no one had mentioned when the expected crossing was to take place and so Mike would be able to prepare them for the inevitable.

By lunch time, the whole ship was a hive of activity. Work was forgotten, the Second Mate was alone on the bridge, the Third Engineer and a donkey man in the engine room. Everyone else was preparing for the afternoon's entertainment and those that were not doing anything constructive were keeping an eye on the whereabouts of those who were unwillingly going to provide the entertainment.

Around 1430 hrs Phil and Mike noticed several people heading towards the No 3 hold. Dressed in swimming trunks and wearing wigs made from brushed out strands of rope, with their bodies painted in different colours they looked ridiculous. But the two boys realised quickly that this was the search party looking for all the first-timers. They decided that they would hide until they found out what was happening.

Grabbing a torch they headed for the after mast house and the ladders leading down into the holds. As they walked out onto the deck, a second search party was heading down the afterdeck on the port side. They threw themselves on the deck and crawled to the mast house, so remaining undiscovered.

Quickly they knocked the dogs of the waterproof door and climbed inside, putting the dogs back on behind them so as not to leave clues. This done, with the aid of the torch they made their way into the tween deck, climbed onto the top of the gunny bales and started to make their way to the No 3 hold.

The heat in the hold was stifling as they made their slow progress forward, crawling along the top of the bales. Eventually they could hear noises, the shouts and cheers of the people assembled on the hatch top above them and the shouted obscenities of their victims. A stream of light lit up one of the bales in front of them. They realised this was one of the massive cowl ventilators that forced air into the hold to reduce the temperature. Crawling underneath it, they were able to get some cooling air, but also hear every word of what was going on up on deck.

The search parties were being briefed to go and find the first-timers who had not yet been brought before King Neptune. Mike and Phil's names were top of the list. The boys listened to the wild performance above them before realising that with a little effort they could actually climb one at a time into the ventilator and so see what was happening on deck.

Phil went first and then slithered back down into the hold with tales of the wild excesses above them. Paint, grease, electricity, scissors, water and razors featured heavily. After hearing Phil's description Mike was not certain that he wanted to look, but never the less did so. He decided after doing so that he would have preferred not to have bothered.

The Captain, who had obviously put an enormous amount of work into his costume, sat on his throne at the side of the specially created pool. He was resplendent in a long brushed out rope wig with a grass skirt, and a huge crown. His magnificent looking trident must have been made especially in the engine room. Directly across the pool was a metal chair into which each of the first-timers was to be strapped. This was connected to a lighting cluster socket that the Electrician, similarly dressed in costume, was controlling.

Kirton, clearly inspired by the Captain, was also in full costume and relishing his position as one of the sadistic torturers. He was wielding a large pair of scissors on the victim's hair, whilst his counterpart, the Second Engineer was applying large handfuls of yellow engine grease to a junior engineer. Other crewmembers were applying black grease, paint and, in the Cook's case, feathers. At the same time, the Electrician was cranking up the electricity flowing through the frame of the chair, creating even more misery.

Eventually the victim, totally unrecognizable, was ejected from the chair into the pool. He struggled as he tried to see and find the pool edge. Eventually he was dragged out and lay on the deck, where he tried in vain to clear the grease from his eyes with grease covered hands. At last, he made it onto his feet and dragged himself towards the accommodation to clean up.

The search parties returned with the Radio Officer, another junior engineer, two stewards and two seamen, all of who were similarly dealt with. Once again Phil and Mike's names were read out and the search parties set out to find them, returning fifteen minutes later with the news that they could not be found. They were told to try again, and to issue the direst threats if the two did not surrender themselves immediately.

For the next few minutes, Phil and Mike could hear the searchers shouting all around the ship and discussed what they were to do. They decided reluctantly that they would not escape retribution. No matter how long they hid, they would eventually be found. They knew that even Paul and Tony would be lined up against them. Taking all this into consideration they climbed the nearest ladder leading to the main deck and allowed themselves to be found, professing total amazement that anyone had been unable to find them.

The torture seemed to go on forever. He had first been soaked with water containing Teepol which stung his eyes, then grease of different colours came at him from each side, whilst at the same time it felt as if his hair was being dragged out by its roots rather than cut with scissors. Initially he struggled, but then accepted that it was a waste of time and concentrated on it all being over. He was able to drag himself from the pool and headed for the shower. Together with Phil, he used yards of toilet roll and rags in an attempt to rid his body of the grease and paint. Then they decided that the only way they would succeed would be to wash themselves in paraffin. To say that this brought tears to the eyes was an understatement and they climbed into the hot shower as soon as possible with large amounts of soap.

Once they had managed to clean their bodies, they looked at what was left of their hair. Wild, short tufts of hair stuck up all over amid the areas that were now bald and those that were still the same as before. Whilst contemplating what to do, the Fourth Engineer and the three junior engineers, who had suffered a similar fate, joined them. They decided between them that there was only one thing to do. Using scissors and razors, they shaved off the remaining hair until they were totally bald.

At dinner that evening and on deck the next day they were the butt of many jokes from the remainder of the first-timers and the crew in general. But by the following night, all the other victims had shaved their heads, realising that they would not be able to save their previous hairstyles.

After all the excitement of the previous day, life returned to normal. Out came the chipping machines and hammers and with one addition, a spare plastic white cover from his uniform cap fashioned into a cap to protect his white head from the sun, Mike settled down into the normal sea routine.

Slowly the four boys were putting on weight after their illness, but despite this one of the first jobs they had to complete was to make tighter belts to keep up their shorts. No amount of adjustment was capable of taking up all the slack, and they knew that they would have to invest in new pairs when they had a chance to go ashore in Cuba. In the meantime, they could create their belts using clips from old flags and new signal halyard that they spliced onto the clips.

The thoughts of going ashore in Cuba were somewhat premature as they had first to complete their longest ever time without shore leave. Although they would be calling at Durban and Port of Spain for bunkers, they would not have an opportunity to go ashore. They would have to travel 12,000 miles before that opportunity came along.

This represented almost a fifty percent longer gap than either their voyage from Cuba to Japan or Portland to India. On the bright side, it meant that their hair would have grown to a respectable length before they met the public again.

The first few days of the voyage had passed with little or no input from Kirton since the incident with the bow shackle. Mike had ensured that, on the bridge, he got his cocoa on time in the evening and his tea in the morning. Apart from the timing of his star sight, Mike stayed well out on the bridge wing away from him.

Of course it could not last. Ten days out of Calcutta, Kirton decided to resume his physical fitness campaign. He too had suffered whilst in India and had lost weight. As soon as he had finished his sight, he would pick up his weights and march up and down the bridge wing lifting each one in turn in front of him. He would then follow this by lifting to the sides and twisting. Mike ensured that he was on the opposite bridge wing so that he could concentrate on being the lookout, and did not have to catch Kirton's eye.

The idea of always standing on the extremity of the opposite bridge wing worked for about two days. Then Kirton could resist no longer, and came over to Mike to give him the weights. Mike could just about lift them, and with effort push them one at a time into the air. This was not good enough for Kirton, who wanted him to lift both weights out in front of him simultaneously. Mike shook and sweated as he attempted to lift both weights, but knew that he stood no chance of doing it.

Day after day Kirton harangued him, making him work for hours at a time and continually calling him a disgrace and totally unfit for the job. Mike said nothing and continued to lift the weights to the best of his ability. Although he had not suffered as much as Paul and Tony, Mike had still been very ill in Calcutta and was at the lowest weight he had been since becoming a teenager. The constant lifting was making him feel quite ill and dizzy, but he kept himself going by thinking that one day Kirton would go down to the deck below whilst Mike had the weights in his hands.

On the plus side, the combination of the weight lifting and the need to put on some weight gave Mike a wonderful appetite. Each breakfast he would go through the cereals, curried eggs or kedgeree, bacon, eggs and flapjacks and toast to follow. By lunch time he was ready for a full lunch. After a few days of this, he started to worry that he may become like Kirton and be obsessed with his body.

They arrived in Durban on the Saturday, on what was the coldest day that they had experienced since passing the Aleutians back in June. The Pilot was in his blue uniform and looked startled to see them all still in their tropical whites. The response was almost immediate, and an order came down from the bridge to change into the uniforms they normally only wore in the northern hemisphere.

Their time in Durban was almost the same as in Miri, longer only by the time it took to enter and leave the port itself. Very quickly, the fuel lines were connected, food that looked considerably more appetizing than the last came aboard followed by yet more paint and they were on their way. The Pilot having disembarked, they had a chance to read their mail before starting the weekly cleaning ready for the Captain's inspection on the following day. It looked to all intents that they could enjoy a peaceful weekend.

Disaster struck late on the following evening. The oldest of the four donkey men had started his watch by checking on the ship's boiler. Exactly what happened next was not certain, but the boiler suffered a blow-back and a huge ball of flame engulfed the donkey man, burning him terribly. The Fourth Engineer, together with his junior, immediately went to his assistance and called the Chief Steward as the first aid officer. With great difficulty, they manoeuvred the man, who was in terrible agony, on a stretcher to the hospital bay where the Chief Steward could apply dressings.

A decision had to be taken urgently on the best course of action, and the Captain was summoned. The Chief Engineer and the Chief Steward wanted the donkey man landed at the nearest port, which would be Port Elizabeth, so that he could be treated professionally. If not Port

Elizabeth, then Cape Town, a further 500 miles away. The Captain was non-committal and promised to make a decision as soon as possible.

Within a short time, news of the accident spread around the ship. It became generally assumed that the ship would put into port to land the unfortunate crewmember. The Captain meanwhile kept a low profile and made several calls to the company's head office back in the UK, and to the local agents.

Time went by to the extent that they realised they would not be going into Port Elizabeth, because of the cost of the exercise. Then it became apparent that for the same reason they would not go into Cape Town either. The ship's company was incensed at the lack of compassion or interest in the fate of the man. He was still in terrible pain, despite being given what pain relief the Chief Steward could administer.

Representations from most sections of the ship were made to the Captain, but he was adamant that there would be no change in the ship's itinerary. The donkey man would be landed ashore when the ship reached Port of Spain in Trinidad, a further five and a half thousand miles away. The decision was greeted with almost universal derision that a man should be expected to suffer so much for so long. Morale, which had not been particularly good since arriving in India, suffered a further lowering.

Whether it was to boost his terribly flagging popularity or not was difficult to know, but the Captain made sudden concessions to the Chief Engineer, Chief Steward and Kirton. The passenger cabins, which had remained empty from the time *La Cordillera* was first built, and which had proved to be extremely vexatious to a succession of ship's companies, suddenly came to prominence.

By comparison with the other accommodation, they were palatial with delicate green leather armchairs and settee, beautifully finished light ash woodwork and comfortable bunk beds. First the Chief Engineer, followed by Kirton, moved in, followed eventually by the other departmental heads. As a gesture, it may have possibly succeeded in keeping them on side, but did nothing to improve the Captain's standing with the remainder of the crew.

CHAPTER 24

They rounded the Cape two days later and started the long haul across the South Atlantic towards the West Indies. With the possible exception of a lighthouse on the eastern extremity of Brazil, they did not anticipate seeing any land until they arrived at Port of Spain in around two weeks' time.

Almost immediately they entered the Atlantic, they started to see the world's biggest seabirds, the albatross. These huge birds drifted effortlessly on the thermals, swooping down occasionally to take a fish or to examine rubbish that had been thrown over the side. Their incredible size and beauty was a contrast with the last large birds they had met, the Hooghly vultures.

Whilst Mike knew that the wingspan of these beautiful birds was in the region of ten to twelve feet, it remained difficult to imagine this size as they circled, above and around them. Only seeing one close-up would give a sense of scale and he pondered on what this would be like. He did not have long to wait before finding out.

Two evenings later, just before midnight, Paul and Tony woke him to come and see what was on the afterdeck. Phil was still on the bridge, having just called Paul, and was therefore unaware of the sudden disturbance. Mike dressed quickly and headed out onto the deck. He was still half asleep, but awakened rapidly when he saw the reason for his call. Standing only six feet from him was a baby albatross that had obviously decided to examine the ship closely and now could not get sufficient wind under its wings to take off again. Whilst it did not look distressed or afraid, a look at the size of the wings and beak put off anyone from moving any nearer towards it.

Within minutes, word of the visitor's arrival had spread and several seamen and engineers joined the assembled throng. They huddled by the No 4 hold, away from the bird, whilst various options on what was to be done were discussed. Having had to read *The Ancient Mariner* on more than one occasion, Mike's only interest was that it should be returned to its normal environment as soon as possible. Things were bad enough on the ship without having the death of an albatross hanging around them. Everyone agreed on this, but who was going to lift it onto the ship's rail so that it could take off properly?

Presently the sound of footsteps on the metal deck could be heard, and it became clear that someone was walking down the starboard alleyway, straight towards the bird. For a minute, the spectators were hushed as Phil came into sight carrying the silver plated teapot from the bridge. With his mind obviously on the end of his watch and the thought of his welcoming bunk, he walked past the bird in a way only seen in cartoons. Two steps past he froze, looked back, shouted, dropped the teapot and ran the length of the afterdeck. The crowd dissolved in fits of laughter. The teapot never really recovered.

Eventually a blanket was produced and three volunteers threw it over the bird to pin its wings. While it was temporarily rendered blind, they could lift it onto the rail. Without looking back or giving the appearance of having experienced anything unusual, the bird swooped off the rail towards the sea and was gone, skimming the surface before rising and disappearing into the darkness. The lightness of the moment cheered up the crew and helped them to concentrate more on the voyage and their impending return to Cuba, rather than the injured donkey man.

Within a few days, they were nearing the equator again and the sun beat down on them remorselessly. Kirton was still picking on Mike and having him exercise with his weights in the early part of his watch. As a new way of getting his fitness regime through to Mike, he decided to have him chip some particularly thick areas of rust on the deck between the two main accommodation areas, alongside No 3 hold.

But this was to be no ordinary chipping. The rust was so thick and heavy that it needed a very big hammer to smash it up. After being shown the work, Mike headed for the forecastle and returned with a fourteen-pound sledgehammer. Immediately he started to smash the rust areas, with a reasonable amount of success. Kirton sneered at what he had done and headed for the engine room. He returned with a twenty-eight pound hammer that was used on the spanner that removed the main piston retaining nuts. Giving the deck several smashes with the hammer, he threw it towards Mike and told him to get on with it properly.

Mike started to hit the deck whilst Kirton watched him, gleefully. Within a few minutes, he was panting for breath and the sweat was pouring off him. He lost his grip on the hammer handle and so hit the deck at the wrong angle, jarring his arm and shoulder. Within the hour, Mike was coming very near to collapse due to the heat of the midday sun and the exertion of lifting and swinging the massive hammer.

Kirton, who had returned to inspect the work, possibly realised that he had gone too far and walked away towards the ladder leading to the accommodation. Just as he did Mike swung the hammer and it slid from his fingers, flying through the air to the shout of "You bastard," from Mike. It landed inches behind Kirton. He turned immediately and looked at Mike, but did not say a word. He gave Mike no more grief for the remainder of the voyage.

Mike anticipated problems on the following morning when he relieved Paul and made the tea, but none were forthcoming. He took his tea to the far end of the bridge wing and concentrated on drinking it and watching the horizon around him. It was clearly going to be another scorching hot day and over on the starboard quarter the sun was showing stunning signs of putting in an appearance.

He glanced occasionally at Kirton to see whether he was going to produce the weights, but today there was no sign of them. He received a gruff "Get the chronometer," from him as he came out onto the bridge wing with his sextant, but that was the full extent of their communication. After marking the time for him, Mike returned to the bridge wing. For the first time since leaving India, he allowed himself to give some thought to what was going to happen next.

They were aware already that they were heading for Port of Spain where they would take on sufficient fuel to last them until they knew the full extent of their movements. From there, they had discovered that their first port in Cuba would be Cienfuegos, a small port on the southern coast. After which they would discharge in a further eight ports around the coast, finishing in Havana, the capital.

At this point, once again, the rumourmongers took over. The favourite was to stay in Cuba after completing the discharge of the gunny bales and then load sugar for Japan. Upon completion of unloading, they would follow their earlier route to Portland and then back to India where they would load gunny bales again. Against this theory was the fact that the sugar shipping season was believed to be over until next year.

Second favourite was to load grain again in the USA and take it directly to India. This had a lot of credence. One of the Engineers claimed that he had asked his wife to ring the company head office for information, and that was what she was told. The outside bet was on collecting a grain cargo and taking it to Europe. Whilst everyone preferred this option, they considered it unlikely and refused to contemplate it seriously. Against both these theories was the fact that it was doubtful if the head office even knew themselves where they would be going next.

He thought for a while of home and the letters he had received in both Calcutta and Durban from his brothers and sister and Jono telling of the great times they were having during the summer holidays. The owner of the developing and printing company had called. Was Mike going to look after the daily film collection? The motorcycle was back on the road and they could use Mike full time in the processing lab. Just the mention of the motorcycle had made Mike very wistful. The thought of that plus six weeks holiday made him wonder what he was doing there.

His thoughts were interrupted by the Bosun arriving on the bridge to discuss the day's work with Kirton. They would arrive at Port of Spain the next day, so he wanted as much of the ship as possible spruced up. All areas of the deck where chipping had taken place needed completion, and the final coat of deck paint needed to be applied. The main accommodation blocks needed a coat of white paint. This was akin to painting the Forth Bridge. It had been originally started months ago, but forgotten for other work. Now it would continue throughout their time in Cuba.

As always, the apprentices drew the short straw. They would be painting the deck areas. One of them would work with a roller on a pole whilst the other three would work with brushes and paint kettles painting around every bollard, stanchion, deck housing and accommodation block. A straight line where the heavy red deck paint met the white or black paint was vital. Admittedly, at the end of the day the area they had painted looked impressive, but, as usual, they were destined to have to have a preliminary wash in paraffin before entering the shower.

Early next morning they arrived in Trinidad. At last, the donkey man could be landed and taken to hospital for specialist treatment. A large number of the crew gathered as he was taken ashore, still in considerable pain and heavily bandaged. A constant stream of invective from his friends was aimed at the bridge. Captain Eyre-Walker kept a very low profile, as indeed he had done since the accident occurred, seventeen days ago.

Port of Spain came and went like Miri, Yokohama and Durban. The agent came aboard together with the usual crowd of officials and hangers-on, the fuel line was connected, the tanks pumped full and they were ready to go. The crowd of officials who had sat in the Captain's cabin throughout the bunkering clutched their cigarettes and spirits, and departed as quickly as they had arrived.

The Pilot boarded, and at the end of a very short pilotage he disembarked. Full speed ahead was rung, and the course was set for Cienfuegos. They were left to reflect that it would have been very pleasant to go ashore, the weather was very hot and there was an attractive spicy smell to the air. But in five days' time they would be ashore again in Cuba. It was a thought that added a spring to the step of the majority of the crew and helped to erase the memories of the last few months, and India in particular.

The voyage to Cienfuegos was a nervous one. It was the hurricane season and already two major hurricanes had passed through the area leaving trails of devastation. There was a warning of a third storm brewing to the south of them but its path was currently somewhat unpredictable. So far, they had been very fortunate. The voyage from Durban had been the fastest yet at a speed of just over thirteen knots, with no bad weather.

Their good luck held. Astonishingly, after four days of an average speed of slightly over fifteen knots, when they walked outside the accommodation their nostrils were filled with the sweet smell of sugar. They had arrived in Cienfuegos.

CHAPTER 25

They gently edged alongside the quay in Cienfuegos. On first glance the quay was all there was to Cienfuegos. There appeared to be little else in the way of storage or normal port facilities. In fact, it made Vishakhapatnam look like a large modern port. With the exception of the mandatory officials, there was no sign of any other life. It was Saturday, and a large amount of wheeling and dealing had to be completed and many palms greased before a decision to work on Saturday and Sunday would be made.

Eventually an understanding was achieved. As if by magic, vans and ramshackle cars appeared from nowhere disgorging several gangs of stevedores. The hatch covers were removed. The first bales were discharged onto the old lorries and driven away to sugar plantations or somewhere similar. They were to find that with the exception of Santiago, Manzanillo and Havana, most of the ten ports would be very similar. A sufficient stock of bales for their own sugar production would be unloaded at each port.

The longest stay at any one port would be five days, with most completed in two days' work and an overnight sailing to the next port. It meant also that the cargo had to be checked meticulously. That inevitably meant one apprentice on each of three holds, one on night watch and a deck officer on each of the other holds. This, hopefully, would ensure that the total cargo tally matched the figure given in Calcutta. For a change, it was an easy job for the apprentices, but extremely soporific as they sat watching the cargo hook swing backwards and forwards across the hold.

For the first time for weeks, they were able to go ashore that evening. On the face of it, there was nowhere to go. Apparently, just out of sight there was a bar, which doubled once again as a brothel. Within an hour from the time work stopped, a crocodile of crewmembers headed into the distance, with only one, or maybe two, things on their mind.

They had noticed prior to leaving the ship that an armed security guard was aboard, but had thought very little of it at the time. He was there to defend the ship should any terrorist or freedom fighter decide to attack. The movement to overthrow President Batista had grown dramatically in the months since their last visit. Castro's troops would suddenly swoop down and attack at will to obtain anything that would be useful to them in the mountains.

It was difficult to gauge whether the rebels were supported or not in this area. Slogans and posters covered the walls they found when they eventually reached the bar. Anyone asked whom they supported would look all around them furtively before replying one way or the other. The general consensus was that Castro was likely to triumph against the increasingly unpopular Batista.

The cubalibras flowed thick and fast that evening as the crew made the most of their first night back on dry land. Those who had availed themselves of all the bar's services had nearly spent up, and they still had another twenty-four days to go. As the boys returned to the ship they passed many of their colleagues along the way. They wondered how many would turn out for work the following day.

The absence of people for work during the next few days became a major problem, causing the Captain to make the decision that no more subs would be issued for the duration of their time in Cuba. This decision incensed the crew who saw it as a challenge to their civil liberties. They had earned the money, but were not being allowed to spend it. Drastic measures were needed to ensure that they could continue to enjoy themselves.

First, a large combination rope disappeared. Then it was stores of all sorts, culminating in a chipping machine being exchanged for a case of rum. Every locker had to be secured each night. Every item of equipment that was not in use was stowed away as the perpetrators exacted revenge on the Captain. Seeing the crew going ashore, it was obvious that they were involved, but proving it was very difficult.

They moved on quickly to Manzanillo, one of their three

major ports. There the bars lined the waterfront, and the quality of the working girls improved out of all recognition. They could have expected to experience far more problems, but it seemed for a while that the situation dramatically improved. More people were reporting for work first thing in the morning, and not necessarily looking like walking corpses. Manzanillo was the zenith of the crew's behaviour, but Santiago, their next port and one of the majors, would be the nadir.

The Captain and other senior officers had not realised something that the crew already knew. Santiago was the home of Bacardi, and their distillery lay just up the road from the ship. It was customary to show visitors around the distillery and to allow them to sample the different types of rum. Parties toured on a regular basis each day. The fact that they could go ashore and get totally plastered each day appealed to the crew and it became a waste of time calling them in the morning.

Initially the distillery did not understand that the finer points of anejo and viejo rums were not being appreciated and the tours continued. Each day crewmembers returned with their Bacardi that they had purchased for around $1.50 a bottle. Each day, on all four days, they would be back again for another tour.

If Santiago marked a disappointing low in the behaviour of the crew, then a week of night watch at Guantanamo would prove to be Mike's personal nadir. They had already been ashore in Guantanamo earlier in the voyage, and knew that apart from the bar/brothel there was nothing there. Maybe it was because their bodies could not stand the continuous excesses of women and beer, but the crew en-masse stayed aboard. The remaining apprentices went ashore.

At 1900 hrs, having applied liberal amounts of mosquito repellent and clad only in shirt and shorts, Mike strode out on deck to begin his long night's work. He first went forward and checked the ropes, ensuring that they were tight and that the rat guards were in place. Then he walked slowly aft to do the same and realised that the crew were having a party outside their accommodation.

"Have a drink Mike," shouted one or two of the crew. Although the apprentices were regularly warned not to fraternize with the crew, they all enjoyed a good relationship. Mike replied that he would have a small one. The Bacardi splashed into the glass followed by a large amount of Coke and he sipped it slowly, making it last while he chatted with them.

Aware that Kirton was likely to be on the prowl, presently Mike moved on back to the forward accommodation. By this time, the engineers and Radio Officer had come out onto the deck to enjoy a drink on what was a very pleasant, hot evening. "Have a drink Mike," said the engineers who were drinking the South African Castle lager they had purchased from the Captain's bond instead of the local Cuba Libras. Mike took a bottle and sat down with them for a few minutes.

After the beer, Mike headed for the forecastle and started the whole routine all over again, arriving eventually on the afterdeck where the crew's party was becoming livelier. "Have another drink Mike," they chorused as he arrived back, most of them unaware that he had been away. "Just a small one," said Mike not wishing to seem ungracious. Once again, the Bacardi splashed into his glass, but with rather less Coke, as they were running out. Besides which, the Coke here cost more than the Bacardi.

Again Mike headed for the foredeck, but was stopped by the engineers. They pressed another bottle of lager into his hand and talked to him for some time. By now, it was approaching midnight. It was time to cook his meal and he headed for the galley, where the food had been left out.

Normally the galley range was quite easy to fire up. You put a lighted piece of paper into the firebox, turned on the oil injectors, and then turned on the fan. This would cause it to burst into life and you would be able to cook on it quite quickly thereafter. On this occasion, Mike was having problems. First, he turned on the fan too early and had burning paper everywhere. Then he flooded it with oil, causing a huge conflagration when it finally burst into life.

He put it down to tiredness, and in the end managed to cook his meal of bacon, eggs, beans and toast. It did not look particularly pleasant, but to Mike's palate it was fine.

As soon as he had finished his meal, he headed out onto the deck again, stopping for a short time to chat to the engineers before going aft where the crew welcomed him again. Both parties insisted on him having a drink and so not wishing to appear anti-social, he did. At about 0030 hrs, he stopped for a short rest and sat on one of the No 4 hold hatch boards. He remembered nothing more after that.

Tony, Paul and Phil arrived back on board at 0100 hrs. They had enjoyed a pleasant evening at the local bar and were now ready for their beds prior to another day of cargo tallying. As they came to the door to the accommodation by hold No 4, they noticed Mike stretched out on a hatch board. In fact, it was the only hatch board above a nearly empty hold. One move either way would mean someone picking up the pieces at the bottom of the hold. They dragged him back onto the deck and along the alleyway until they reached their bathroom. Depositing him in the shower, still dressed, they turned on the cold tap and went to their beds.

Around four hours later at 0500 hrs, Mike woke up. Eventually he dragged himself out of the shower, which was still running. He felt awful. His head felt as if someone was using a sledgehammer on it and he had the urge to be violently sick. Suppressing the urge, he staggered out on deck, trying desperately to remember what had happened. The cool breeze reacted with his soaked shirt and shorts causing him to start sobering up very quickly. His first thought was to check the deck and the moorings in case anything had happened, but he could see no problems.

By 0630 hrs, when it was time to call all the apprentices and crew, he had managed to pull himself together and hoped to be able to get into his bunk as soon as possible. His colleagues were not going to let it go that easily. They extracted the Michael from him as much as possible. They told him what an idiot he was, and how close he had come to ending it all. Mike did not really need telling, he felt so grim. He vowed he would never do anything like it again. That promise was one he stuck to religiously for the rest of his time at sea.

He had hoped that he had heard the last of his previous night's work, but at dinner there were subtle comments. A number of the engineers mentioned that the night watch must be a very tiring job. He watched Kirton's ears prick up. He knew he had better be careful that evening, as Kirton would be wandering around.

During the course of the night, Kirton put in several appearances, asking whether Mike had checked the ropes, the rat guards, all the deck lockers etc.. He had, and for the rest of his watch made sure that no one could fault his performance.

If he needed any further incentive, he got it in the early hours of the morning. He had tried not to rest anywhere in case he should go to sleep. He was still feeling fragile from the night before. Around 0300 hrs, he sat down on a chair that had been left on deck for tallying. He did not think that he nodded off, but was woken by the feel of something moving around his feet that were clad only in a pair of flip-flops. As had happened during the visit to Manzanillo, a large rat had just run backwards and forwards across his feet. Nothing could have galvanised him into action more. He spent the rest of the night on his feet.

The rest of his time on night watch passed without incident as they moved around the coast from Guantanamo to Antilla and then to Nuevitas. In fact, he had only one night left before going back onto day work. The night started like all the others. Members of the ship's company headed for the bars/brothels and he was left to walk the decks and chat to anyone that appeared, passing the time until he was ready to cook his meal.

Most of the crew came back to the ship in the early hours of the morning, without causing any disturbance, but at around 0230 hrs he was aware of raised voices on the quay. McLeish was on the quay arguing with a taxi driver. This able seaman was known for his love of drink. He had been logged a day's pay several times by the Captain for his drunken behaviour. Docked pay was always recorded in the ship's log.

McLeish had also been in serious trouble when he failed to turn up in time for the sailing from Guantanamo on the earlier visit. He did in fact turn up just as she headed out of the port and joined the ship on the pilot boat. This time he reached some sort of agreement with the taxi driver and raced up the accommodation ladder heading for his cabin. He returned two minutes later with a carton of cigarettes.

As usual, he had spent all his money on drink. Luckily, the taxi driver seemed quite happy to receive 200 cigarettes instead of his fare. Unfortunately, just as the driver was taking the cigarette carton a policeman walked around the corner of the warehouse. He did not like what he saw and the taxi driver quickly returned the cigarettes to McLeish. Having the sense to realise he was in trouble, McLeish sprinted for the accommodation ladder. The policeman raised his rifle, shooting into the air. As he ran up the ladder Mike shouted to him "Run Jim, they're only blanks," as a bullet ricocheted off the bulkhead alongside him.

Mike hit the deck like a sack of coal, not moving for several minutes until he heard voices on the quay. He peered, gingerly, over the rail to see two policeman. Between them with his hands in the air was McLeish. Another taxi had drawn up, and out of this one stepped the Second Mate.

The Second Mate had also enjoyed a good evening ashore.

He took great exception to the two policemen taking McLeish away with them. The police were not prepared to compromise, or accept the usual bribes of cigarettes, so the Second Mate dug his heels in even further. After a heated discussion for about ten minutes, the Second Mate and McLeish were taken away to the local jail, but first he shouted to Mike to call the Captain.

Mike raced up the two ladders to the Captain's cabin and knocked loudly on the door. A sleepy "Come in," came from inside and Mike entered.

"The police have arrested the Second Mate and McLeish, Sir," said Mike. "Thank you," said the Captain and, for the time being, that was that.

As morning broke the panic started. The Captain headed for the telephone on the quay, and within a few minutes, a taxi arrived bearing the ship's agent arrived. They emerged together thirty minutes later and both headed for the town and the jail. Presumably, fines were paid or palms were greased, because when they arrived back at the ship a second taxi carrying the Second Mate and McLeish also pulled up.

That was Mike's last night watch in Cuba. Taken all round it had been quite eventful. They sailed to Caibarien that evening, and he started back on the cargo tallying the next morning. Somehow, it did not seem the same. The ship was emptying quite fast now, and thoughts once again were turning to where they were going next. They only had two more ports to go after Caibarien, Sagua and Cardenas, before they arrived in Havana. A decision would certainly have been made by the time they reached there.

Sagua and Cardenas passed quickly and quietly. In general, no one had any money left, and if they did they were saving it for Havana. In particular, the cigar smokers were looking forward to the huge ranges of cigars to be obtained there, and so the ship became a comparatively sober one. They arrived in Havana on Friday, which meant a weekend in port. The decision had already been taken not to work cargo on Sunday, so they expected to leave again on Tuesday. But for where?

The answer to the question came not long after their arrival in Havana. From there they would sail across the Gulf of Mexico to Galveston where they would load another grain cargo and proceed to LEO. Last time Mike had to ask where was Leo, this time it was possibly the best news they could have. Only one thing could top it, and that would be confirmation of an English port. It was still very possible, despite the pessimists who fancied Rotterdam, Hamburg or Antwerp.

The curtain of gloom that had enveloped the ship since Portland miraculously lifted. People were singing and whistling again. But would it last? Whilst the four apprentices were thrilled at the prospect of the possibility of Christmas at home, a sudden awful realisation occurred to them. They would be in Galveston in about three and a half days after leaving Havana. By the time they arrived in Galveston they would have to complete rigging the shifting boards.

Normally it would take three days to clean out the holds, then four to five days for the rigging, depending on sea state. Now they were to be expected to do both jobs in three days. Suddenly tallying the cargo was forgotten. They worked in the tween decks ensuring that all the steelwork was in good condition and the bottle screws were well greased, ready for the rush as soon as cargo discharge was complete. They laid out the shifting boards and feeders in order so that time could be saved once the rigging commenced. No time would be lost there, but nothing could start until each of the holds was cleared of cargo and dunnage.

By Monday, the first two holds were empty and work could commence. Dunnage was collected and stowed in the tween deck, and the hold deck swept and emptied. Next bilge boards were covered with paper and battened. The initial work had started during the morning and finished at midnight. Although totally exhausted, they knew that this was the shape of things to come for the next three days. Even the crew, for a change, was working the same hours, but they were paid overtime for doing it.

One by one, the holds were emptied on the Tuesday and they continued to work at the same pace, stopping only for meal breaks and the occasional smoko. When the last of the cargo was about to be discharged, they battened down the holds, lowered the derricks and prepared for departure. They left Havana as night fell. Ahead of them lay three of the hardest days they would ever experience, but just possibly they were heading in the right direction.

CHAPTER 26

As soon as they cleared Havana, they returned to the holds and worked through until midnight again. The watches were forgotten, and the three Mates had to survive on their own whilst on watch. On the next morning, they started work again at 0500 hrs.

Once again, they split into two teams and set off into the holds. The dunnage in this hold still had to be collected, with the usual splinter problem, and stowed away in the virtual darkness of the tween deck. Then by the poor light of clusters in the dark hold, they started sweeping. The dust flew everywhere, in huge clouds virtually obscuring what light there was. They emerged for breakfast choking, spluttering, and black where the dust had stuck to their sweating bodies.

After breakfast, they opened a tiny portion of the hatch so that they could heave buckets of dirt and rubbish up on a line and dump it over the side. This was extremely hard work. The full weight of the load was some forty feet below, and they were tired anyway. When the bilge boards in this hold had been lifted, they discovered a large amount of sugar from the previous voyage that needed removing. The sugar mixed with the sweat from the bales had turned into a syrup that stuck to them, and then attracted all the other filth of the hold. This added many hours to the work.

By lunch time, the bilges on one side were empty, and the boards back in place ready to be covered in paper and battens. They stopped for lunch and dragged themselves up the long vertical ladder with difficulty, heading for the No 4 hold and the galley. As soon as they had eaten, they collapsed on the hatch top until the Bosun told them it was time to start again.

Worked continued on the other bilge. They had all taken turns in heaving out the rubbish, and their hands were sore and calloused as a result. They lowered a heavy roll of paper into the depths of the hold, and they all set about running off lengths of paper so that they could nail the battens to the boards. By dinner time they were totally exhausted as they headed once more to the galley.

The rigging of the steelwork started immediately after dinner in the No 2 hold, where the apprentices were. A larger portion of the hatch was uncovered, giving light and fresh air. A derrick was raised again, so that the central upright could be lifted into position. Because they had laid out all the necessary pieces in the tween deck, the beam and central upright, stays and bottle screws went up quite quickly, and they were able to drop the derrick and cover the hatch again before midnight.

Those that were down in the hold debated whether they had the energy to climb out of the hold, or whether it would be easier to sleep on the bilge boards. They decided to make the effort. With great difficulty and many rest stops, they made it. On one of the other company ships, an apprentice who was similarly exhausted had let go of the ladder whilst he was climbing out of a hold and plunged to his death.

When they showered before hitting their bunks, the water ran black for some time before they could claim to be clean. By the time Mike made it to his bunk Phil was fast asleep. Thirty seconds later so was Mike.

Until now, they had enjoyed the lee of the land, but the wind was starting to pick up and the ship had begun to roll. Initially it had been quite gentle, and had not caused any inconvenience to the work on the previous evening. Now she started to roll around fifteen to twenty degrees, and ahead of them they had the dangerous job of fitting the shifting boards themselves.

At 0500 hrs, they set out again, in the darkness, to No 2 hold. Astern of them was the merest promise of daylight. Although it was difficult to remain upright on the wooden ladder, hanging onto the wire stay whilst turning the bottle screw with a spike, they managed it.

They were now ready for the boards. The weather was very similar to that experienced on the way to New Orleans earlier, and the same problems could be expected. In their favour, they were now experienced and worked well as a team. Against that, they were exceptionally tired after the continual work of the past seven months. The first board was slid out into the centre of the hold while everyone tried to cling on. It was grabbed and slid into the slot without too much difficulty. The next few were more tricky, and jammed halfway down. It had to be time for breakfast.

The wall was complete around lunch time. The decision was taken to try to get all the holds to this point, as it was unlikely they would have time to rig the feeders as well. After lunch, they would start on No 1. That had already been swept, and the bilge boards covered. This would give them the possibility of having two holds with the shifting boards rigged, plus the one the crew had nearly completed.

After lunch, they set about putting in the tween deck beam and the central upright. This was the same job that had come close to dragging Mike and Paul into the hold on the first voyage. It promised to be just as interesting this time. Because of the way the huge steel beam had to be dragged from the side of the tween deck until it hung vertically over the hold, it was always a dangerous job. It was considerably more dangerous with the ship's rolling.

They agreed that if they had trouble controlling it they would all let go, rather than some hero hang onto it. They timed the lift so that the weight was fully taken on the winch whilst she was rolling to starboard, and took the strain at each end to avoid a wild swing as the ship rolled to port. Clinging onto it for grim death, two of them turned the beam and walked slowly around the forward edge of the hold, while the other two attempted to stop it swinging away from them. After two or three rolls to each side, they tried lowering it and hit the slots first time. A sigh of relief and a smoko followed.

The central upright came next. Although it was nowhere near as heavy as the beam, it would still be a major problem as it hung like a huge pendulum. Providing they could keep their balance, the people holding the bottom could control it. They had someone clinging to a beam directly above them with their knees, whilst holding two very large nuts and bolts, and an even bigger spanner. From that distance, the spanner or the bolts dropping could mean instant death to someone below. The nuts would cause immense physical damage. No one wanted to consider what would happen if the person above fell.

Largely because the crew were objecting to working at night, it was decided at dinner time that the job would become a job and finish. The apprentices had to finish fitting the boards in No 1 hold. During this evening, they experienced one of the highlights of the voyage. Phil, who had never been known to swear, hit his foot with one of the sledgehammers. For a moment, the whole hold was silent as they waited for a stream of expletives.

"Drat that nasty hammer," said Phil. In spite of the fact that they were so tired, the hold dissolved into fits of uncontrollable laughter.

Despite approaching a state bordering on collapse, they pushed themselves on for a chance of seeing their bunks a little earlier and succeeded. They had one hold left to fit boards in, and feeders in all holds on the final day before their arrival in Galveston. They stood little or no chance.

They started their final day at 0500 hrs in No 3 hold. The crew team, who had more people, had still not finished their second hold. They would be finishing that before starting to rig the feeders. It became more obvious that there was no chance of the feeders being built. The true story behind the whole operation became apparent. The American stevedores were quite happy to rig all the shifting boards and feeders providing that the holds were ready for them. They would pay a substantial bonus to the ship if they had completed some, or all, the rigging. For the ship, one could read Captain and Chief Officer, with possibly the Second and Third Mates taking some of it.

Not for the first time, the apprentices were sickened by it. They had risked life and limb in an attempt to be ready for cargo, when it was known that local carpenters would do the work. Loading would not commence until the Monday, two days after their arrival.

They dragged themselves to their bunks that night, once again sadder and wiser. They hoped that their final destination would be an English port so that they could get away from this ship, the Mate, and Captain because of their deceit and treachery. Once again, their pockets would be lined at the expense of the totally exhausted apprentices. The crew was not too worried. They earned substantial amounts of overtime to make up for their excesses in Cuba.

The following morning, Saturday 1st November, they arrived back in Galveston. It was their first real taste of an English speaking country since leaving Portland back in the beginning of June. It still looked drab and uninteresting by comparison with New Orleans and Portland, but it had considerable appeal because it may be their chance of a voyage home.

Once again, they endured the interminable administration connected with their entry into the USA. They were rewarded with a mail delivery from shocked relatives and friends who were replying to the letters from India telling of their horrendous time there.

The holds had been stripped of their covers and hatch boards prior to coming alongside. As soon as the official procedures were completed and pratique had been granted, they had permission to use the foreign port. They were invaded by an army of carpenters, all wearing large tool belts with every conceivable tool imaginable in them. Slings of large plywood sheets were lifted aboard. There was to be no messing around with the existing feeder boards. They would build brand new ones. Cynically Mike thought where the plywood sheets would end up after discharge was complete, and who would pocket the money.

The carpenters came with the most incredible array of power tools, which they could only have dreamt of in England. By the end of the day, the feeders were mostly complete and required only finishing off on Sunday. They departed almost as quickly as they had arrived. That was the signal for three of the four apprentices to go ashore to the nearest diner, and gorge themselves on milk shakes and strawberry shortcake to improve their spirits.

Loading began first thing at 0800 hrs on Monday. The grain spewed into holds No 2 and 4 covering everything with dust, but nobody really cared. The countdown to the day when the news they were hoping for had started.

By Thursday, all the holds were full and only required trimming and the feeders filled. On the Friday morning, the men with the surfboards shot the grain into the corners and then filled the feeders. The crew were left to replace the hatch boards and batten down ready for sea. Partly through lack of money, but primarily because of exhaustion, they had not been further ashore than the diner. Now the hopes that had been so badly dashed in Portland were raised again. There was a whole new feeling to the ship as it left Galveston, and headed out into the Gulf of Mexico.

It was now 7th November and, given a reasonable crossing, they should be in radio-telephone contact with the head office in two long weeks. During this time, whether they were going to the UK or Europe, Kirton would want the whole ship painting inside and out. The owner would be bound to visit the ship and Chief Officers were judged by the state of the ship at the time of the owner's visit.

Sure enough, the next morning they broke out all the paint kettles, brushes, rollers, trays, rags and white spirit. Painting started on the forecastle head while the good weather and seas lasted. They were down to the accommodation by the time they entered the Atlantic. The weather initially precluded them from working on the main deck, so the focus went to the bridge and lower bridge decks, and then the boat deck.

Even the lifeboats were swung out before the weather turned, so that the davits could be painted. Although they had regularly held lifeboat drills during the voyage, this was the first time that the boats had been swung out. It was a worrying time for all of them. The davits were of a gravity type. When a lever was pulled, the boat should roll down the ramp of the davit and so swing out over the side. One by one, the levers were pulled and in every case the boat refused to move. Only a session with blowlamps, sledgehammers, and grease would eventually persuade them. Whilst the apprentices were not surprised, the thought that when abandoning the ship they would have to find hammers and blowlamps did nothing to reassure them.

The boat deck was a huge area, mainly of white paint interrupted by huge cowl ventilators for the accommodation and engine room, the engine room skylights, and the lifeboat davits. Here also was the largest area of wooden deck on the ship. This had not been cleaned or maintained during the long voyage. The deck needed holystoning, and the apprentices were nominated to do it. Holystoning consisted of pushing a large block of soft sandstone in a long handled metal frame backwards and forwards along the deck. With the aid of a specialized detergent and water, the wood of the deck came up like new.

At this stage in the voyage, one more mind-numbing job was going to make little difference, so they set about the work and spent the next three days completing it. When they had finished, they were impressed. They returned to their painting with just a touch more pride in their work. After painting came varnishing, then they moved into the accommodation as the weather became colder. All the rails on the bridge and lower bridge needed scraping by dragging the edge of a piece of glass along the rails until the old varnish had gone. Then a new coat was applied.

The weather eventually broke, and she began pitching into the heavy seas with waves breaking over the decks. All further deck work was impossible before they arrived off the English coast. A few suicidal trips were needed to bring back supplies of cream paint, varnish and the usual accessories, but they would now concentrate on painting the accommodation.

Speculation as to their destination was rife. No one really wanted to consider the possibility of them going home in case it did not happen. Rotterdam had become the outright favourite. Various members of the crew suggested that if this were the case, then they would have as big a sub as possible and jump ship, heading on a ferry to the UK. This thought found favour with the four boys, but they knew that they would not do it.

That night on watch, Mike considered his future. He did not want to think too much about the possibility of going home. But what if they did go home? Would he happily sign on for another voyage like this one? From what his Father had told him, he didn't expect life as an apprentice to be easy, but sixteen to nineteen hours a day smacked of something from a bygone age.

On the bright side, he had experienced three American ports, as well as Japan, Cuba and the Panama Canal. He had literally travelled around the world at seventeen. He was slimmer and fitter than he had ever been in his life. He was sun tanned, and his recently acquired crew cut would go down well if they did go home.

On the down side, they had Kirton. He had done his best to make their lives miserable over the past nine months. They had been stuck in India for seven weeks, fighting illness for most of the time, which would always colour his view of that country.

How likely was it that things would be as bad on another ship? He thought back to the original Chief Officer, and what he had said about his future within the company. If he signed full indentures, would he see more of the new ships in the company? Would his career really progress as he had suggested? In six weeks' time, he would have completed a quarter of his apprenticeship. Could he stand three more years like this one? He had definite reservations about that. As long as they arrived home soon, he knew that he would not give up his only dream career.

On the following day, they would be within radiotelephone reach of the UK. The aerials had suddenly shot up on the boat deck, each one vying to be the highest. One had even been connected to a signal halyard, and hoisted up the main mast. Mike knew without being told that their first job in the morning would be to cut down all the aerials, only for them to be put up again later in the morning.

By the time the morning came, the only thought or conversation for everyone aboard was the question of their destination. Every conceivable excuse was made to ensure that they were near a radio. The most popular people were those with the most powerful radios. Bremen had joined Rotterdam as a strong favourite, as it was the port from where the car ships sailed. The plan might be that they would load cars for the United States and then return with another grain cargo.

Suggestions of voyages that would keep them away for at least another year depressed everyone. Then at midday the many and varied radios were able to pick up the conversation between the ship and London. The conversation was long, and they had difficulty at times keeping the signal, but right at the end came their destination. Liverpool.

The prayers of the majority had been heard and answered. The pain was gone. The problems solved. Suddenly life looked rosy again. The air of euphoria on the last occasion that they heard the same news was insignificant compared to the one pervading the ship now. They were going home. These words kept echoing over and over again as they tried to concentrate on their work, but with little success. Within two days, on the 24th, they would be in Liverpool. They would be paid off and be given their travel warrants. By Tuesday or Wednesday, they might be sitting in their own homes. Even now, Mike could not really take it in.

Being Saturday, they set about the cleaning of the

wheelhouse with a will. The wooden deck was scrubbed so hard that you could have eaten off the finished surface. The brass-work was polished until every tiny piece shone, even the exterior telegraph. The smell of Brasso and Mansion Polish hung heavily in the air. Even Kirton and the Captain were heard to mention how good it looked. On the Sunday, they gave the cabins the same treatment. When it came around to Captain's inspection, he nodded approvingly as he inspected the two cabins and the bathroom.

Mike looked forward to his watch that evening. He would have one of the first views of the UK. They crossed Cardigan Bay and would be picking up the coast of North Wales prior to turning into Liverpool Bay. Already fishing boats and other ships leaving Liverpool could be seen and he strained his eyes to try to see the lume of one of the lighthouses, which presently he was able to report to the Third Mate.

As he stood in the corner of the bridge wing with his pint mug, he was conscious of the chill November wind, but he did not feel cold. He was far too excited to worry about the temperature. To him it was a glorious crisp, winter's evening, in the heavens, the stars were visible in their thousands and around him were the lights of home. This would probably be the last time he would stand on this bridge wing where he had spent so much time as they circumnavigated the world. His mind went back to all the thoughts of home he had enjoyed whilst there. In a day or two, he would be seeing them all and the nightmare of a voyage would be forgotten.

The watch passed very quickly, and when he was relieved at midnight he was loathe to return to his cabin, but he would be up early to prepare for entering port. Several people were in a similar state. They settled down for what might be their last chance of a conversation together.

After the short night they were all back on deck just before 0700 hrs. The ropes had to be dragged out, the derricks raised and all the usual preparations made. He saw Kirton huddled on the forecastle head with the carpenter, where he had been since not long after the Pilot came aboard. He thought to himself that if he was really lucky, this could be the last day he would have in his company. Already the problems of the last nine months were slipping from his shoulders.

The tugs that were to guide them into the dock system were made fast, and slowly she swung towards the shore and the lock that signalled the entrance. Passage through the lock was swift due to the state of the tide. Very soon, she was being manoeuvred into Huskisson Dock where, what seemed like an age ago, he had seen *La Pradera*. Bow and stern lines, together with combinations and springs, were run out and made fast. Then they heard the most glorious sound of all as the telegraph rang, for the last time, "Finished with engines." They were home.

CHAPTER 27

By mid-morning the pay off was under way. One by one, the seamen, donkey men and stewards dragged their enormous piles of luggage to the accommodation ladder, and from there into the waiting taxis. The apprentices shook hands and waved goodbye to many of them, knowing they would never see them again. All the engineers other than the Chief, Third and a junior engineer followed them. The three of them would be standing by the ship until relieved. As they shared the accommodation block, they were more sorry to see them go. They wished them all the best, and that they would see them again.

The apprentices were told that they would have to wait until the next day, when their replacements arrived, before they could go on leave. This was due to the lack of seamen and officers, the Second and Third Mates having gone as well. The new Mate was due on the next day. That would mean a final farewell to Kirton, a moment Mike had wished for throughout the past nine months. In addition, the new Captain would arrive. In the meantime, the Bosun was still around to chase them, but he was getting ready to go as well.

Mike had mentioned to him a day ago about leaving friends on the ship and he had immediately imparted one of his usual pieces of wisdom. "Remember son," he said, "There are no such things as friends at sea, only compulsory Board of Trade acquaintances". Mike had thought that a bit cynical, but realised years later that it was more or less correct.

Early the following morning they saw on the quay, resplendent in doeskin uniform, an apprentice. Philip Orozovsky was the first of their replacements. As they had the furthest to go, it was decided that Tony and Phil would be relieved and go home. Paul and Mike helped them to a taxi with their luggage, promising to write and keep in touch, knowing that the chances were that this was the last they would see or hear of each other. Nevertheless they meant it sincerely enough.

Shortly after they had bade farewell to Tony and Phil, the new Captain arrived and they carried his cases up to his cabin. Captain Van Galder was everything his predecessor was not. Small, clean-shaven and quietly spoken, but gave the impression that he could be a difficult man. Mike did not really care, as he would be on his way shortly, and would be having nothing to do with him.

Kirton's replacement arrived next. With still no sign of any more apprentices, Paul and Mike were starting to become slightly nervous about their prospects, and considered leaving as soon as the Captain and Kirton had left. Presently the apprentices were asked to carry the senior officers' entire luggage down to the quay, as they were to share a taxi to Lime Street. This they did gladly in the hopes that they would never meet them again. Churlish to the last, Kirton got into the taxi without a word. As he stood above him on the gangway, Mike wished he had the pin from the shackle lost in the Hooghly, for this would have been a great time to drop it over the side. The Captain thanked them for carrying the luggage down, and for their help during the voyage, and wished them all the best for the future.

As they returned to the ship, Captain Van Galder was walking towards them and announced to their horror that he did not know when their replacements would be arriving, but on no account were they to leave before they did. All the euphoria they had felt during the past two days was wiped away in a flash. There was now obviously, in the Captain's mind, the possibility that they would have to sail in the ship on its next voyage.

Mike, in his excitement, had called his Mother that morning and told her he would be home within the next few days. Now, as in Portland, all this was to be taken away from him. Paul felt the same. He had been very ill in India and the thought of this day was one of the things that pulled him through. Now he too was feeling that unbearable fate was conspiring against them to keep them there. He was adamant that it would not succeed, no matter what the cost to his career

Late in the afternoon, a further apprentice arrived, and Paul as the senior of the two needed no bidding. He asked the taxi to wait as he and Mike carried his bags to it, then he too was gone. Mike had the feeling that he would see him again. He was sorry to see him go.

By mid afternoon on the next day, Mike was frantic. There was still no sign of his relief, and he was becoming obsessed with the possibility that he would be still on the ship when she sailed. The cargo discharge was well under way and would be completed within the next two days. He made the decision. Regardless of the effect on his career, he was leaving. He walked along the quay to the phone box, where he called for a taxi. Keeping a sharp lookout for the taxi, he was back on the quay within fifteen minutes with all his luggage.

The taxi arrived promptly, and he was quickly in it and away. He allowed himself a look backwards at *La Cordillera*, which, unknown to him, he would never see again. Then he concentrated on arriving at Lime Street station and the train to Hull. By good luck, he had timed his escape to perfection. He was on his way to Manchester and then across the Pennines within fifteen minutes.

As somehow he knew he would be, Mr Bampton was on the taxi rank in front of the platform and came forward to help him with his baggage. The conversation as they headed for his home was far more animated than it had been previously, until he asked when Mike was going back. Only then did the enormity of what he had done start to sink in. The chances were that if the head office were in touch with Captain Van Galder, he would not be going back, not shortly nor ever. Mike for a moment became subdued, but raised his spirits as they pulled into St Stephens Road. He was not going to let this cloud his time at home.

His Mother, brothers and sister greeted him as he arrived, and within minutes he was sitting in an armchair with a cup of tea with real milk. All the stress fell from his shoulders as he gave out presents to everyone and started telling them all the things that had happened in the past nine months. Looking back he realised he had told them nothing of the unpleasant things that had happened, only the good. He was becoming a typical seafarer already, concentrating only on the good news.

Two days later a large envelope, addressed to him, arrived in the post; it bore the franking stamp of Buries Markes and contained his indentures. He was to be offered full indentures and a four-year apprenticeship backdated to January. This gave him enormous relief. Within the next few weeks, he would be receiving an appointment to another ship. Although he was enjoying his leave immensely, he could not help thinking what would he get next? Would it be something modern like *La Pradera*, or even *La Colina*, or old like *La Pampa* or *La Estancia*?

Gradually he had met all his friends and caught up with the news and gossip, amongst it was one piece of news that he could have well done without. Julia was still heavily involved with Derek, meaning that he would have to make an effort to find another partner for his forthcoming welcome home party. He immediately set his sights on Jacqui who he had hoped to date a long time ago but did not think he stood a chance. His luck had changed dramatically, as Jacqui's eyes lit up at his invitation. She became his constant companion for the duration of his leave.

Three weeks had gone by, and he had settled nicely into shore life as Christmas approached. Life could not have been more perfect. He had his family around him, a stunning girlfriend and the Christmas and New Year festivities fast approaching. As he reflected on this, he picked up the pile of Christmas cards that the postman had just delivered. Amongst the cards was a letter addressed to him once again bearing the Buries Marke's house flag. Surely not before Christmas, he thought as he opened it and read the contents.

"Please report to *M/V La Colina* in Port Talbot on 31st December 1958, a rail warrant is enclosed."